Hiking
New York

A Guide to the State's Best Hiking Adventures

Fifth Edition

Rhonda and George Ostertag
Revised by Randi Minetor

FALCONGUIDES

ESSEX, CONNECTICUT

FALCONGUIDES®

An imprint of Globe Pequot, the trade division of The Rowman & Littlefield Publishing Group, Inc.
4501 Forbes Blvd., Ste. 200
Lanham, MD 20706
www.rowman.com
Falcon and FalconGuides are registered trademarks and Make Adventure Your Story is a trademark of
The Rowman & Littlefield Publishing Group, Inc

Distributed by NATIONAL BOOK NETWORK

Photos by Rhonda and George Ostertag unless otherwise noted
Maps by Melissa Baker and The Rowman & Littlefield Publishing Group, Inc.

British Library Cataloguing in Publication Information available

Library of Congress Cataloging-in-Publication Data
Names: Ostertag, Rhonda, 1957– author. | Ostertag, George, 1957– author. | Minetor, Randi, reviser.
Title: Hiking New York : a guide to the state's best hiking adventures / Rhonda and George
    Ostertag ; Revised by Randi Minetor.
Description: Fifth edition. | Guilford, CT : Falcon Guides, [2024] | Includes index. | Summary: "This
    updated guidebook features seventy-five of the best trails the Empire State has to offer-from
    the 4,000-foot peaks of the Adirondacks and the lore of Rip Van Winkle's Catskills, to the
    glacier-gouged landscape of the Finger Lakes region"—Provided by publisher.
Identifiers: LCCN 2023056652 (print) | LCCN 2023056653 (ebook) | ISBN 9781493077342
    (paperback) | ISBN 9781493077359 (epub)
Subjects: LCSH: Hiking—New York (State)—Guidebooks. | Trails—New York (State)—Guidebooks. |
    New York (State) —Guidebooks.
Classification: LCC GV199.42.N65 O88 2024 (print) | LCC GV199.42.N65 (ebook) | DDC
    796.5109747—dc23/eng/20231208
LC record available at https://lccn.loc.gov/2023056652
LC ebook record available at https://lccn.loc.gov/2023056653

♾™ The paper used in this publication meets the minimum requirements of American National
Standard for Information Sciences—Permanence of Paper for Printed Library Materials, ANSI/NISO
Z39.48-1992.

Contents

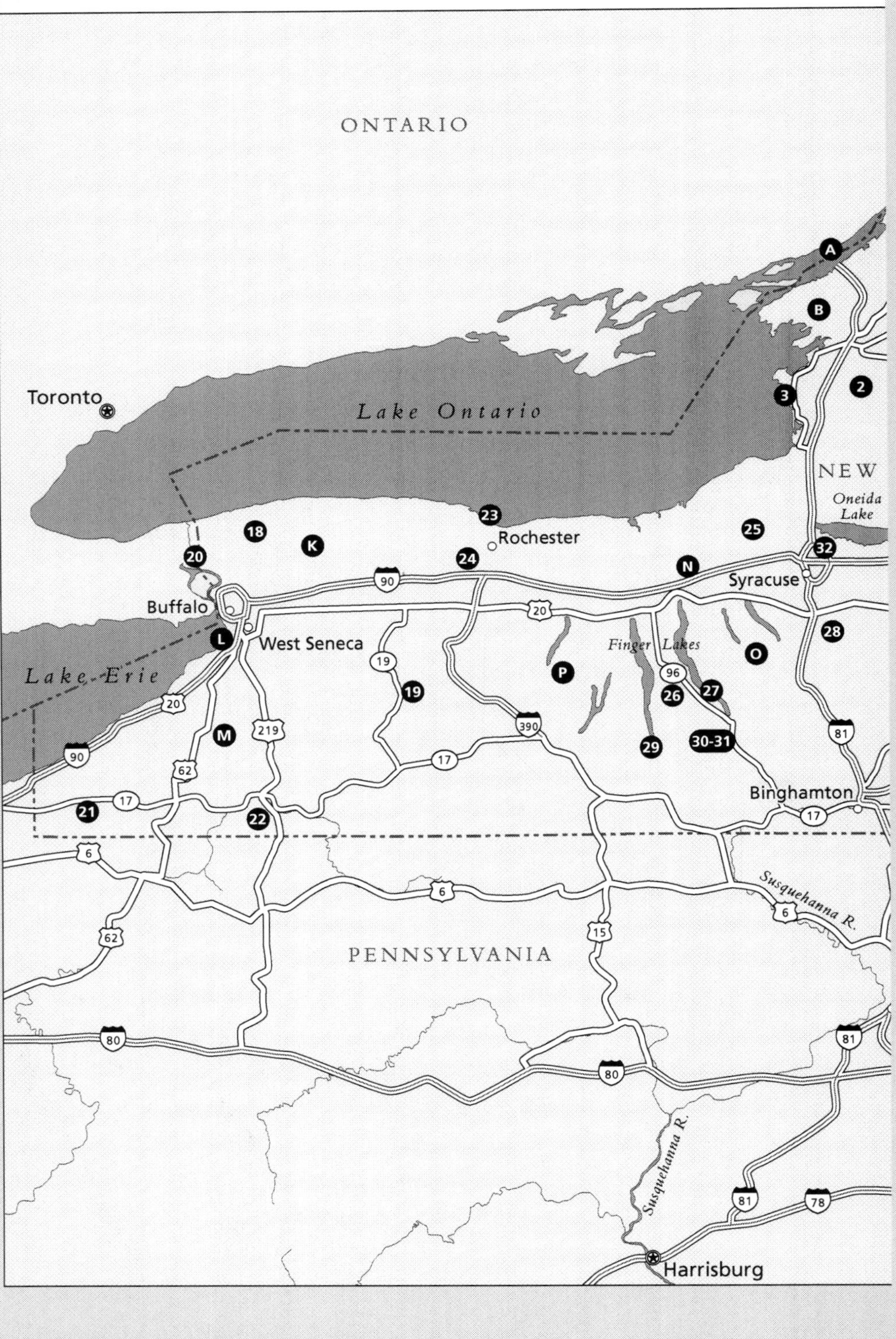

ONTARIO

Toronto

Lake Ontario

A

B

3

2

NEW

Oneida Lake

23

Rochester

25

32

18

20

K

24

90

20

N

Syracuse

Buffalo

L

West Seneca

19

19

19

Finger Lakes

O

28

P

96

26

27

Lake Erie

20

M

219

390

17

29

30-31

81

90

62

6

Binghamton

21

17

22

17

6

6

Susquehanna R.

80

62

15

PENNSYLVANIA

81

80

80

81

Susquehanna R.

81

78

Harrisburg

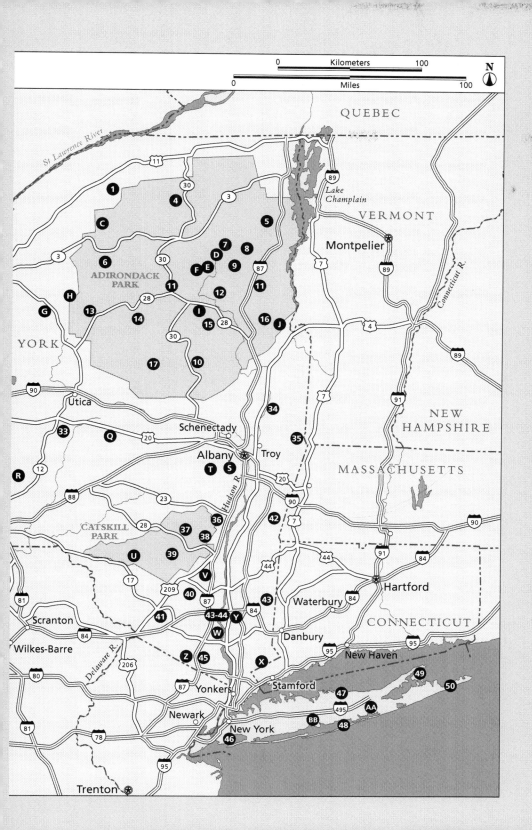

Acknowledgments

Many thanks to the trail associations and individual volunteers who blaze and maintain the trails, the preservationists who work to save New York State's prized natural and cultural areas, and the many landowners who have allowed the state trail system to grow and endure. Many trails would slip from existence without their cooperation.

As the reviser of this fifth edition of *Hiking New York*, I also thank the team at Falcon, who always produce such beautiful books, for the energy and care that I know went into this edition. Special thanks to my agent, Regina Ryan, and to Mason Gadd, acquisitions editor at Falcon, for giving me the opportunity to bring a native New Yorker's perspective to this complex and comprehensive overview of the state's extraordinary hiking experiences.

Introduction

From the Adirondack lakes and peaks to the falling waters of the Finger Lakes Region, from the heritage of the Erie Canal to the lore of the Catskills, New York State offers hikers unforgettable experiences. The trails selected for this book explore premier parks, forests, mountains, gorges, flatlands, swamps, beaches, and reserves. You will travel to sparkling waterfalls and daunting cliffs, New York's highest summit and others of comparable beauty and challenge, and to valley floors blanketed in wildflowers or fallen autumn leaves.

The advance and retreat of four glacial masses over a period of 2 million years sculpted the face of New York State, gouging out north–south lakes, scouring valleys, and depositing rock debris. These ages of excavation, coupled with the state's legendary weather patterns, have created a first-rate playground for those who love to explore the outdoors—much of it a short train ride from New York City or a half day's road trip by car from the "Thruway cities" of Buffalo, Rochester, Syracuse, and Albany. The state boasts thousands of miles of trails, from short nature walks to lengthy converted canal and train corridors, to outstanding rugged wilderness hikes. In this book we attempt to bring you a representative sampling of some of the best, but we did leave some for you to find. After all, discovery is one of the joys of hiking.

Through these pages, you will inhale mountain air from atop the flat ridges of the Allegheny hills, the blinding white quartzite ledges of the "Gunks" (the Shawangunks), and the chiseled peaks of the Adirondacks. You will admire the jeweled waters of the Great Lakes, the Finger Lakes, and the Genesee, Mohawk, Hudson, and Saint Lawrence Rivers, and you will enfold yourself in wilderness solitude.

Outcrop vistas, clear coursing streams, beaver ponds, marshes, pine barrens, rolling hardwood forests, alpine stands of fir and spruce, meadows, and even desert plains will spice the journey. You will walk in the footsteps of past presidents and literary giants, generals, and agricultural pioneers. The pivotal battles for independence and the rising tide of the Industrial Revolution add their tales to the terrain's story. Exploring New York's open spaces can be a welcome escape from the congestion of its celebrated cities, bringing you the opportunity to forge closer connections to nature, land, and self.

As you explore the state's wilderness areas, you may see that many New York trails have undergone recent reconstruction to keep up with the ravages of major storms, climate alterations, and other factors that can destabilize rock walls and hillsides. Additional switchbacks, stone steps, walls, underpinnings, course redirection, and more may change the exact route of a trail—and by its very nature, a book cannot keep up with these. A fine and willing volunteer corps keeps the trails passable for all of us, devoting their time, sweat, and knowledge to protect the state's hiking resources. The New York–New Jersey Trail Conference, the Adirondack Mountain Club (ADK), the Appalachian Mountain Club (AMC), the Finger Lakes Trail Conference (FLTC), and the Long Island Greenbelt Trail Conference, to name a few, not only advocate,

Mount Jenkins delivers sweeping Adirondack views.

maintain, and improve trails but also produce excellent maps. We are the beneficiaries of their fine work, so please consider supporting these groups through the purchase of their maps in addition to the ones in this book. Updated at least annually, their maps may hold the most current information on the lay of the trail, land ownership, shelters, facilities, and obstacles.

Weather

For the most part, hiking in New York is a three-season pursuit, with many trails doubling as winter cross-country ski routes and snowshoe trails. Spring and fall offer a preferred mix of mild temperatures and low humidity. Summer can bring extremes in both categories, as well as dramatic afternoon thunder and lightning storms.

Generally speaking, the climate for New York falls in the humid continental zone. Within that broad classification, the state has three weather regions: the milder and more humid southeastern lowlands, the chillier mountain uplands (Adirondack and Catskill Mountains), and the Great Lakes Plains of the northwestern state, where lake-effect weather can mean heavy winter snowfalls and increased wind year-round.

Always check current weather forecasts before setting out on any trail. This is especially true for long hikes and overnight outings. Do not discount the unexpected: Pack on the side of caution and know what to do in case the weather turns bad. (See the "Your Safety on the Trail" section later in this introduction.)

Rainbow Falls hurries water to its joining with the Ausable River.

Flora and Fauna

With its variations in elevation and terrain, New York rolls out a rich leafy and floral tapestry. More than half of the state is covered in forest, with an outstanding representation of 150 tree species. Hardwood forests predominate, but the canopy varies: Lower elevations and southern reaches have transitional hardwood compositions of beech, birch, basswood, sweet gum, magnolia, hickory, maple, and oak, while red maples, which can like it wet or dry, claim northern swamps and decorate much of the Adirondack region. Sugar maples are common, producing the maple sugar for which New York is famous. The state's higher reaches support a rare-to-this-latitude boreal spruce and balsam fir complex filled out by mountain ash, white pine, and paper birch. Above timberline, only the most stubborn species thrive.

Meadow plains parade out such species as dame's rocket, Canada and gray goldenrod, black-eyed Susan, common and swamp milkweed, butterfly weed, and Joe Pye weed, giving way to New York and white wood aster in fall. Viburnum, sarsaparilla, bunchberry, baneberry, Solomon's seal, azalea, rhododendron, and mixed ferns shower the forest floor and midstory. Wetlands bring together pickerelweed, rose mallow, common yarrow, snakeroot, boneset, cattail reeds, rushes, high-bush blueberry, and common water hemlock. Altogether, this glorious tapestry of shape, shade, and texture fashions a sensory-rich frame for the state's pathways.

Populating New York's niches and habitats are some 600 species of mammals, birds, reptiles, and amphibians. White-tailed deer are the most common large mammal sightings. Because of their numbers, deer have become nuisances in towns and dangers on roadways—so lower your speed and watch the roadsides to reduce the chance of deer collisions., especially before dawn and after dark

Black bears also reside in the Empire State. When backpacking, take necessary precautions and suspend all foodstuffs, garbage, and smelly accessories from trees; in the Adirondacks, vault containers are required to protect both you and the bears. Check the fact sheet at www.dec.ny.gov/docs/regions_pdf/bcbears.pdf for the best advice from the NY Department of Environmental Conservation on camping in New York's bear country.

Although trapped nearly to extinction in prior centuries, beavers again flourish in the state. Their constructions have a tendency to rewrite trails, to the consternation of hikers and the frustration of guidebook authors. But the animals' industry improves fisheries and water quality, and you have to admire their perseverance. Moose, another animal that had nearly vanished from the state in the 1860s, has made a comeback in recent decades, with the Department of Conservation reporting adequate numbers to boast a successful population.

More likely critter encounters include woodchucks, mice, rabbits, raccoons, and muskrats. More than 450 species of birds either pass through New York on their way north or remain to breed in the state's widely diverse habitats. Eastern bluebirds, the state bird and once a species of concern, have strengthened their numbers since the

1960s. Songbirds, migrating kettles of hawks, woodpeckers, loons, ducks, shorebirds, and wild turkeys reward birders on trails. The cry of the loon is as much a sound of the wilderness here as the howl of the wolf or the coyote in the West.

Frogs, toads, newts, salamanders, and slithering snakes can disturb the water and part the grasses, or hop or scramble across trails before hikers' eyes. Rattlesnakes find limited habitat in a few of the state's rocky realms. Thriving fish populations claim both warm and cool waters.

Even when the menagerie goes unseen, we can rejoice in the songs, tracks, rustles, splashes, and subtle clues of the life around us. As stewards of the flora and fauna, we need to minimize both our trace and that of our doggie companions when we hike the trails.

BUGS

New York endures a tormenting mosquito and blackfly season, especially in the Adirondacks. Less troublesome in dry years, the insects can be unbearable from late May through the end of June if the spring has been unusually wet. Keep in mind that some mosquitos can spread diseases, including West Nile virus, zika virus, and even dengue fever, eastern equine encephalitis, and malaria in a few isolated cases. Your best bets for protection are long sleeves and long pants or clothing treated in advance with insect repellent made for this purpose. If it's just too hot for such precautions, the New York State Department of Health recommends using an insect repellent that contains significant amounts of DEET or picaridin. Here's what the DoH has to say about botanical oils and other natural repellents: "Insect repellent products containing botanical oils, such as oil of geranium, cedar, lemongrass, soy or citronella, are also available. Because most botanical oils are not regulated the same as the active ingredients above, they have not been tested for their potential to cause health effects or their effectiveness as a repellent. However, the information available on these products indicates that they generally have limited effectiveness in repelling ticks and insects."

Ticks

Ticks are a major issue in New York State, and not just in the wilderness—they are now present in city parks and even in the backyards of suburban homes. Deer ticks may carry diseases like Lyme disease, a chronic illness that can be life-altering. The best defense is prevention: On any hike wear long pants and a long-sleeved shirt. Apply a repellent that contains permethrin to your clothing and on exposed skin—this is the only insect repellent that truly repels and even kills ticks (don't bother with homeopathic substitutes). At the end of your hike, do a spot check for ticks (and insects in general). If you do find an attached tick, grab the head of the tick firmly with a pair of tweezers as close to the skin as possible, and free it from the skin with a gentle, even pull. Clean the affected area with an antibacterial cleanser and then apply triple antibiotic ointment. Monitor the area for a few days. If irritation persists, or if a white spot or red "bullseye" ring develops, see a doctor. If you experience symptoms after a hike like headache and a stiff neck, loss of facial muscle tone or a droop on one side of the face, severe swelling in the knees or other large joints, or intermittent pain in tendons, muscles, or bones, see your doctor as soon as you can.

Wilderness Restrictions/Regulations

Although this book concentrates primarily on public land offerings, trails across private, trust, and conservancy lands extend hiking opportunities. To continue this privilege, we must assume full responsibility for our own well-being whenever we cross onto privately held land. Heed all posted rules and exercise your best no-trace wilderness manners. Keep to the trail, leave gates as they were found, and police your actions and those of your animal, if indeed pets are allowed. In all cases, if you pack it in, pack it out.

This book indicates if and where trails cross onto private lands—but ownership changes or a landowner may withdraw the privilege of through-travel. Respect such closures. At privately operated resorts or reserves, fees or suggested donations may be requested for the use of their trails.

Trails traversing lands managed by state, county, and federal agencies shape the core of this book. Of the state-operated properties, state park sites (overseen by the New York State Office of Parks, Recreation and Historic Preservation) typically show greater grooming and development and possess more facilities. At most state parks, you can expect to pay a seasonal entrance fee. Many of us who hike avidly and use the outdoors find the purchase of the New York State Parks Empire Passport, an annual day-use pass that provides unlimited access to most state parks, many New York State Department of Environmental Conservation (DEC) forest preserve sites, and other lands, easily pays for itself.

The DEC manages the vast acreage of state-owned lands, much of it state forests: planted stands and natural woods open to selective harvests and multiple-use recreation. Here they provide basic facilities: backcountry shelters and privies, trail registers, and parking lots. By contrast, the state forest preserves at Adirondack Park and Catskill Park feature protected woodlands closed to harvest and other revenue-making enterprises but open to various recreational pursuits. State wildlife management areas primarily promote and sustain waterfowl and wildlife populations, with hunting and fishing, birding, and hiking being compatible recreations. Multiple-use areas serve a gamut of year-round recreational users.

Trail parking and use are generally free for DEC lands, although some nature centers and day-use areas require fees. The DEC does have an extensive trailhead registration program. Take the time to sign in and out and comment on the condition of the trail and its markings. The collected information figures into the allotment of funds for trail improvement and expansion.

In a few areas, land agencies issue trail or camp permits to help monitor and manage the trails and to minimize overuse. On DEC lands, single-site stays of longer than three days and camping parties that exceed ten in number do require permits, and these can be picked up at the overseeing DEC office for the particular trail. To protect the integrity of the wild, keep your party size small.

Lean-tos are available on a first-come, first-served basis. Remember, you must share these shelters with other parties. For more detailed rules and regulations, visit the DEC website: www.dec.ny.gov.

Trail Navigation

With the predominance of leafy forests, some manner of blazing or marking—paint, diamond, or disk—guides you along most New York trails. The DEC uses both color-coded and user-coded disks to mark routes. In several areas the agency offers independent trail systems for foot, horse, and mountain bike use. On some private lands, blaze patterns may exist for one-directional travel only, so be sure to consult a map before plotting your course, and carry the map on your hike. Cairns and stakes are other manners of marking a route. A double-blazing pattern typically warns of a change in direction. Often the top blaze is offset to the right or left to indicate the direction you turn.

Because intervals between blazes can vary greatly, make a point to familiarize yourself with the blazing frequency on the trail you are walking. An uncommonly long lapse between blazes may indicate that you have strayed off course, in which case you should backtrack to the last known marker and look again. If reasonable short searches do not turn up the next marker and the trail, the wise course of action is to turn around and return to the trailhead. Autumn adventures require you to be especially alert because fallen leaves can completely conceal the tracked paths. For wilderness backpacking, you may want to bring a GPS device that uses batteries and satellite navigation (rather than cellular, as this can be nonexistent in the backcountry), and a solar charger to keep it running when you need it most.

Several long-distance routes crisscross New York on the way to other states, each with a signature blaze color. Just over 90 miles of the Appalachian Trail (white blazes) trek across the state's southeastern corner, while the blue-blazed North Country Trail, stretching from Vermont to North Dakota, uses a number of New York trails to advance its route across the state from east to west. Most recently, the new Empire State Trail, established in 2017, creates an official route from New York City to Buffalo and from Albany to the Canada border by creating connections between many existing trails.

Your Safety on the Trail

Hiking in New York involves all kinds of unforeseen circumstances: wet ground, slippery rocks, precarious precipices, muddy embankments, icy ridges, long downhill slopes, and scrambles up and over boulders. Weather can change with little preamble, and a sudden drop or rise in temperature can turn a pleasant day into a precarious situation. Some hikes appear to pose no hazards at all, but the majority require at least a small amount of risk. You'll want to be ready for whatever situation you may encounter.

Wear appropriate footwear. Ankle support can make all the difference when you're hiking on rocky trails and rockhopping across streams. There's nothing worse

Solitude and society can be found along the Appalachian Trail.

than having your hike or vacation spoiled by a sprained ankle you got when your foot unexpectedly slipped off a ledge—and I speak from experience. If the hike you've chosen includes a creek walk, wear your favorite old sneakers or a pair of waterproof boots—but not flip-flops or other open-toed shoes. Protect your toes from rocks hidden below the surface of the water by wearing close-toed or amphibious shoes.

Note: A properly fit pair of boots should feel comfortable from the first day you wear them—they should not need "breaking in." Buy your boots from an outfitter with knowledgeable sales staff to be sure you're getting the best advice.

Bring clothing for changeable weather—including a waterproof rain jacket or poncho—even on a sunny day. In New York State, storms can pop up in the mountains in minutes, turning a sunny morning into a soggy downpour. If you hike in winter, dress in layers that you can remove during the uphill stretches and put back on to keep from getting chilled once you've cooled down.

Bring food and water. If you're going on a long day hike, bring at least one full meal and some salty/sweet snacks like trail mix. Much of the hiking in this book involves uphill stretches, which can lengthen the time you're on the trail. You're going to need more water than you think, so plan on a pint per hour and bring at least an extra hour's worth. You may be tempted to refill your water bottles on the trail from the stream you're following to the falls, but waterways often carry waterborne bacteria and protozoa that can cause serious illnesses. If you want to depend on streams for your water supply, it's imperative that you carry some type of water filtration system.

Know where you're going. Bring this book with you, and find or download additional maps as indicated in each hike description. Learn to use a compass, and bring one along—or bring a GPS device if you're comfortable with that technology.

Protect against bugs. See the section in this introduction about bugs and ticks, which can carry diseases and spread them to humans. A new threat, the Asian long-horned tick, has recently arrived in New York State and may carry exotic diseases as well.

Wear sunscreen, even on a cloudy day. While most of the hikes in this book take you through forested areas, you will find yourself in bright sunlight when you reach summits, open meadows, and waterfalls. Snow is also a powerful sunlight reflector, so if you're hiking in winter, apply sunscreen to any exposed skin before you start out.

Never hike alone. First, it's not nearly as much fun as hiking with a buddy. Second, see or read *127 Hours.* You just never know when you're going to turn your ankle—or get your arm caught in a crevice—and find yourself stuck miles from the nearest road.

Read the signs. Nature preserves and state parks post signs to alert you to potential hazards within their boundaries, and it's always better to know what to expect. New York State has its fair share of wilderness obstacles—watch out for poison ivy, ticks, mosquitoes, timber rattlesnakes—yes, that's a remote possibility—and black bears.

Stay on the trail. You will be safer from poison ivy and bugs if you stick to the beaten path, and the forests and fields you cross will be safer as well. Stepping off the path can damage fragile ecosystems, like native vegetation and wildflowers. Resist the urge to cut across switchbacks or take unmarked, unauthorized shortcuts.

Wade or swim only where it's safe. The vast majority of waterfalls produce a great deal of force as they tumble down into plunge pools. These pools can have underwater ledges that can trap swimmers beneath them, or entangling vegetation that can wind itself around your arms or legs and keep you submerged. The water's force itself can push you down or pull you into a dangerous whirlpool. Safe swimming areas are usually marked as such in parks; if there's no swimming or wading allowed, rest assured there's a good reason.

Use a walking stick. Having a third point of contact with the ground can help you maintain your balance, brace you against falls, and find your best footing when you can't see below the surface. A walking stick or a pair of ski poles can be invaluable for winter hiking and for treks on steep, rocky trails. Creek walks can involve stepping into murky water with little to no idea what's on the bottom of the stream, as well as walking on slick slabs of rock that turn out to be less stable than they appear.

Avoiding Theft and Vandalism

Unattended hiker vehicles are vulnerable to theft and vandalism, but the following steps can minimize your risk:

- When possible, park away from the trailhead at a nearby campground or other facility.
- Do not leave valuables in the vehicle. Place keys and wallet in a button-secured pocket or remote, secure compartment in your daypack, where they will be ready for your return.
- Be suspicious of loiterers—never volunteer the details of your outing.
- Never pick up hitchhikers.
- Be cautious about the information you supply at the trailhead register. Withhold information such as license plate number and duration of stay until you are safely back at the trailhead. Instead notify a trusted friend of your trip details and notify that friend promptly upon return.

Backcountry travel includes unavoidable risks. Know yourself and your abilities, and let independent judgment and common sense be your ultimate guide to safe travel.

How to Use This Book

Each region begins with an introduction, where you're given a sweeping look at the lay of the land. After this general overview, chapters feature specific hikes within that region.

To help you choose the right hike for you and your party, each hike chapter begins with a hike summary, giving you a taste of the hiking adventure to follow. You'll learn about the trail terrain and what surprises the route has to offer. Next you'll find the rundown: where the trailhead is located, the nearest town, hike length, approximate hiking time, difficulty rating, elevation change (the difference between a trail's elevation extremes), best hiking season, type of trail terrain, what other trail users you may encounter, trail contacts (for updates on trail conditions), and trail schedules and usage fees.

The **approximate hiking times** are based on a standard hiking pace of 1.5 to 2 miles per hour, adjusted for terrain and reflecting normal trail conditions. The stated times will get you there and back, but be sure to add time for rest breaks and enjoying the trail's attractions. Although the stated times offer a planning guideline, take into consideration your personal health, capabilities, and hiking style, and make this judgment for yourself. If you're hiking with a group, add enough time for slower members. The amount of carried gear also will influence hiking speed. In all cases, leave enough daylight to accomplish the trip safely.

In **Finding the Trailhead,** we supply dependable directions to the trailhead from a nearby city or town, right down to where you'll want to park your car. Following that, the hike description is the meat of the chapter. Detailed and honest, it's the authors' personal experience and carefully researched impression of the trail. While it's impossible to cover everything, you can rest assured that we don't miss what's important. In **Miles and Directions,** we provide mileage cues to key junctions and trail name changes, as well as points of interest. The selected benchmarks allow for a quick check on progress, and serve as your touchstone for staying on course. Finally, **Hike Information** offers local sources for learning more about the area and may suggest things to do nearby or places to camp.

How to Use the Maps

For your own purposes, you may wish to carry a copy or a cell phone picture of the map and cue sheet to help you while hiking. Otherwise, just slip the whole book in your pack and take it with you. Enjoy your time in the outdoors and remember to pack out what you pack in.

The route map is your guide to each hike. It shows the accessible roads and trails, water, landmarks, towns, and key navigational features. It also distinguishes trails from roads, and paved roads from unpaved roads. The selected route is highlighted.

The included maps are not intended to replace more detailed agency maps, road maps, state atlases, and/or topographic maps, but they do indicate the general lay of the trail and its attractions to help you visualize and navigate its course. We have provided links to detailed maps created by the land management agencies that you can download and print. In addition, organizations like the Adirondack Mountain Club, the Appalachian Mountain Club, and the New York–New Jersey Trail Conference create some of the best hiking maps you will ever own. They're available for purchase from these organizations at very reasonable rates.

Trail Finder

Trail Name	Backpackers	Young Children	Older Children	Dogs	Nature Lovers	History Lovers	Waterfalls	Peak Baggers	Vistas
1. Stone Valley							•		
2. Inman Gulf Hiking and Nature Trails		•	•		•				
3. Lakeview Natural Beach Hike		•	•		•				
4. Jenkins Mountain Hike			•					•	
5. Poke-O-Moonshine Trail			•					•	•
6. High Falls Loop	•			•	•		•		
7. Mount Marcy/Van Hoevenberg Trail	•				•			•	•
8. East Branch Ausable River Loop					•		•	•	•
9. Blue Mountain Trail			•						•
10. Murphy Lake Trail		•	•	•	•			•	
11. Pharaoh Mountain and Lake Loop	•			•	•			•	•
12. Stony Pond Trail	•		•	•	•				
13. Middle Settlement Lake Hike	•			•	•				

Trail Name	Backpackers	Young Children	Older Children	Dogs	Nature Lovers	History Lovers	Waterfalls	Peak Baggers	Vistas
14. West Canada Lakes Wilderness Hike	•		•	•	•				
15. Siamese Ponds Hike	•	•	•		•				
16. Tongue Mountain Range Loop	•			•	•			•	•
17. Jockeybush Lake Trail		•	•		•				
18. Erie Canal Heritage Trail		•	•			•			
19. Letchworth State Park		•	•		•	•	•		•
20. Niagara Falls State Park			•		•		•		•
21. Fred J. Cusimano Westside Overland Trail	•			•	•				
22. Allegany State Park, Red House Headquarters—Eastwood Meadows Loop			•	•	•				
23. Genesee Riverway Trail			•	•	•	•	•		
24. Genesee Valley Greenway	•		•	•	•	•			
25. Beaver Lake Nature Center		•	•	•	•				
26. Interloken National Recreation Trail	•		•	•	•				
27. Taughannock Falls State Park		•	•		•		•		

Trail Name	Backpackers	Young Children	Older Children	Dogs	Nature Lovers	History Lovers	Waterfalls	Peak Baggers	Vistas
28. Onondaga Trail	•			•	•				
29. Watkins Glen State Park		•	•			•	•		
30. Buttermilk Falls State Park		•	•				•		
31. Robert H. Treman State Park			•			•	•		•
32. Old Erie Canal Heritage Trail		•	•			•			
33. Beaver Creek Swamp Loop			•	•	•				
34. Wilkinson National Recreation Trail		•	•			•			
35. Taconic Crest Trail			•	•	•				
36. North–South Lake Loop			•		•				•
37. Indian Head Mountain Loop	•				•			•	•
38. Overlook Mountain Hike	•		•		•	•		•	•
39. Slide Mountain Loop			•			•		•	•
40. Minnewaska State Park Preserve		•	•		•				•
41. Bashakill Wildlife Management Area		•	•		•				
42. Taconic State Park			•	•	•			•	•

Trail Name	Backpackers	Young Children	Older Children	Dogs	Nature Lovers	History Lovers	Waterfalls	Peak Baggers	Vistas
43. Hudson Highlands State Park: Cornish Estate/Undercliff			•		•	•		•	•
44. Breakneck Ridge Trail								•	•
45. Pine Meadow Lake Loop			•		•				
46. Jamaica Bay NWR: West Pond Trail		•	•		•				
47. Rocky Point Pine Barrens State Forest			•	•					
48. Fire Island National Seashore	•	•	•		•				
49. Mashomack Preserve		•	•		•				
50. Hither Hills State Park			•		•				

Map Legend

Municipal

≡⟨90⟩≡ Interstate Highway

≡⟨219⟩≡ US Highway

≡⟨177⟩≡ State Road

────── Local/County Road

= = = = Dirt Road

├──┼──┤ Railroad

·· — ·· — ·· State Boundary

•—•—•—• Power Line

Trails

■■■■■■ Featured Trail

- - - - - - Trail

Water Features

⬭ Body of Water

≈ Marsh

〜 River/Creek

≋ Waterfall

o⌐ Spring

Symbols

≍ Bridge

▲ Backcountry Campground

■ Building/Point of Interest

⊛ Capital

▲ Campground

⊤ Lighthouse

✕ Mine

🅿 Parking

▲ Peak/Elevation

🄰 Picnic Area

▦ Scenic View

🮲 Tower

o Town

➊ Trailhead

❓ Visitor/Information Center

Land Management

▭ State Park

Thousand Islands– Seaway Region

The Thousand Islands (actually more than 1,800 islands), the Saint Lawrence River Seaway, the eastern shore of Lake Ontario, and the low-lying forests west of the Adirondacks come together on the Canada border to form one of the state's most delightful regions for hiking.

The Iroquois Confederacy dubbed this place Manitouana, or "Garden of the Great Spirit," an apt name for this union of water and woods. From its shimmering blue expanses and racing waters to the seemingly boundless wilderness and recreational beaches, the Thousand Islands has something to satisfy every wanderer—even a rare "alvar" habitat, austere barrens with a peculiar linear vegetation pattern that only occurs within a small arc running from northern Michigan to this remote part of New York.

History here blends the cultures of Native Americans and French, British, and American settlers, and a number of sites capture tales of local battles in the War of 1812—some of which ended in heroic victories for American soldiers. More recent arrivals, the Amish have a handful of communities in Saint Lawrence County.

Raquette River, Stone Valley Recreation Area

Maple sugaring, a practice since colonial times, continues to be a cornerstone of the region's agricultural business each spring. The tasty products entice visitors throughout the year, often sold side by side with New York's bountiful apple harvest. Dairies, wineries, farms, ranches, and orchards complete the rural landscape.

The changeable weather associated with the Great Lakes charges the air with excitement, bringing added intensity to the region along with a long season of winter white. The notorious lake-effect snow is measured in feet, not inches. During the second and third weeks of October, autumn turns the woods amber and crimson, making fall one of the prime seasons for long woodland hikes and expansive, azure-sky views across the St. Lawrence Seaway.

1 Stone Valley

In the towns of Colton, Pierrepont, and Parishville, this moderately difficult wooded trail rounds an exciting 3.2-mile stretch of the Raquette River through a hemlock-beech forest. Gorges and scoured potholes create waterfalls, rapids, and chutes as the river rushes past islands and overhanging cliffs.

Start: At the northwest trailhead off Browns Bridge Road

Distance: 7.8-mile loop, including spur

Approximate hiking time: 4 to 5 hours

Difficulty: Moderate, with some wet or uneven footing and log crossings

Elevation change: 250 feet up and down on a rolling trail

Trail surface: Forest floor, crushed gravel, grass, some connecting road

Seasons: Open year-round, best May–Oct

Other trail users: Snowshoers, cross-country skiers, and kayakers (during specific powerhouse scheduled water releases at the dam)

Canine compatibility: Dogs allowed; leash recommended during summer high-use times

Land status: Brookfield Power, Saint Lawrence County, and the town of Colton lands, with a few private parcels on the river's east side

Nearest town: Colton

Fees and permits: None

Schedule: Open daily dawn to dusk

Map: Stone Valley Cooperative Recreation Area map: www.stlctrails.com/trails/trail/stone-valley-trail

Trail contact: Saint Lawrence County Planning Department, 48 Court St., Canton; (315) 379-2292 weekdays only; www.stlawco.org/Departments/Planning

Special considerations: There is a working dam on this site. Even during periods of low water, sudden releases from the dam can make the water rise rapidly. Stay on the trail, and don't climb out onto rocks in the river. If you hike during hunting season, wear blaze orange.

Finding the trailhead: From the intersection of NY 56 and NY 68 at the southern end of the hamlet of Colton, go north on NY 56 for 3.6 miles and turn right (east) onto Browns Bridge Road (NY 24). Go 0.5 mile and turn right to enter the northwest trailhead parking lot near the powerhouse in 0.1 mile; this site offers the best parking. Find additional access in Colton at the Raquette River bridge. GPS: 44.584117, -74.958106

The Hike

Thanks to a partnership between the Laurentian Chapter of the Adirondack Mountain Club, the St. Lawrence County Youth Conservation Corps, and landowners Brookfield Renewable Power, St. Lawrence County, and the town of Colton, the Stone Valley Cooperative Recreational Area—an obvious labor of love—provides the public with a well-maintained, clearly interpreted trail that begins with four fascinating waterfalls in under a mile. More than simple drops from one level to the next, these waterfalls feature narrow chutes, potholes that create exciting waves and rapids, and islands in the middle of the river. The surrounding hemlock, maple, and beech

Hemlock roots reach for nutrients at Stone Valley Recreation Area.

forest creates a sense of wilderness that you might not expect so close to a power plant, providing close encounters with birds, butterflies, and other wildlife and a level of silence New Yorkers find only in the north country.

Arrows, blue trail markers, red access trail markers, and small plaques explaining the geologic and cultural history of the area mark this route. The trail rounds the powerhouse site, following service roads and grassy tracks through open woods, bramble-shrub clearings, and forest plantations. Watch for deer tracks in the soft dirt, and for frogs, toads, ruby-throated hummingbirds, ruffed grouse, and other woodland critters.

There's a marker pointing you left along an old woods road after a half mile or so. The path descends and rounds toward the river, crossing a soggy drainage and some corduroy where creative stepping may be needed. At 1 mile the spur to O'Malley Brook Overlook travels a pine-maple slope, overlooking a series of beaver dams on a river tributary. Soon you reach a Raquette River overlook and beach, where you see 15-foot O'Malley Brook Falls. The side trail ends with a loop; return to the main trail.

Beyond the overlook spur, the true river hike begins, rolling along the wooded slope for a grand upstream tour. Where you first meet the tannin-darkened river, it flows broad and slow, coursing between rock and fern banks. Upstream it cuts a more volatile figure as the trail undulates between shore level and 100 feet above the stormy water. At 2 miles you'll pass a deep pool known both as Lucy's Hole and "The Gut."

A steep ascent and descent precedes The Narrows, where long bedrock fingers squeeze the water into channels of river fury. As you proceed upstream, the sights become more dramatic: 15- to 18-foot falls, tilted bedrock slabs, worn chutes, and potholes reveal the impact of centuries of rampant flow. Side drainages arrive as waterfalls, adding to the visual bonanza. Above The Tub (a 12-foot-diameter river pothole hidden here by a stone lip), the river spills in serial drops, losing 25 feet in elevation over a 100-foot distance.

As the Raquette River becomes gorge-like just before the power company dam, the trail veers away from the river, climbing above the stone ruins of a tannery. Cross the footbridge over a penstock (a water conduit) and turn left on a dirt road, entering Colton. For the loop, you will cross the road bridge over the Raquette River and take the first left, past the Colton Fire Department. The foot trail resumes at a pair of millstones. As the east-shore trail alternates between terrace slope and river level, expect some uneven footing.

The downstream return offers new perspectives on the river. You will skirt a soggy meadow bottomland that separates the path from the river. At the upcoming intersection with a woods road, turn left. Where the trail curves right to edge a bedrock slab at the river, steel anchor pins embedded in the rock recall the nineteenth century when lumberjacks floated logs on the river to downstream mills. Side trails branch right to Lenny Road.

Large potholes riddle the bedrock ridge that shapes The Tub. During spring floods, this rock transforms into a roaring cataract of churning stones. After The Narrows, the trail makes a steep uphill charge and travels the upper slope for a spell before plunging back to river level. Plaques identify marble outcrops (common in the Adirondack lowland), glacial erratics, and fossils. Past Lucy's Hole, you come to a series of deep pools, more evidence of time and rushing water in action.

After the O'Malley Brook footbridge, cross a woods flat on the dirt road to pick up the trail on the left. The trail now hugs a terrace 50 feet above the river before ending at Lenny Road. From there, you will complete the loop via road and road bridge, returning to the trailhead.

Miles and Directions

0.0 Start from the southwest corner of the northwest trailhead parking lot. Follow the marked service road south.

0.1 Turn left on the trail, finding a trail register with brochures. Sign the register.

1.0 Bear right at the trail fork and quickly turn left on the marked O'Malley Brook Overlook spur.

1.5 Return from the overlook spur to the main trail and continue the loop (turning left).

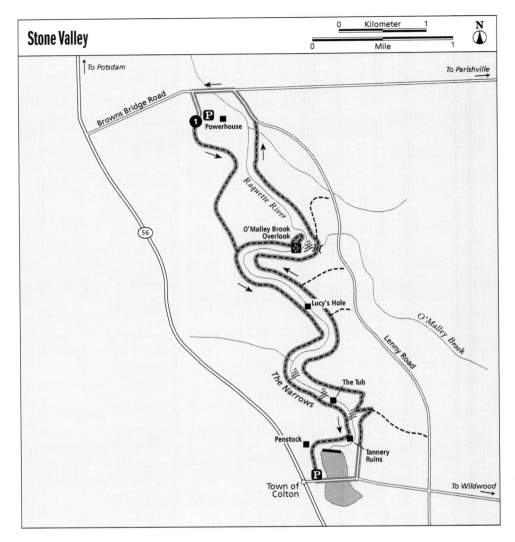

0　　　Kilometer　　　1

0　　　　　Mile　　　　1

N

To Potsdam

To Parishville

Browns Bridge Road

1　Powerhouse

Raquette River

56

O'Malley Brook
Overlook

Lucy's Hole

O'Malley Brook

Lenny Road

The Narrows

The Tub

Penstock

Tannery
Ruins

Town of
Colton

To Wildwood

2.0 Reach Lucy's Hole.

3.8 Enter Colton and turn left to cross the road bridge over the Raquette River.

4.0 Turn left on the first paved road and hike past Colton Fire Department to resume on foot trail.

6.3 Cross the O'Malley Brook footbridge.

7.1 At Lenny Road, turn left and walk to Browns Bridge Road, where you'll turn left to cross the river bridge. Turn left on the road near the powerhouse. When you reach the register, remember to sign out.

7.8 End back at the northwest trailhead.

Hike Information

Local Information

Saint Lawrence County Chamber of Commerce, 101 Main St., Canton; (315) 386-4000; www.visitstlc.com

Local Events/Attractions

Higley Flow State Park, on a fettered stretch of the Raquette River south of Colton, offers swimming, canoeing, and fishing. Higley Flow State Park, 442 Cold Brook Dr., Colton; (315) 262-2880; https://parks.ny.gov/parks/higleyflow/maps.aspx.

Colton Country Days, each July, roll out an old-fashioned frog-jumping contest, barbecue, band concert, ice cream social, and fireworks. Town of Colton, (315) 262-2810; www.townofcolton.com.

Accommodations

Higley Flow State Park campground, open Memorial Day weekend through Labor Day, has 128 campsites. Reservations: (800) 456-2267; https://newyorkstateparks.reserveamerica.com/camping/higley-flow-state-park/r/campgroundDetails.do?contractCode=NY&parkId=420.

Organizations

Laurentian Chapter of the Adirondack Mountain Club, http://adklaurentian.org

2 Inman Gulf Hiking and Nature Trails

South of Watertown, three nature and hiking trails line up end-to-end for a single south rim tour that overlooks 5 miles of Inman Gulf. This Tug Hill State Forest area wins over visitors with its ancient river drainage, sheer shale walls, a waterfall, diverse forests, wildflowers, fall foliage, and wildlife.

Start: At the west trailhead (parking area 1)

Distance: 5.5 miles one-way (11 miles round-trip, or complete as a shuttle hike by parking a second vehicle at one of the 5 parking areas along the route)

Approximate hiking time: 2.5 to 3.5 hours one-way

Difficulty: Moderate

Elevation change: The trail shows about a 200-foot elevation change.

Trail surface: Earthen path

Seasons: Spring through fall

Other trail users: Mountain bikers, hunters, snowshoers, cross-country skiers (no mountain bikers or skiers allowed on the hike's Oak Rim Trail segment)

Canine compatibility: Dogs permitted on leash (bring water for your dog)

Land status: New York State Department of Environmental Conservation (DEC), except a small private piece along the Oak Rim Trail

Nearest town: Adams Center

Fees and permits: None

Schedule: Open daily dawn to dusk

Maps: www.dec.ny.gov/docs/regions_pdf/tughill2.pdf

Trail contact: New York State DEC, Region 6, Lowville Office, 7327 State Route 812, Lowville; (315) 376-3521; www.dec.ny.gov/lands/8001.html

Special considerations: Beware of unstable crumbling shale edges; stay on the trail.

Finding the trailhead: From the intersection of NY 177 and US 11 at Adams Center south of Watertown, go east on NY 177 for 6.4 miles and turn north onto Lowe Road at Tremaines Corners. In 1.4 miles bear left and continue 0.2 mile more to Williams Road/Old State Road. Turn right (east) on Williams Road, going another 0.2 mile to reach parking area 1, with space for a half dozen vehicles. Four additional parking lots sit farther east along Williams Road, allowing you to shorten the hike's length or choose an alternate starting point. GPS: 43.83849, -75.878258

The Hike

The geologic feature of Inman Gulf extends 9.6 miles between Barnes Corners and the Sandy Creek confluence in Rodman. This west-to-east (upstream) hike along the south rim offers a restorative woods walk, with periodic overlooks of the impressive, 250-foot-deep chasm, where the Gulf Stream flows at the bottom, alternating between shimmering riffles and still, black pools. A variety of DEC trail marker disks, paint blazes, and cairns mark the route, while wooden plaques identify trailside trees. White-tailed deer, barred owl, and common raven may appear for surprise encounters.

The Oak Rim Trail launches the hike, leading you into a mixed conifer/deciduous forest. In moist pockets, dame's rocket and jewelweed replace the woods' flora in spring and summer. As the trail approaches the chasm rim, you can get a

Rich forest cloaks the steep slopes of Inman Gulf.

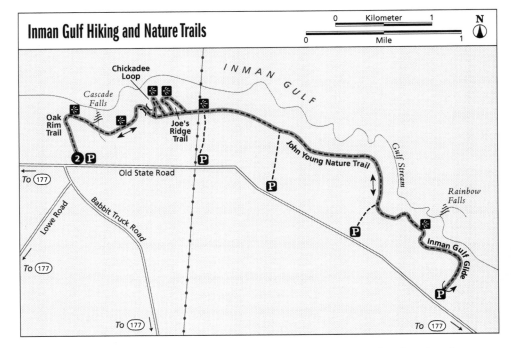

Inman Gulf Hiking and Nature Trails

quick, restricted look at Inman Gulf—but a better view lies just ahead at the view-point's bench, where you can stop to admire the best up-canyon view of the entire hike. For this banner look, the fluted cliffs and steep wooded walls of Inman Gulf meet in a V. A rim to the rear peeks through the pointed gap.

After a rock-hopping stream crossing, follow a small drainage downstream to overlook Cascade Falls, plummeting in a steep cataract over tiered rock before racing into the gulf. At an ancient red oak, a broad, tree-framed down-canyon view is sure to slow your step, especially in fall. More views across and into the twisting gulf urge you onward. Hemlocks claim the rim; oaks cling to the cliff's edge, and mixed deciduous trees fill the deep chasm.

Chickadee Loop offers a 0.2-mile side trip along a small ridge, leading to a view of a tight downstream bend and the steep shale cliff of the north wall. Where Chickadee Loop rejoins the main trail, you again have an option of either following the main trail or taking another side trip on Joe's Ridge Trail, which heads left. This 0.3-mile side loop passes through a natural mineral lick where deer commonly gather, to ascend yet another thin pull-apart ridge (perhaps isolated by the ancient Gulf Stream). This side tour likewise offers a front-row seat to Inman Gulf, while the main trail gets lost in the cheap seats.

The rim-hugging tour then resumes with stolen glances of the gulf through the hemlock boughs, and later through the branchwork of oak, beech, and aspen. Cross an open utility corridor, bypassing the side trail to Williams Road and parking area 2. Rim travel now shows gentle gradients. Depending on the season, brightly colored mushrooms and virtually colorless Indian pipe may sprinkle the forest floor.

After the John Young Nature Trail replaces the Oak Rim Trail as host, you pass through an ice-age depression formed when the Gulf Stream flowed at or near the top of the forest plateau. Gulf views become more teasing.

The Inman Gulf Glide brings home the tour. It briefly follows an overgrown woods road, crossing a drainage to return to the rim. Verdant vegetation claims the southern wall. The highlight on this stretch is the tree-framed view of Rainbow Falls, a 60- to 80-foot white veil that spills from a treed drainage on the north wall. When full, the waterfall rages.

Soon a lower terrace distances the trail from the gulf. Where the trail curves away from the gulf as it approaches parking area 5, it passes through a rather uniform plot of mature, cultivated white and red pines. The last part of this route offers no additional gulf views, so out-and-back hikers often choose to turn around here rather than proceeding all the way to the last parking area.

Miles and Directions

0.0 Start from the west trailhead (parking area 1) and follow the Oak Rim Trail into the woods.

1.4 Cross a bridge, reaching the Chickadee Loop junction. **Option:** Proceed forward on the Oak Rim Trail or turn left on Chickadee Loop, a 0.2-mile crescent-shaped side trail that returns to the Oak Rim Trail farther east.

1.5 Reach the Joe's Ridge Trail junction. **Option:** Proceed forward on Oak Rim Trail or turn left, adding a 0.3-mile side trip on Joe's Ridge Trail.

2.2 Cross a utility corridor, continuing east along the south rim. A side trail here leads right to Williams Road and parking area 2.

2.9 Continue straight on John Young Nature Trail.

3.9 Continue straight on Inman Gulf Glide.

4.4 View Rainbow Falls.

5.0 Follow the trail as it curves into a pine plantation on the way to parking area 5. **Bailout:** Out-and-back hikers may prefer to turn around here. If you've parked a second vehicle at parking lot 5, keep going.

5.5 End at the easternmost trailhead (parking area 5).

Hike Information

Local Information

The Greater Watertown North Country Chamber of Commerce, 1241 Coffeen St., Watertown; (315) 788-4400; www.watertownny.com

Local Events/Attractions

Whitewater rafting on the churning Black River in Black River Gorge is popular. Rapids bear such descriptive names as "Cruncher" and "Rocket Ride." Outfitters run the river Memorial Day through Columbus Day; May and June have the most powerful flows. Whitewater outfitters operate out of Watertown and Dexter.

3 Lakeview Natural Beach Hike

In Jefferson County, 20 miles southwest of Watertown, this hike offers a relaxing stroll along a limited-access natural barrier beach on Lake Ontario. The trail sits within 3,461-acre Lakeview Wildlife Management Area and explores a small part of the largest freshwater barrier beach in the state. Stroll along a natural white-sand beach and spit, view protected vegetated dunes, overlook Floodwood Pond, and spot a wide variety of migrating seabirds and shorebirds in spring and fall.

Start: At beach parking, Southwick Beach State Park
Distance: 6.5 miles out-and-back
Approximate hiking time: 3 to 4 hours
Difficulty: Easy
Elevation change: None
Trail surface: Sand
Seasons: Open year-round, with the best hiking spring through fall
Other trail users: Birders, fishers, inland hunters
Canine compatibility: Dogs permitted on leash. When entering through the state park, your dog must be leashed and you must have proof of your dog's rabies shots or a current dated collar tag.
Land status: New York State Park and NY Department of Environmental Conservation (DEC)
Nearest town: Henderson
Fees and permits: Access to the Natural Beach hike is via Southwick Beach State Park, a fee area.

Schedule: Lakeview WMA is open year-round, dawn to dusk. Southwick Beach State Park is open early May through Indigenous Peoples' Day in October. When the park is gated, access is walk-in only; do not block the entry when parking.
Map: www.dec.ny.gov/docs/wildlife_pdf/lakeviewmap.pdf
Trail contacts: New York State DEC, Region 6, 317 Washington St., Watertown; (315) 785-2263; www.dec.ny.gov/outdoor/9328.html Southwick Beach State Park, 8119 Southwicks Place, Henderson; (315) 846-5338; https://parks.ny.gov/parks/36/
Special considerations: This is a natural beach, not a bathing beach, so you may not swim, picnic, camp, build fires, or play radios. To protect the fragile dunes, cross only at the designated elevated boardwalks. Heed all posted rules for both the beach and the state park. Deer and waterfowl hunting occur inland in season; if you hike during these seasons, wear blaze-orange clothing.

Finding the trailhead: From I-81 south of Watertown, take exit 40 and head west on NY 193 for 8.3 miles to the Southwick Beach State Park entrance. For a beach hike alone—and better parking—start at the state park's beach parking lot. For an inland start, follow the nature trail that heads south at the Southwick Beach entrance station. GPS: 43.764641, -76.214639

The Hike

An ideal hike for exercise walking, daydreaming, and nature study, this beach route travels the northern 3-mile spit of Lakeview Wildlife Management Area (WMA). The more remote southern spit is inaccessible, save by boat. This hike begins in Southwick

The tranquil shore meets Lake Ontario along Lakeview Wildlife Beach.

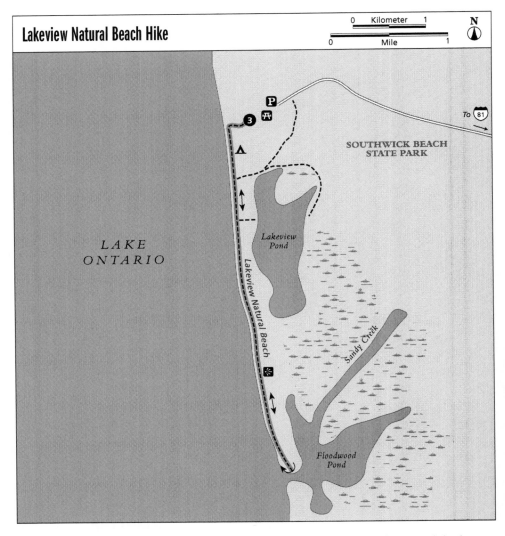

0   Kilometer   1

0   Mile   1

N

To 81

SOUTHWICK BEACH
STATE PARK

P
3

*LAKE
ONTARIO*

*Lakeview
Pond*

Lakeview Natural Beach

Sandy Creek

*Floodwood
Pond*

Beach State Park, known in its 1920s heyday as a bustling recreational area with bath-houses, a midway, a dance hall, a roller coaster, and a ballfield. Now, a much quieter developed beach for swimming and sunbathing abuts the WMA's natural spit.

The compressed, fine-grained sandy beach beckons, its sands embellished by wave-deposited lines of duckweed and tiny mussel shells. In early morning the cottonwood trees shading the park campground above the beach toss long shadows across the sand. Walkers soon see signs indicating where the developed beach ends and the Lakeview WMA natural beach begins. A low berm or flattish dune now backs the strand, but cottonwoods still claim the back swale.

The first boardwalk over the dune marks the entrance to the Lake Ontario Dune Trail. This nature trail offers an alternative start (or ending) for this hike; it begins near the park entrance station, passing among hardwoods. A second trail arrives from the east and merges with the nature trail before it reaches the beach. That trail begins at the Lakeview Pond trailhead off Pierrepont Place (west off NY 3, south of Southwick Beach State Park). It provides yet another start option for this hike and a good option in the off-season.

The rhythmic lapping and tranquil blue of the lake provide a soothing backdrop in clear weather, but storms rolling in across Lake Ontario churn out a more exciting scene. Across the broad blue expanse, a power plant spews steam. Makeshift wind shelters may dot the beach.

A second walkover leads to Lakeview Pond, and later an elevated platform lifts you above the thicket to view the Sandy Creek wetland. The WMA's Sandy and South Sandy Creeks support steelhead trout and Chinook salmon, making this a popular place for anglers. White-tailed deer, red fox, and beaver are possible inland wildlife sightings.

Along the beach, herring and ring-billed gulls bob in the shallows and race along the strand, as common and Caspian terns cut and dive into the water after silvery fish. Spring and fall migration can bring a wide variety of shorebirds, while overwintering ducks can include bufflehead, common goldeneye, hooded, and red-breasted merganser, and long-tailed duck. Eventually the dunes grade higher into humps stabilized by trees and vegetation. Some of the dunes get to be 30 feet high, but there is little loose sand except on the low seaward brow and between the discrete bunches of dune grass. At times small yellow beetles cling to everything, including anyone who lingers too long.

The river outlet of Floodwood Pond signals the end for northern spit travel. Across the outlet stretches the inaccessible southern spit. Driftwood-strewn sands and beachgoing red-winged blackbirds precede the outlet. Among the gray, weathered driftwood, you may discover tiny cottonwoods taking root or the dizzying tracks of shorebirds. By following the outlet upstream, you can return the way you came, or extend the hike as far as the mouth of Floodwood Pond, though large beds of reeds shape pond viewing.

Miles and Directions

0.0 Start at beach parking for Southwick Beach State Park. Hike south on the beach from the bathhouse/concession building.

0.2 Enter the Natural Beach area. Continue south on the beach spit.

0.5 The nature trail arrives from dunes via boardwalk.

1.0 Reach the walkover to Lakeview Pond.

2.4 Reach the elevated viewing platform at Sandy Creek wetland.

3.2 Reach the Floodwood Pond outlet. Backtrack north to beach parking.

6.5 End back at Southwick Beach State Park.

Options

For this hike, you may choose instead to start on the nature trail, which begins near the state park entrance station. Follow the path south, passing in turn an abandoned orchard, some impressive beech trees within a hardwood grove, and a small waterfall at the Filmore Brook crossing. An access path from the Lakeview Pond area arrives on the left, before the hike turns right (west) to arrive at the beach via a boardwalk. Stay on the boardwalk to protect sensitive dune habitat. The nature trail joins the beach hike at the 0.5-mile mark. Before starting out on the nature trail, it's a good idea to ask rangers about the trail's condition. You will want to watch out for poison ivy, especially when hiking with little ones. Similarly, the nature trail can vary the hike's return.

Additional trails explore the inland area of the WMA, including a 3,800-foot trail to a South Sandy Creek viewing platform. Reach WMA parking areas and a kiosk along NY 3 south of the state park; review the WMA map on the DEC web page.

Hike Information

Local Information

The Greater Watertown North Country Chamber of Commerce, 1241 Coffeen St., Watertown; (315) 788-4400; www.watertownny.com

Local Events/Attractions

You'll find swimming and sunbathing on the adjacent beach of **Southwick Beach State Park.** Southwick Beach State Park, 8119 Southwicks Place, Henderson; (315) 846-5338; https://parks.ny.gov/parks/36/.

The 454-mile Great Lakes **Seaway Trail National (and New York State) Scenic Byway** follows the shores of Lakes Ontario and Erie and the Niagara and Saint Lawrence Rivers before drifting into Pennsylvania. The drive passes museums, historic sites, Niagara Falls, lighthouses, trails, natural and recreation areas, farm markets, and wineries. In the hike's vicinity, it follows NY 3. Visit www.discoverupstateny.com/visit-regions/seaway-trail/, or for a detailed pictorial description of the entire route, see Randi Minetor's book *Scenic Driving New York*, available from Globe Pequot.

Accommodations

Southwick Beach State Park campground, open early May through Indigenous Peoples' Day, has one hundred sites. Reservations: (800) 456-2267; https://newyork stateparks.reserveamerica.com.

Honorable Mentions

A Wellesley Island State Park

Wellesley Island State Park serves as a splendid introduction to the beauty of the Thousand Islands. Reclaimed from its days as farmland, this island now showcases mixed deciduous woods, abandoned field and pasture, rocky shores, and hilltop knolls. Panoramic views take in the Saint Lawrence River, Thousand Islands, and Canadian shore. In the southwestern portion of the park, a 600-acre peninsula and nature preserve hold 8 miles of interlocking trails that welcome short excursions. The easy 4-mile Round-the-Peninsula Trail stitches together several of the named paths for a first-rate tour of the island, its terrain, and locale. Begin at the Minna Anthony Common Nature Center, where maps and brochures are available. The trails are open during daylight hours, and park fees are required.

From Watertown, go north on I-81 for 26 miles, and take exit 51 for Wellesley Island State Park (after the Thousand Islands Toll Bridge). Following signs, turn right in 0.1 mile, and again turn right onto NY 100 in another 0.5 mile. Go 0.5 mile more and turn right onto Cross Island Road. The park entrance is in 1.6 miles. Follow the signs to the nature center and trails. GPS: 44.316555, -76.020454. For information, contact Wellesley Island State Park, 44927 Cross Island Road, Fineview; (315) 482-2722; https://parks.ny.gov/parks/wellesleyisland/details.aspx.

Shoreline oak overlooks the Saint Lawrence River.

B Chaumont Barrens Preserve

Because of its rare and sensitive nature, we have classified this Nature Conservancy preserve northwest of Watertown as an honorable mention, but the natural offering is without peer. Here you will discover a rare alvar landscape, where the austere barrens show an unusual but naturally occurring linear vegetation scheme. Intense glaciation, recurring cycles of flood and drought, and strong winds have shaped this severe landscape of limestone bedrock fissures, marine fossils, rare native grasslands, rubbly moss gardens, and shrub savannas. Only a fistful of alvar sites exist in all of North America. They occupy an arc from northwest Jefferson County in New York through Ontario, Canada, into northern Michigan.

An easy 2-mile self-guided loop examines the mystery and beauty of this globally significant habitat. Keep to the trail, using stepping stones where available, and beware of cracks, fissures, and hidden holes. Leave pets at home, and obey The Nature Conservancy's (TNC's) rules and closures that protect this fragile treasure. Summer temperatures can be hot, so carry water. The trail is usually open from early May through mid-fall from dawn to dusk, but the exact dates depend on the area's flooding cycle.

From I-81 at Watertown, take exit 46/Coffeen Street and follow NY 12F west for 2 miles. Turn right (north) on Paddy Hill Road/NY 12E, crossing over the river. Turn left to stay on NY 12E all the way to the village of Chaumont (8.4 miles from the NY 12F junction). In Chaumont take the first right on Morris Track Road/NY 125; go 3 miles and turn left on unsigned Van Alstyne Road, just beyond a small cemetery on the right. A board with an arrow indicating Chaumont Barrens points out the turn. The preserve entrance and parking are on the left in 1.1 miles; closures are posted at the parking lot. GPS: 44.101530, -76.074050. For information, contact The Nature Conservancy, Central and Western New York Office, 274 North Goodman St., Suite B261, Rochester; (585) 546-8030; www.nature.org/en-us/about-us/where-we-work/united-states/new-york/.

The Adirondacks

Carefully preserved for its scenic value as well as its many benefits to the state's environment, New York's Adirondack range holds a distinctive place among the nation's many mountainous regions. These mountains form a circular dome 160 miles across and a mile high, shaped over the course of 5 million years—but the rocks that compose these peaks are more than 1,000 million years old, making them some of the oldest mountains on the continent. The Adirondacks remained largely untouched by human endeavor until the whole-sale harvest of white pine and eastern hemlock by the construction and paper industries from 1870 to 1890, denuding the mountainsides and spurring erosion and other destructive forces. When local residents, politicians, and industry worked together to protect 6 million acres of mountains and forests by creating Adirondack Park, they legislated that no more land within the "Blue Line" around the park could be sold or leased. State-owned land within the boundary will be protected in perpetuity, keeping millions of acres of wilderness from being logged or mined to the point of becoming an eroded wasteland.

Situated at the transition zone between the eastern deciduous and boreal forest ecosystems, the Adirondacks play host to a rich assortment of flora and fauna.

Sugar maples lift leaves skyward along Blue Mountain Trail.

Sphagnum bogs, river floodplains, spruce wetlands, agricultural lands, hardwood and conifer forests, and exposed rock realms invite a wide variety of plants, birds, and animals. The region's careful protection has kept its inventory of native plant and animal species mostly intact, even as climate change warms the area for longer periods in spring and fall.

For seekers of chiseled mountains, remote wooded valleys, crystalline streams, enticing lakes, and expansive views, the Adirondacks fulfill the quest, providing a much sought-after outlet for challenge and adventure, renewal and escape. Two visitor information centers—one at Paul Smiths, the other at Newcomb—can help launch you on your way.

The High Peaks Region, which includes all peaks over 4,000 feet in elevation, receives the greatest amount of boot traffic, but superb trails explore the entire region. Venture to pristine lakes for fishing or swimming, or seek out streams, cascades, and waterfalls. Wildflower-dotted beaver meadows, whisper-quiet forests, and thrilling promontories with panoramic views of the lake-and-forest tapestry provide something for hikers at every level. Plus, the region produces one of the showiest fall color changes you'll find anywhere.

4 Jenkins Mountain Hike

Paul Smiths Visitor Interpretive Center (VICs), on the campus of Paul Smiths College/The College of the Adirondacks, provides some of the area's finest nature trails. The Jenkins Mountain Hike is the longest of these, and it explores forest, glade, and glacial drift before reaching a summit vista. If your time is short or if you wish to extend your visit, more than ten nature trails at the VIC introduce hikers to mixed forests, meadow openings, and a beaver pond.

Start: At the entrance road to Paul Smiths VIC

Distance: 8.2 miles out-and-back for the shortest, most direct route (Logger's Loop to blue-blazed Jenkins Mountain Trail)

Approximate hiking time: 4 to 5.5 hours

Difficulty: Strenuous

Elevation change: The trail climbs 800 feet to a summit elevation of 2,477 feet.

Trail surface: Service road and rocky or earthen path

Seasons: Open year-round; hiking is best in spring, summer, and fall

Other trail users: Snowshoers, cross-country skiers, birders

Canine compatibility: Leashed dogs permitted (clean up after pet), no dogs in winter

Land status: Paul Smiths College

Nearest town: Saranac Lake

Fees and permits: Trail fees required in winter.

Schedule: Building hours: 9 a.m. to 5 p.m. daily, except Thanksgiving and Christmas. Trails: daylight hours.

Map: www.adirondackvic.org/TrailMap.html

Trail contact: Paul Smiths VIC, 8023 Highway 30, Paul Smiths; (518) 327-6241; www.paul smithsvic.org

Special considerations: There is no camping on VIC land. The lean-tos on the property are day-use-only facilities. There is no bait fishing on VIC waters. Pack in, pack out.

Finding the trailhead: From the NY 30/I-86 junction at Paul Smiths (26 miles north of the hamlet of Tupper Lake, 13 miles west of Saranac Lake), go north on NY 30 for 0.9 mile and turn left (west) to enter the VIC. GPS: 44.449777, -74.259543

The Hike

Paul Smiths VIC boasts a fine collection of nature trails, but for those with an appetite for greater challenge and a quest to get above it all, the site's Jenkins Mountain may best fill your time. Uphill from the parking lots, this straightforward hike to the summit follows the gated service road, which becomes Logger's Loop, west off the VIC entrance road for just under 2 miles. The road offers a good walking surface and mild grade. Maple, beech, birch, and the occasional conifer shape a partial canopy. Hobblebush and brambles claim the road shoulder.

Locator boards for cross-country skiers and 0.5-mile incremental markers may assist you in tracking your progress. Where the route crosses over Barnum Brook, you'll spy the snag-pierced marsh to your right. The path heading left along the

Jenkins Mountain delivers sweeping Adirondack views.

brook's west shore leads to Barnum Brook Trail; keep to the service road. After meeting the red Fox Run Trail, follow the blue blazes for the site's Jenkins Mountain Trail.

Past a privy, the hike's foot trail section begins. It traverses a glacial-drift ridge that parts a fern glade from a beaver pond. Beech, maple, and birch clad the ridge. A beaver lodge, a neatly constructed beaver dam, and the north summit of Jenkins Mountain can contribute to views.

Round the point of the glade and continue advancing along and over similar low glacial ridges. Sarsaparilla, fern, and club moss accent the rock-studded forest floor. A few black-cherry trees appear in the forest ranks. After crossing a small drainage, the trail enters a long straightaway at the base of Jenkins Mountain. Deer, songbirds, woodpeckers, and toads the size of fingertips can stall your pace for a closer investigation.

Setting up for the final mile, the trail ascends fairly steeply and then enters a switchback between boulders and outcrop ledges. Where the trail hugs the line of Jenkins Mountain Ridge, the grade moderates. Stepping stones may assist your footing in a small jewelweed meadow.

Just beyond the 4-mile marker, you reach the summit. The summit outcrop presents a 180-degree southwest panorama, with tower-topped Saint Regis Mountain claiming center stage. The Adirondack High Peaks, Long and Black Ponds in the valley bottom, and a rolling wooded expanse complete the view. Fog may lift from the ponds and paint the drainages between the mountains. The return is as you came.

Miles and Directions

0.0 Start from the VIC entrance road and head west on the service road (what becomes Logger's Loop). (**Option:** Hikers may alternately start on the Barnum Brook nature trail, and from the Barnum Brook Trail follow the blue blazes for the Jenkins Mountain Trail, bypassing a big chunk of service road travel, for a 9 mile out-and-back hike to the summit.)

0.4 Cross Barnum Brook.

1.6 Reach a trail junction and continue forward on Jenkins Mountain Road. ***Note:*** The Long Pond Trail (green) heads left here to Long and Black Ponds.

1.8 Foot trail replaces road.

4.1 Reach the summit outcrop. Return by same route.

8.2 End back at the trailhead.

Options

The **VIC nature trails** offer alternative or additional hiking through mature mixed forest, pine forest, and wetland habitats. The trails range between 0.5 mile and 4.5 miles in length. The 1-mile Barnum Brook Trail starts at the entry trailhead, while the 3-mile Heron Marsh Trail starts out the visitor center's back door and visits Shingle Mill Falls.

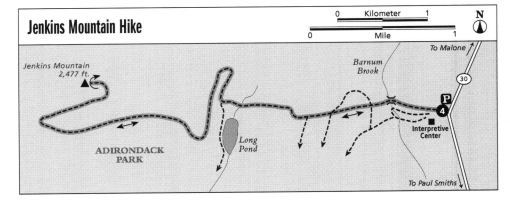

The **Barnum Brook Trail** travels a wide gravel-based trail (accessible by wheel-chair) and a handsome boardwalk and bridge spanning the tea-colored water of Barnum Brook. Enfolding the trail is a stunning woods of big pines, maple, beech, birch, black cherry, red spruce, and balsam fir. Trail observation decks overlooking Heron Marsh, Barnum Brook's mirror-black outlet pool, and a beaver lodge will win you over.

The **Heron Marsh Trail** tours along the shore of extensive Heron Marsh. Side loops and spurs lead to marsh vantages and an observation platform. Birders will want a scope, binoculars, and field guide to fully enjoy this hike. Bittern, great blue herons and green herons, osprey, and many species of ducks may be visible, depending on the season. This loop also accesses Shingle Mill Falls. Spilling over a natural bedrock sill, the falls powered mills for early settlers. Mature mixed conifers and young deciduous woods fill out the tour.

Hike Information

Local Information

Saranac Lake Area Chamber of Commerce, 39 Main St., Saranac Lake; (518) 891-1990; www.slareachamber.org

Local Events/Attractions

The Wild Center, the natural history center of the Adirondacks, offers outdoor trails through 31 acres of forest, as well as exhibit halls with live animals and fish, and a panoramic indoor theater. 45 Museum Dr., Tupper Lake; (518) 359-7800; www .wildcenter.org.

Accommodations

Meacham Lake (Department of Environmental Conservation) Campground, about 10 miles north on NY 30, is open from mid-May through Indigenous Peoples' Day in October and has 224 sites. Reservations: (800) 456-2267; https://newyorkstate parks.reserveamerica.com/camping/meacham-lake-campground/.

5 Poke-O-Moonshine Trail

This short, straightforward hike climbs an eastern Adirondack peak, passing through mixed woods and topping outcrops before reaching the rocky summit and a 1917 fire tower that's on the National Historic Lookout Register. Granite-gneiss cliffs, mixed forest, a lean-to, and the elevated tower view of the Lake Champlain–High Peaks neighborhood urge hikers skyward. Peregrine falcons judge the peak's cliffs wild enough for nesting.

Start: At the northern trailhead of the Ranger Trail
Distance: 2.4 miles out-and-back
Approximate hiking time: 1.5 to 2 hours
Difficulty: Moderate due to terrain and steep gradient
Elevation change: The trail ascends 1,300 feet to a summit elevation of 2,180 feet.
Trail surface: Rocky or earthen path
Seasons: Best for hiking late spring through fall
Other trail users: Rock climbers, hunters
Canine compatibility: Dogs permitted on leash
Land status: New York State Department of Environmental Conservation (DEC)
Nearest town: Keeseville
Fees and permits: None

Schedule: No time restrictions
Map: http://cnyhiking.com/Poke-O-Moonshine.htm
Trail contact: New York State DEC, Region 5, 1115 NY 86, Ray Brook; (518) 897-1200; www.dec.ny.gov/lands/106486.html
Special considerations: Peregrine falcons nest on the mountain cliffs. During nesting season (Apr 1 through mid-July), hikers should pass respectfully, opting for the Observers' Trail. This trail begins about a mile south on US 9 for a 5-mile out-and-back hike. Also, climbers may not have access to all routes. Peregrines are territorial and will defend nests, even against humans. Check at trailheads about which climbs may be closed.

Finding the trailhead: From the junction of NY 9N and US 9/NY 22 in Keeseville, go south on US 9 for 7.2 miles, turning right (west) to enter Poke-O-Moonshine Day-Use Area to access the northern trailhead. From I-87, take exit 33 and go south on US 9 for 3.1 miles to reach the northern trailhead. GPS: 44.401886, -73.502910

The Hike

This sometimes steep, eroded trail scales the wooded flank of Poke-O-Moonshine Mountain, which owes its peculiar name to a dichotomous profile of fractured cliff and summit rock slabs. To the Algonquin Indians, these features suggested a descriptive name, combining the words *pohqui*, meaning "broken," and *moosie*, meaning "smooth." Through the passage of time and the inexperienced ear of the white settlers, the Algonquin name eventually corrupted into "Poke-O-Moonshine."

The trail charges steeply up the slope cloaked in sugar maple, birch, and beech. Oaks, rare interlopers in the Adirondacks, rise among the bigger trees. The side trails of climbers branch off to round below the cliffs to the right. Sarsaparilla and ferns

Poke-O-Moonshine Lookout keeps history alive.

dot the rock-studded forest floor. Although boots have broadened the trail, the slope retains its soil, which is not always the case in this region.

The trail veers left at the base of a cliff to top a ledge for an early view of the highway corridor below and the ridges stretching east to Vermont. White pine, hemlock, striped maple, and oak prefer these rockier reaches. A madrigal of bird whistles, pipes, and caws competes with the drone of wheels on the roadway.

Where the trail moves inland from the edge of the cliff, so should you. The effects of weathering combined with the canted surface could cause you to lose your footing. Soon the trail narrows and the grade moderates, following a drainage crowded with nettles, trillium, and red-flowering raspberry. As the drainage steepens, so does the trail.

In a saddle clearing, a rock fireplace and old foundation hint at the onetime lookout cabin. If you skirt the site to the left, you will reach the current overnight lean-to and privy. The trail to the fire tower bears right at the cabin ruins to ascend an eroded, spring-soaked slope. The south trail, the Observers' Trail, meets up near the cabin ruins and shares the final leg to the summit.

Just above the saddle, you come upon a bald outcrop sloping up to the left. This affords fine views of ski-run-streaked Whiteface Mountain, as well as a ragged skyline of rounded and conical peaks. If you are staying overnight at the lean-to, this outcrop is ideal for stargazing, especially during the annual Perseid meteor showers, which peak around August 11 or 12.

BUILT FOR SPEED

The peregrine falcon, a high-nesting hunter built for speed, is an endangered species protected under federal and New York State law. The peregrine falcon population was nearly wiped out by DDT, and by the 1960s there were no breeding pairs left in the state. Reintroduction and natural reproduction have returned these birds to the New York skies, with at least seventy-seven pairs breeding across the state.

New York City, with its human-made high-rise structures, is one of the other major peregrine nesting areas in the state, along with cityscapes in Rochester and Buffalo, state parks in the Capital District, and just about every bridge across the Hudson River. Adults weigh about 2 pounds, with adult males being one-third smaller than their female counterparts. The sharp-eyed birds can plunge at speeds of 200 miles per hour, snapping up their feathered prey midflight. When not in diving descent, the 15- to 20-inch birds are recognized by their wingspan of more than 3 feet, dark wings, barred underparts, a dark face with yellow-ringed eyes, and sharp talons at the ends of yellow feet.

In the Adirondacks, nesting peregrines are found at such sites as Chapel Pond and Whiteface. The peregrine nest, or scrape, is a shallow gravel depression on a suitable high ledge, where three to five eggs are laid. Incubation lasts about one month, and chicks remain at the nest until they fledge about forty-five days later.

Additional outcrops follow, but they neither improve upon nor significantly alter the view. The trail advances in upward spurts. Where it tops out, follow the ridge to the right. Cut through a corridor of low-stature white birch and striped maple before emerging on the summit outcrop near the fire tower, which shoots up five flights.

Adopted by the Protect the Adirondacks group and jointly rehabilitated by volunteers and the DEC, the tower welcomes visitors to climb to its lookout cab. The joint endeavor preserved both the landmark and its fine elevated vantage point. Within the tower cab, locator boards identify key features in the panoramic view: Lake Champlain, Burlington, Vermont, and the Vermont mountains in the east. Volunteer stewards staff the tower in summer.

The bald summit knob serves vista seekers as well. From here, the long, shimmering platter and dark-treed islands of Lake Champlain dominate the view to the east-northeast; Whiteface Mountain rises to the west. Smaller lakes, rural flats, and the ridge and cliffs of Poke-O-Moonshine Mountain complete the panorama. Lichen and mineral leaching streak the cliffs green, orange, and black. Mountain ash grows below the summit. When you are ready to surrender the mountaintop, the return is as you came.

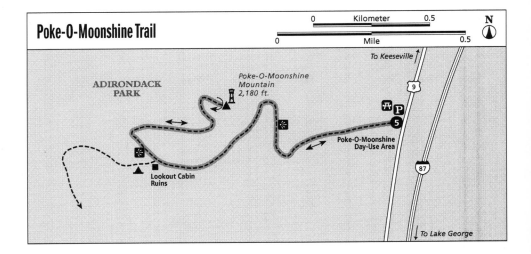

Poke-O-Moonshine Trail

Miles and Directions

0.0 Start at the northern trailhead. Ascend the forest slope.

0.7 Pass the ruins of the onetime lookout cabin.

1.2 Reach the summit tower and turn around.

2.4 End back at the trailhead.

Options

For an alternative, longer hike (5 miles out-and-back), start at the southern trailhead, the **Observers' Trail.** It offers a more graduated ascent before meeting up near the cabin ruins. The trail begins west off US 9, a mile farther south. GPS: 44.389226, –73.507429

Hike Information

Local Information

Lake Champlain Region, 814 Bridge Rd., Crown Point; (518) 597-4649; www.lake champlainregion.com

Local Events/Attractions

Noblewood Park, a 63-acre park and nature preserve on Lake Champlain where the Boquet River empties into the lake, offers nature trails, 3,500 feet of sandy beach, 2,500 feet of river frontage, large wetlands, and nesting falcons, all near a virgin forest. Park entrance is off NY 22 (east of Poke-O-Moonshine). Noblewood Park, Willsboro; www.townofwillsboro.com/noblewood-park.html.

Ausable Chasm, 12 miles south of Plattsburgh on US 9 (exit 34 off I-87), offers night lantern tours, boat tours, rafting, tubing, camping, and nature trails among massive 500-million-year-old stone formations. Tours take place daily from mid-May through Indigenous Peoples' Day from early morning until 4 p.m.; the full site is open year-round for hiking. Ausable Chasm, 2144 US 9, Ausable Chasm; (518) 834-7454; www.ausablechasm.com.

Organizations

Adirondack Mountain Club, 1002 Adirondack Loj Rd., Lake Placid; (518) 523-3441; https://adk.org

6 High Falls Loop

This clockwise loop into Five Ponds Wilderness in the Cranberry Lake Region traverses a diverse area of marsh, hardwood forests, conifers, and blowdown, visiting the Dead Creek Flow of Cranberry Lake, High Falls, and the Oswegatchie River drainage. The blowdown is the legacy of the great windstorm of 1995, but the new forest is rapidly returning and is like a thicket in places. Wildflowers, wildlife, or a burst of fall color can enhance the journey.

Start: At the eastern trailhead (the Plains Trail)
Distance: 16.8-mile loop, with spurs to overnight shelters
Approximate hiking time: 9 to 11 hours, but you'll move faster when the blackflies are out
Difficulty: Strenuous
Elevation change: The trail has a 200-foot elevation change.
Trail surface: Levee, foot trail, old truck grade, and beaver bypasses and dams
Seasons: Open year-round, but late summer and fall are best for hiking
Other trail users: Hunters, snowshoers, cross-country skiers
Canine compatibility: Dogs permitted on leash
Land status: New York State Department of Environmental Conservation (DEC)
Nearest town: Star Lake

Fees and permits: None
Schedule: No time restrictions
Maps: www.dec.ny.gov/docs/lands_forests_pdf/mapfivepondswild.pdf
Trail contact: New York State DEC, Region 6, Potsdam Office, 190 Outer Main St., Suite 103, Potsdam; (315) 265-3090; www.dec.ny.gov/lands/34719.html
Special considerations: Come prepared for biting insects; netting and repellent are recommended. Avoid after heavy rains or during high water. You will find pit toilets at the overnight shelter sites at Janack's Landing and High Falls. Designated campsites also serve the route. There is no camping within 150 feet of any road, trail, or water, except at the designated sites. The usual DEC rules for camping and permits are enforced.

Finding the trailhead: From the junction of NY 3 and CR 61 (the Wanakena turnoff), 8 miles west of Cranberry Lake and 6 miles east of Star Lake, turn south on CR 61 and proceed 1 mile, twice keeping right to cross the Oswegatchie River bridge. Continue east on South Shore Road. You will locate the western trailhead (the High Falls Truck Trail) on a southbound dead-end road in 0.1 mile, its trail parking next to tennis courts in another 0.1 mile, and the eastern trailhead (Plains Trail) 0.4 mile farther. GPS: 44.133415, -74.915139

The Hike

For a clockwise loop, follow the Plains Trail as it traces a former logging railroad grade, which later narrows. Young forest frames the route, along with wind-snapped trees. Ahead where the trail parts a beaver marsh, wet spots may require a hop across or navigating via married logs. The snag skyline, blackwater reflections, and clumps of greenery add to viewing; listen for much lively birdsong in the abundant trees.

Dead Creek hosts enchanted woods along High Falls Loop.

A rich, shady cathedral of maples edges Dead Creek Flow—part of Cranberry Lake—and open-water views alternate with treed buffers. You may spot a common loon or great blue heron visiting the creek bed. Although the scenery suggests a leisurely Sunday pace, the mosquitoes may call for double time. Spans over the inlet flows keep feet dry, except where beaver-raised waters overflow the log passages.

If taking the detour to Janack's Landing, a rustic boardwalk and trail lead to the landing, its engaging lake view, and its overnight shelter on the peninsular knoll. Here lady's slippers decorate the forest floor in season. From the landing trail junction, the loop gradually ascends, passing within a mixed-age woodland of maple, cherry, and birch. Where the trail to Cat Mountain heads left, continue following the loop on your way to High Falls.

A vast zone of blowdown rubble next claims the loop. Although the trail itself is clear, you have to marvel at the power of the microburst

In the summer of 2006, the DEC completed the trail between West Inlet and Dead Flow, the final link in the long-distance trail encircling Cranberry Lake—a hike of more than 50 miles. Here the loop arcs right and eases down to the Glasby Creek crossing, an area of scenic cascades and beaver-broadened segments. The trail traces the lake's east shore in an easy-to-follow bypass along the base of Threemile Mountain, but this section can be hot and humid, with an open skyline, snags, thick shrubs, and briars. Continue downstream.

Lady slipper graces the forest floor in Adirondack Park.

that took place here in 1995. Cross the disrupted area until you reach High Falls junction, then head left to visit High Falls, a 20-foot-tall cascade near the head of the Oswegatchie River. The tannin-colored water spills between and over the bulging and sloped outcrops of pink granite, streaked by varnish and mottled by lichen. Away from the riotous falls stretches a tranquil river; there's a shelter back in the woods.

Resume the loop and follow the High Falls Truck Trail, passing through scenic woods of white pine and mixed hardwoods before entering a tamarack-pine area and, later, a grassy meadow. Glasby Creek threads through the meadow to a plank bridge that crosses the stream. The setting continues to change as you follow the Oswegatchie River downstream, with more overlooks and fine scenery.

The levee parts two more beaver ponds, but generally the old route allows fast, dry travel. Where the blue-marked Sand Lake Trail heads left, remain on High Falls Truck Trail. Red disks, some faded or decayed into remnants, may help mark the primary route. More levee and beaver sites follow, as well as designated campsites where the trail overlooks a horseshoe bend on the Oswegatchie.

The red DEC markers make a more regular appearance as the truck route passes through a recovering forest habitat. In another mile or so, you'll cross an old stone bridge; it sits at a canted-bedrock waterfall on an Oswegatchie tributary. At the truck-trail junction beyond the stone bridge, keep right for the red-marked loop.

As the hike completes its passage along the vast Oswegatchie River marsh, it skirts High Rock. The grade then trends northward, crossing a pair of brooks and slow-moving Skate Creek to emerge at the barrier and register for the western trailhead. From here, return to South Shore Road and follow it east to end back at the Plains Trail parking.

Miles and Directions

0.0 Start from the eastern trailhead and follow the Plains Trail into forest.

3.1 Reach the Janack's Landing junction and proceed forward for loop. **Option:** A 0.2-mile detour left leads to the grassy point of Janack's Landing and its overnight shelter.

4.0 Reach the Cat Mountain junction. Follow the red-marked loop as it arcs right.

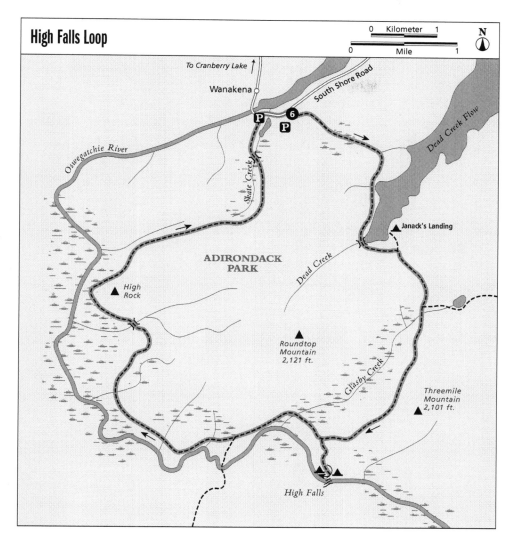

6.6 Reach the High Falls junction. Hike left to visit the falls, and keep left (upstream) at the fork.

7.0 Reach High Falls. Backtrack to the loop and turn left on High Falls Truck Trail.

8.4 Reach the Sand Lake Trail junction. Proceed forward, remaining on High Falls Truck Trail.

11.8 Cross an old stone bridge.

12.2 Reach a truck-trail junction. Keep right for the red-marked loop.

16.2 Reach the barrier/western trailhead. Round the gate and hike north to South Shore Road.

16.3 Reach South Shore Road; turn right (east) and follow the road back to your vehicle.

16.8 End at the eastern trailhead.

HUNTING SEASON

Hunting is a popular sport in the United States, especially during rifle season in October and November. You can still hike in these months in many areas, but take a few precautions:

- Learn when the different hunting seasons start and end in the area in which you'll be hiking.
- During these seasons, be sure to wear at least a blaze-orange hat, and possibly put an orange vest over your pack.
- Don't be surprised to see hunters in camo outfits carrying bows or muzzle-loading rifles in-season.
- If you feel more comfortable hiking without hunters around, choose state and local parks where hunting is not allowed.

Hike Information

Local Information

Saint Lawrence County Chamber of Commerce, 101 Main St., Canton; (315) 386-4000; www.visitstlc.com

Local Events/Attractions

Boating and trout fishing are popular on **Cranberry Lake,** a prized water source tucked in a 50,000-acre wilderness webbed by trails. Drive the area's roads to see some of the most spectacular fall foliage in the Northeast; contact Saint Lawrence County Chamber of Commerce, or pick up Randi Minetor's book *Scenic Driving New York*, which provides detailed directions and route descriptions.

Accommodations

Cranberry Lake (DEC) Campground, 230 Lone Pine Rd., off NY 3 in Cranberry Lake Village, is open mid-May through mid-October and has 173 sites. For information: (315) 848-2315 or www.dec.ny.gov/outdoor/24460.html. Reservations: www.reserveamerica.com.

Organizations

Adirondack Mountain Club, 1002 Adirondack Loj Rd., Lake Placid; (518) 523-3441; https://adk.org

7 Mount Marcy via Van Hoevenberg Trail

In the High Peaks Region, this demanding all-day or overnight hike arrives from the north and offers the shortest approach to Mount Marcy—the highest point in New York State (5,344 feet). The first recorded ascent came in 1837, and a continuous stream of feet has followed. To the native Iroquois Confederacy, the mountain was known as Tahawus, or "Cloud Splitter," an apt name. Completing this challenge brings a well-earned reward: one of the finest, sweeping High Peaks panoramas in the Adirondacks. Rare arctic-alpine habitat, abundant wildlife, and scenic brooks make the reward even sweeter.

Start: At the Loj trailhead
Distance: 14.8 miles out-and-back
Approximate hiking time: 9 to 11 hours
Difficulty: Strenuous due to length, terrain, and gradient
Elevation change: The trail has a 3,200-foot elevation change, attaining Mount Marcy's summit at 5,344 feet.
Trail surface: Rocky or earthen path
Seasons: Open year-round but best summer through fall
Other trail users: Snowshoers, cross-country skiers
Canine compatibility: Leashed dogs permitted. This is a well-used trail, so leave high-strung dogs at home.
Land status: Adirondack Mountain Club and New York State Department of Environmental Conservation (DEC) land
Nearest town: Lake Placid
Fees and permits: Adirondack Loj charges for trail parking.

Schedule: No time restrictions
Map: https://mtvanhoevenberg.com/wp-content/uploads/sites/6/2020/12/OSC_trails-2.pdf; maps are also available at bookstores throughout the region
Trail contact: New York State DEC, Region 5, 1115 NY 86, Ray Brook; (518) 897-1200; www.dec.ny.gov
Special considerations: The final 0.5 mile to the summit requires a rock scramble. Come prepared for chilly winds and cool summit temperatures, and be alert to weather changes. Camp only at the lean-tos or designated tent sites. Camping and fires above 4,000 feet are prohibited. In the High Peaks, all food must be stored in bear vaults (bear-proof containers); suspending food is no longer adequate. The current maximum group size for overnight use is 8, and 15 for day use. The DEC asks for your voluntary compliance in keeping off the trail during the mud season in spring.

Finding the trailhead: From the junction of NY 73 and I-86 in the village of Lake Placid, go east on NY 73 for 3.2 miles and turn right (south) on Adirondack Loj Road. Go 5 miles to reach the entrance station for the Loj. Find the trailhead at the opposite end of the lower parking lot from the High Peaks Visitor Information Center. Because parking lots can fill in summer, off-season and midweek visits are advisable. GPS: 44.183130, -73.963857

Cairn marks the heights of Mt. Marcy.

The Hike

Follow the wide, well-trampled, blue-marked trail, passing through a mixed conifer-deciduous forest and crossing over the Mr. Van Ski Trail. Ongoing improvements including reinforced steps, foot planks, levees, and stepping stones have reduced the mire and erosion that once characterized the Van Hoevenberg Trail.

Passing through planted pines, cross the footbridge over the Heart Lake outlet, followed soon after by the footbridge over MacIntyre Brook. Despite the popularity of this hiker highway, wildlife sightings can reward early morning hikers. Owls, deer, bats, and even a pine marten may surprise you.

Past the junction with the yellow trail to Algonquin Peak, maple, birch, small beech, hobblebush, and striped maple surround the path. In another mile ascend along rushing Marcy Brook, sequestered deep in a draw. Campsites occupy the balsam fir and birch woods. Ahead the trail crosses the picturesque wooden Marcy Dam. In the past campers suspended their food supplies from the dam, but bears figured out how to haul up the goodies, so resist temptation here; comply with the use of bear vaults.

Cross-pond views feature Mount Colden; Avalanche, Phelps, and Table Top Mountains; and the slopes of Wright Peak and Algonquin. Over the shoulder looms Whales Tail Mountain. The popularity of the lean-tos and the ranger station here bring bustle to the area.

Following the rocky terrain of Phelps Brook upstream, you come to the high-water bridge. During low water, cross 500 feet upstream via the rocky streambed itself. The tour continues upstream on the opposite shore, but Phelps Brook slips from sight. At the junction with the red Phelps Mountain Trail, continue forward; dense spruce and fir narrow the aisle.

A mile from the first crossing, cross a bridge back over Phelps Brook, finding a steeper climb and larger rocks. Shortly the trail turns away from the brook, as a winter-use trail continues upstream. Small-stature trees weave an open cathedral as you climb stone steps and short log ladders.

Passing designated camp flats, cross Marcy Brook upstream from Indian Falls. You can't see the falls from the crossing; for a top-of-the-falls view, take an immediate right on the foot trail heading downstream 100 feet to a broad outcrop, washed by the brook at the head of Indian Falls. Here the falls spill through a cliff fissure, offering a striking view out to Algonquin and the MacIntyre Range.

Resuming the hike, at the junction at 3,600-foot elevation, bear left with the blue disks, temporarily enjoying a more relaxed grade. Bunchberry, moss, and whorled aster carpet the ground in season. A section of corduroy trail here may be particularly muddy in spring; it's followed by a steep, rocky ascent with stones aligned as stairs.

In a high meadow, the imposing peak of Mount Marcy comes into view with its open summit outcrop and the silver snags piercing its fir mantle. Toy-sized hikers wind skyward. This eye-opener alerts you to the climb still ahead. Canted exposed outcrops alternate with corduroys as the trail draws into an alpine opening. Views build, with nearby Mount Haystack being particularly arresting.

An arctic-alpine habitat claims the upper reaches of Marcy, so keep to the prescribed route, now a rock scramble. From the summit plaque, one last scrambling burst takes you to the top. The view is both glorious and humbling. During summer months a High Peaks Summit Steward provided by the Adirondack Mountain Club watches over Marcy, educating hikers about this sensitive site.

A LASTING LEGACY

Henry Van Hoevenberg, known as "Mr. Van," the affable outdoorsman known for his signature leather hat and leather wardrobe, opened the area's first Adirondack Lodge in 1890 and blazed many of the Heart Lake–area trails. He laid out the trail to Mount Marcy that now bears his name; it continues to be the most direct and shortest route to the cloud-flirting peak. Van Hoevenberg named Mount Jo, the small but substantial peak rising above Heart Lake, for his bride-to-be, Josephine. He played a key role in shaping wilderness recreation in the Adirondacks as we know it today. The Van Hoevenberg lodge burned down in a forest fire in 1903 and was eventually replaced by the circa-1927 Adirondak Loj, built and named by Melvil Dewey, who preferred this more rustic spelling of "Lodge." Dewey served as chairman of the Lake Placid Club, which preceded the Adirondack Mountain Club in ownership of this property and facilities.

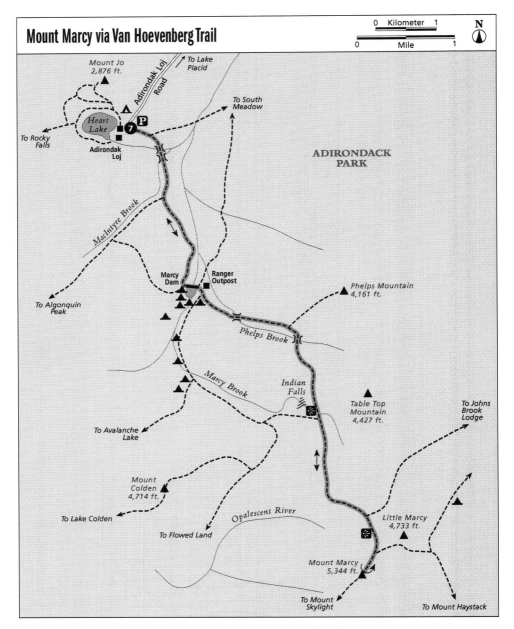

0   Kilometer   1

0   Mile   1

N

Mount Jo
2,876 ft.

Adirondak Loj
Road

To Lake
Placid

To South
Meadow

Heart
Lake

7

P

To Rocky
Falls

Adirondak
Loj

**ADIRONDACK
PARK**

MacIntyre Brook

Marcy
Dam

Ranger
Outpost

Phelps Mountain
4,161 ft.

To Algonquin
Peak

Phelps Brook

Marcy Brook

Indian
Falls

Table Top
Mountain
4,427 ft.

To Johns
Brook
Lodge

To Avalanche
Lake

Mount
Colden
4,714 ft.

To Lake Colden

Opalescent River

Little Marcy
4,733 ft.

To Flowed Land

Mount Marcy
5,344 ft.

To Mount
Skylight

To Mount Haystack

Sweeping views include many Adirondack landmarks: the regal MacIntyre Range, the ridges north to Canada, the Green Mountains of Vermont, Lakes Champlain and Placid, Boreas Ponds, and Lake Tear-of-the-Clouds, the highest lake source of the Hudson River. The Hudson–Saint Lawrence River Divide passes over the top of Mount Marcy. Crystals and lichen adorn the rock. When you're ready to descend, return the way you came.

Miles and Directions

0.0 Start from the Loj trailhead and follow the blue Van Hoevenberg Trail.

1.0 Reach a trail junction. Bear left, staying on the blue trail. *Note:* The yellow trail leads to Algonquin Peak.

2.2 Cross wooden Marcy Dam, bear right along the shore, and at the junction in 500 feet, head left for Mount Marcy. *Note:* The trail to the right leads to Avalanche Lake and Lake Colden.

2.5 Cross the high-water bridge on Phelps Brook. (During low water continue upstream 500 feet to cross on the rocky streambed.)

4.2 Cross Marcy Brook and continue forward. **Option:** Upon crossing, an immediate right leads to an outcrop at the head of Indian Falls in 100 feet.

5.8 Reach a trail junction. To the left lies Keene Valley. Head right for Mount Marcy.

6.4 Reach the saddle junction and bear right. Yellow paint blazes and the occasional cairn mark this final leg to the summit.

7.4 Reach the summit. Return by same route.

14.8 End back at the Loj.

Hike Information

Local Information

Lake Placid Convention and Visitors Bureau/Regional Office of Sustainable Tourism, 2608 Main St., Lake Placid; (518) 523-2445; www.lakeplacid.com

Local Events/Attractions

The **Lake Placid Olympic Center** has a museum of Lake Placid Olympic history and four ice rinks open for hockey, figure skating, and speed skating, with open evening skating and skate rentals. Olympic Center, 2634 Main St., Lake Placid; (518) 523-1655; www.orda.org.

At **John Brown Farm State Historic Site,** you can tour the last home and burial site of the famed abolitionist. The home is open from May 1 through October 31, Wednesday through Monday from 10 a.m. to 5 p.m. Grounds are open year-round. 115 John Brown Rd., Lake Placid 12946; (518) 523-3900; https://parks.ny.gov/historic-sites/johnbrownfarm/details.aspx.

Accommodations

Adirondak Loj has lodge accommodations for thirty-eight guests and a food service, plus a campground with thirty-one tent sites, sixteen lean-tos, one yurt, and six canvas cabins. Adirondak Loj reservations and information: https://adk.org/locations/.

Organizations

Adirondack Mountain Club, 1002 Adirondack Loj Rd., Lake Placid, NY 12946; (518) 668-4447; www.adk.org

8 East Branch Ausable River Loop

Within the private Adirondack Mountain Reserve (or Ausable Club, as it is also known), this rolling hiker-trail loop travels the east and west shores of the pristine East Branch Ausable River. Side trips lead to the elevated vantages at Gothics Window and Indian Head and to showery Rainbow Falls. Old-growth hemlocks and tranquil woods shape a soothing backdrop.

Start: At the trail gate
Distance: 9.6-mile loop, including side trips (11.1 miles with the road distance to and from trailhead parking)
Approximate hiking time: 5 to 6.5 hours
Difficulty: Strenuous due to footing and terrain
Elevation change: The trail travels between 1,350 and 2,700 feet above sea level, with the high point at Indian Head.
Trail surface: Earthen and rock-studded woods path
Seasons: Open year-round, best hiking is from late spring through fall
Other trail users: None
Canine compatibility: Dogs not permitted
Land status: Private reserve land
Nearest town: Lake Placid

Fees and permits: All hikers entering the reserve must register.
Schedule: Daylight hours only
Maps: www.dec.ny.gov/docs/lands_forests _pdf/mapadirondac.pdf
Trail contact: New York State Department of Environmental Conservation, Region 5, PO Box 296, 1115 NY 86, Ray Brook, NY 12977; (518) 897-1200; www.dec.ny.gov
Special considerations: Reserve rules include no pets, fires, or camping, and no bicycles on Lake Road. Only reserve members may fish or swim. The reserve has protected this site since 1897, so do your part, practicing the Leave No Trace ethic. "ATIS" (Adirondack Trail Improvement Society) markers may help point out trails.

Finding the trailhead: From Keene Valley, go south on NY 73 East for 2.8 miles, and turn right (west) onto a gravel road opposite the marked trailhead for Roaring Brook Trail to Giant Mountain to find this trail's parking. Because it often fills, plan an early or off-peak time arrival. Do not park anywhere along the gravel road. You must park away from the Ausable Club and not block the club-area road with shuttle drop-offs or pickups. GPS: 44.149692, -73.767799

From the parking area, hike west on the gravel road (the surface later changes to pavement) to reach the Ausable Club (0.5 mile). Turn left on Lake Road Way and descend between the tennis courts. Beyond member parking, reach the register and entrance station at 0.7 mile. Sign in and enter via the fanciful gate.

The Hike

Hike up the closed dirt road past the Ladies Mile Trail, and bear right for the marked East River Trail, coming to the river loop junction at a bridge. Don't cross here—continue upstream along the east bank (you'll return on the loop along the west bank). Mossy stones stud the east bank trail.

Lower Ausable Lake fills a narrow canyon.

After crossing the footbridge over Gill Brook, cross a reserve road and ascend through a high-canopy forest. The trail rounds below an isolated outcrop with splendid views of Wolfjaw Mountain. Where the trail traverses an old-growth hemlock plateau, it ascends some 200 feet above the river before a quick, difficult descent.

On the lower slope, a double waterfall comes into view. The upper 20-foot falls pours through a pinched gorge and feeds a lower 6-foot falls, with a surging channel between and a dark plunge pool. Back on the elevated riverbank, pass room-sized boulders, briefly parallel a pipe that draws water for the club, and pass a river bridge. Upstream the ragged Gothics-Sawteeth skyline appears.

Beaver Meadow soon claims the river bottom, braiding the stream. Below Bullock Dam, Leach Bridge spans the river at the outlet to Lower Ausable Lake. The lake waters and boathouse are closed to the general public, and shore access is limited to the marked trails. Here you cross the bridge for the loop, but to top Indian Head for an overlook, remain on the east shore, coming out at the main reserve road. You'll find the marked trail to Indian Head off this road.

En route to Indian Head, a 115-foot spur heads right to Gothics Window, offering a tree-framed look at the rugged Gothics and high-peak amphitheater. The main trail climbs, with short ladder segments at steep stretches. Taking a right at a three-way junction puts you atop Indian Head—a broad, flat outcrop with a spectacular view surpassed only by the view from the Indian's brow below. Nippletop, Colvin, the curved platters of Upper and Lower Ausable Lakes, the Sawteeth, Gothics, and Wolfjaw complete the panorama.

Back at Leach Bridge, cross the river. Views stretch to the Mount Colvin–Sawteeth gateway at the head of Lower Ausable Lake. Adding the left spur to Rainbow Falls, you find sheer cliffs, the 150-foot misty shower, and a greenery-filled box canyon. When the sun strikes it, a rainbow spectrum autographs the falls. Return to Leach Bridge and hike the West River Trail downstream, passing the trail to Lost Lookout.

The shoreline ramble takes you over rocks, below the cliffs, and through shady spruce–hardwood forest. The trail eases, traversing a beech flat and raised dike. Eastern views span the alder meadow to the Bear Den–Dial Mountain ridge. Cross a couple of drainages and pass a ladder ascent to the Gothics to reach Beaver Meadow Falls, an 80-foot falls splashing over tiered cliff.

Past the double falls on the East Branch, the trail drifts from the river into a realm of old-growth hemlock. Stay on the West River Trail, crossing paired logs over a pretty brook with a 10-foot cascade in a rocky slot. The trail next descends a steep ridge.

Where the trail bottoms out, the West River Trail veers left but generally keeps toward the river. Hike past a spur on the right to Canyon Bridge and meet Cathedral Rocks Loop. You may follow the loop left to visit Pyramid Brook and a falls mostly swallowed by rocks. Staying downstream along the river, return to the river-loop-junction bridge. Here, too, the Cathedral Rocks trail meets up. Cross the river bridge to close the loop and backtrack through the reserve.

Miles and Directions

0.0 Start at the gate past the trail register. Pass through the attractive gate and hike the dirt road into Adirondack Mountain Reserve, passing the signed Ladies Mile Trail.

0.3 Turn right on the marked route for the East River Trail.

0.5 Reach the river loop junction at a bridge. Proceed upstream along the east shore for a clockwise loop. *Note:* The return is via the West River Trail across the bridge.

0.8 Cross Gill Brook footbridge and turn left, following this side brook upstream to cross a reserve road (at 1 mile) and ascend.

2.0 Overlook a double falls on the river.

2.3 Reach a junction. Bear right, staying along the east bank. *Note:* To the left is the main reserve road.

2.4 Reach a junction. Keep left. *Note:* Path heading right leads to the river bridge to Beaver Meadow Falls.

2.9 View Bullock Dam, a plank-topped log stretched the length of the river.

3.4 Reach Leach Bridge and the river loop return junction. **Option:** To add the Indian Head overlook, postpone crossing and remain on the east shore. Ascend sharply left, turn right near a storage shed, and ascend 50 yards on a gravel road to emerge at the main reserve road in 0.1 mile. Follow the main reserve road left 500 feet to the marked trail to Indian Head. Take the indicated trail and stay left, contouring and switching back up the slope. At 3.7 miles a 115-foot spur heads right to Gothics Window. The main trail climbs. At a three-way junction, go right 0.1 mile to top Indian Head (4.3 miles). Backtrack to Leach Bridge.

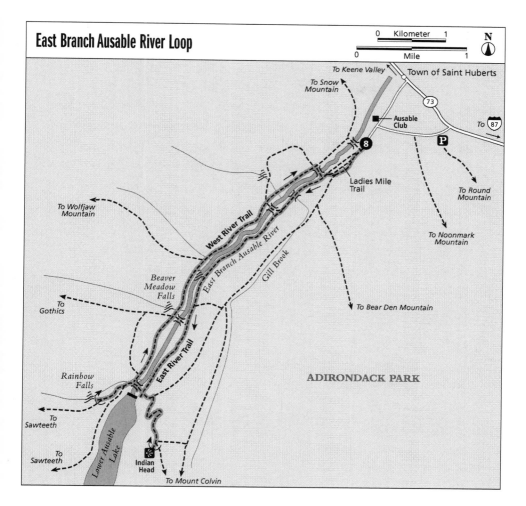

East Branch Ausable River Loop

To Keene Valley

To Snow
Mountain

Town of Saint Huberts

73

Ausable
Club

To 87

8

P

Ladies Mile
Trail

To Round
Mountain

To Wolfjaw
Mountain

West River Trail

East Branch Ausable River

Gill Brook

To Noonmark
Mountain

Beaver
Meadow
Falls

To
Gothics

To Bear Den Mountain

East River Trail

Rainbow
Falls

ADIRONDACK PARK

To
Sawteeth

Lower Ausable Lake

To
Sawteeth

Indian
Head

To Mount Colvin

5.2 Cross Leach Bridge to the west shore junction; the loop's return is to the right. **Option:** To add a visit to Rainbow Falls, turn left. At the dam bear right and, shortly after, again bear right to reach Rainbow Falls (5.4 miles). Return to the river loop at Leach Bridge.

5.7 Reach Leach Bridge. Hike the west shore trail downstream.

6.8 View Beaver Meadow Falls.

8.1 Reach a junction. Proceed forward and remain on the West River Trail at junctions that quickly follow. *Note:* Downhill to the right is Canyon Bridge, the largest of the river footbridges.

8.8 Cross the river bridge and backtrack to the reserve gate.

9.6 Pass through the gate and to return to your car, ascend through club grounds, and turn right.

GETTING INTO SHAPE

Unless you want to be sore—and possibly have to shorten your trip or vacation—be sure to get in shape before a big hike. If you're terribly out of shape, start a walking program early, preferably eight weeks in advance. Start with a 15-minute walk during your lunch hour or after work, and gradually increase your walking time to an hour. You should also increase your elevation gain. Walking briskly up hills really strengthens your leg muscles and gets your heart rate up. If you work in a storied office building, take the stairs instead of the elevator. If you prefer going to a gym, walk the treadmill or use a stair machine. You can further increase your strength and endurance by walking with a loaded backpack. Consider stationary exercises like squats, leg lifts, sit-ups, and push-ups. Other good ways to get in shape include biking, running, aerobics, and, of course, short hikes. Stretching before and after a hike keeps muscles flexible and helps avoid injuries.

Hike Information

Local Information

Lake Placid Convention and Visitors Bureau/Regional Office of Sustainable Tourism, 2608 Main St., Suite 2, Lake Placid; (518) 523-2445; www.lakeplacid .com

Local Events/Attractions

The **Adirondack History Museum,** open weekends from Memorial Day weekend through Indigenous Peoples' Day in October, is a classic small-town museum in the old school building at the corner of NY 9N and Hand Avenue in Elizabethtown. The collection records two centuries in Essex County and is paired with a traditional colonial garden of plants, herbs, and flowers. Contact Essex County Historical Society, (518) 873-6466; www.adkhistorycenter.org.

Organizations

Adirondack Mountain Club, 1002 Adirondack Loj Rd., Lake Placid, NY 12946; (518) 668-4447; https://adk.org
Adirondack Trail Improvement Society, PO Box 565, Keene Valley, NY 12943; (518) 576-9157; www.atistrail.org

9 Blue Mountain Trail

Above the east shore of Blue Mountain Lake, this quick, steep summit ascent reaches a fire tower, retired from duty but open for public viewing, and a cherished 360-degree Central Adirondack view. Besides the sweeping vistas, the trail offers an attractive fir-spruce forest and the historic summit benchmark placed by Verplanck Colvin, an important early surveyor who helped open the Adirondacks to the public.

Start: At the Blue Mountain Trailhead
Distance: 4.0 miles out-and-back
Approximate hiking time: 2 to 3 hours
Difficulty: Moderate due to the sharp elevation gain
Elevation change: The trail travels between 2,200 feet at the trailhead and a summit elevation of 3,759 feet.
Trail surface: Worn rock path with surface hardening and stone-step improvements
Seasons: Open year-round, best for hiking spring through fall
Other trail users: Snowshoers
Canine compatibility: Dogs permitted (The trail is very narrow and the first part is on private land, so leash your dog.)

Land status: New York State Department of Environmental Conservation (DEC) and private land
Nearest town: Blue Mountain Lake (or Indian Lake or Long Lake)
Fees and permits: None
Schedule: No time restrictions
Maps: www.dec.ny.gov/docs/lands_forests _pdf/bluemtnhikemap.pdf
Trail contact: New York State DEC, Region 5, 1115 NY 86, Ray Brook; (518) 897-1200; www.dec.ny.gov
Special considerations: After rainstorms, the worn bed of the rocky trail can become a runoff channel, so watch your footing.

Finding the trailhead: From the intersection of highways 28, 30, and 28N in the hamlet of Blue Mountain Lake, go north on NY 30/NY 28N for 1.4 miles and turn right (east) for the marked trailhead parking lot for the Blue Mountain and Tirrell Pond Trails. GPS: 43.874651, -74.430995

The Hike

From the trailhead parking lot, follow the red disks of the Blue Mountain Trail. The first half of the trail shows refinements of stone steps and parallel plank walks, designed to minimize erosion. The second half shows the eroded bare rock of the historic trail, naked of any topsoil.

The highly accessible Blue Mountain interpretive trail ascends the namesake peak that looms above the east shore of Blue Mountain Lake. Because of the trail's convenient location and relatively short length, it offers newcomers a quick snapshot of the challenge and wilderness discovery of the Adirondacks. Pick up an interpretive brochure from the box near the trail register (if other hikers haven't beaten you to the supply) for information about the numbered features along the trail.

Attractive signs mark trailheads throughout New York forests.

HIKING WITH YOUR DOG

Bringing your furry friend with you is always more fun than leaving them behind. Our canine pals make great trail buddies because they never complain and always make good company.

Before you plan outdoor adventures with your dog, make sure they are in shape for the trail. Take them on your daily runs or walks. Be sure your dog has a firm grasp of the basics of canine etiquette and behavior, and that they can sit, lie down, stay, and come on command. Purchase collapsible water and dog food bowls for your dog. If you are hiking on rocky terrain or in the snow, you can purchase footwear for your dog that will protect the dog's feet from cuts and bruises.

Once on the trail, keep your dog under control. Remember, wildlife needs supersede our pet's sense of fun, and other hikers need to feel safe. Always obey leash laws, and be sure to bury your dog's waste or pack it out in resealable plastic bags.

STORM OF THE CENTURY

The Great Appalachian Wind Storm of November 1950, a cyclonic nor'easter, cut a swath of fear and destruction across the Appalachians, impacting twenty-two eastern and Midwest states and killing more than 300 people before entering Canada. In New York, punishing winds and rain toppled trees, cut power, raised coastal waters, and swamped banks. This storm of the century, at the time the largest recorded windstorm in the Adirondacks, wreaked havoc on more than 400,000 acres.

Before the century was out, though, a second megablow smacked the Adirondacks on July 15, 1995. The declared microburst (a downdraft that causes an outburst at surface level) downed hundreds of thousands of trees, killing five, clogging and wiping out trails, and stranding ninety hikers and canoeists. It prompted the biggest rescue effort in New York State Department of Environmental Conservation history. Although the 1995 storm occupies only a fraction of the 1950 storm footprint, it left 38,000 acres with more than 60% downed trees and another 109,000 acres with 30% to 60% of trees down. The High Falls area (Hike 6) perhaps best reveals the legacy and the recovery.

Tall maple, black cherry, and birch weave the overhead canopy, with fern, viburnum, striped maple, and brambles filling out the woods. Where the trail briefly levels, big yellow and white birch trees dominate. Many of these birches germinated after the Great Appalachian Wind Storm of 1950, which impacted 424,000 acres in the forest preserve.

At the upcoming brook crossing, a small cascade sheets over canted rock. Ahead you can see where trail improvements are gradually overcoming problems of erosion trenches and soggy spots. At times snags open the canopy, but the trail remains mostly shaded. At the next brook crossing, both forest and trail undergo a character change. A higher-elevation forest of spruce, fir, birch, and mountain ash now claims the peak, while the trail narrows, steepens, and grows increasingly rocky.

Steep rock outcrops next advance the trail. You will need to dig in with the toes of your boots on the descent. After rains this section can become a full-fledged creek, with water racing down, around, and over the rocks. At the trail's sides, clintonia, bunchberry, oxalis, and club moss grow. In another half mile, canted bedrock offers a more moderate climb through tight stands of fir and spruce.

The bald summit outcrop holds the five-story, steelframed observatory. You are welcome to ascend the fire tower, but permitted numbers are limited on the structure at any one time. Erected in 1917, the tower was restored by a volunteer committee in 1994, and the DEC has since restored the tower cab for public use. Summit views sweep a bold tapestry that includes Whiteface, Algonquin, Colden, and Marcy peaks;

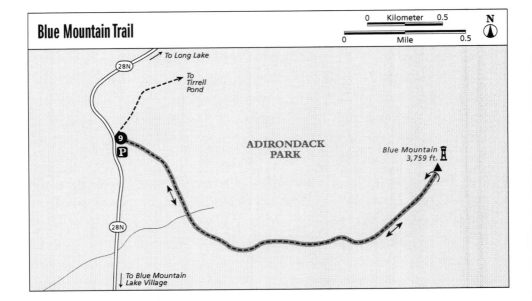

Blue Mountain Trail

Blue Mountain, Eagle, Utowana, and Durant Lakes; Minnow, Mud, South, and Tirrell Ponds; and Blue Ridge. On autumn mornings, handkerchiefs of fog lift from the cobalt platters and drift across the gold, green, and red of the lake basins.

Other summit structures include a cell tower and a DEC communication station. A few paces north of the 35-foot fire tower, look for the summit markings placed by Verplanck Colvin. In the 1870s Colvin's men shot off bright explosions here so that the Adirondack survey teams could triangulate on the peak.

The return descent is as you came.

Miles and Directions

0.0 Start from the Blue Mountain trailhead. Head generally east on the red trail.

0.7 Cross a brook.

2.0 Reach the summit outcrop and fire tower. Return by the same route.

4.0 End back at the Blue Mountain Trailhead.

Options

You might choose to hike the 3.3-mile **Tirrell Pond Trail,** which shares the same trailhead parking area. This yellow-marked wooded trail journeys north before turning east, passing at the northern foot of Blue Mountain. It follows private roads and intersects the Northville-Placid Trail north of Tirrell Pond. Lean-tos occupy the north and south ends of the pond. The pond's beach and views of Tirrell Mountain attract many visitors.

Hike Information

Local Information

Hamilton County Department of Economic Development and Tourism, 102 County View Dr., Lake Pleasant; (518) 548-3076; www.hamiltoncounty.com

Local Events/Attractions

The Adirondack Experience: The Museum on Blue Mountain Lake has twenty buildings on a 32-acre campus filled with exhibits that tell the story of life, work, transportation, and recreation in the Adirondacks since the early 1800s. The site is noted for its historical boat collection. The museum holds many events, including the annual Rustic Fair in September. Open Memorial Day weekend through Indigenous Peoples' Day in October weekends from 10 a.m. to 5 p.m. Admission is charged. Adirondack Experience, 9097 State Route 30, Blue Mountain Lake; (518) 352-7311; www.theadkx.org.

Accommodations

Lake Durant (DEC) Campground, 8301 NY Route 28 & 30, is open mid-May through Labor Day and has sixty-five sites. Reservations: (800) 456-2267; www.reserveamerica.com.

Organizations

Adirondack Mountain Club, 1002 Adirondack Loj Rd., Lake Placid, NY 12946; (518) 668-4447; www.adk.org

10 Murphy Lake Trail

North of Northville, this hike along a time-worn, centuries-old road accesses three sparkling lakes—Bennett, Middle, and Murphy—cradled in the quiet wooded beauty of the southern Adirondacks. Fishing, camping, a historic settlement site, loons, and colorful fall foliage all help sell the trail. Because of its gentle grade and multiple stops, it makes a fine first backpack for the family.

Start: At the Creek Road trailhead
Distance: 7.8 miles out-and-back
Approximate hiking time: 5 to 6 hours
Difficulty: Moderate
Elevation change: From a trailhead elevation of 940 feet, the trail tops the 1,600-foot mark while rounding Middle Lake. It then dips to Murphy Lake at 1,473 feet.
Trail surface: Earthen or grassy old road
Seasons: Open year-round, best hiking is spring through fall
Other trail users: Hunters, mountain bikers, snowmobilers, snowshoers, cross-country skiers
Canine compatibility: Dogs permitted (leash recommended)

Land status: New York State Department of Environmental Conservation (DEC)
Nearest town: Wells
Fees and permits: None
Schedule: No time restrictions
Map: https://adirondackatlas.org/?token=f93925f2ee97af5d44c25a6c09bb091d
Trail contact: New York State DEC, Region 5, 701 South Main St., Northville; (518) 863-4545; www.dec.ny.gov
Special considerations: During the fall hunting season, it's best to avoid the area or, at least, wear blaze-orange clothing. Although snowmobilers can use the trail, their use is generally light because the trail is not long.

Finding the trailhead: From Sacandaga Campground and Day-Use Area (3.4 miles south of Wells), go south on NY 30 for 5 miles and turn left (east) onto Creek Road. From Northville, find the turn for Creek Road 3 miles north of the NY 30 bridge over the Sacandaga River. The marked trailhead is left off Creek Road in 2.2 miles. Parking is on the broad road shoulder. GPS: 43.301948, -74.200176

The Hike

This trail heads north along a former road, ascending with a steady, moderate grade past the register. In some places, the old road is worn deep into the terrain. It probes a tall forest of white pine, hemlock, oak, maple, ash, birch, and aspen. Various ferns, sarsaparilla, and foamflower dot the understory, and mossy boulders and logs lend interest to the forest floor.

Before long, the greenery all but vanishes from the forest floor. Where the incline flattens, big white pines shade the route and soften the road with their discarded needles. The hike next passes a remnant rock wall and rounds a barrier. This trail is closed to all motorized travel except for snowmobiles; the snowmobile markers perform double duty, guiding hikers in the off-season.

Bennett Lake, Wilcox Lake Wild Forest, Adirondack Park

At about a mile, you may see some exposed red soil, hinting at an early-twentieth-century ferric oxide (paint pigment) mine. Although trees and leaf mat have reclaimed the mining settlement, you still may notice unusual mounds, cellar holes, or rusting debris.

A pair of cairns on the right funnel you down a wide trail to Bennett Lake, a camp flat, and a privy. The elongated oval of Bennett Lake rests below a rolling wooded ridge. Aquatic grasses and plants adorn its shallow edge, while insect chirrs fill the air in season. A small boot-compressed beach offers lake access.

A moderate, rocky ascent from the Bennett Lake basin continues the hike. Toads, eastern newts, gray squirrels, and ruffed grouse may increase your wildlife tally, and the haunting cry of a common loon can usually be heard coming from the lake.

Where the trail passes between two low ridges, the comfortable earthen bed returns, and more greenery spreads beneath the trees. At a small drainage, you may encounter a mud hole; bridges typically span the larger runoffs.

After the trail tops out, a side trail veers right, passing through a hemlock grove to reach a Middle Lake campsite. A muddy shoreline with a few logs for footing offers a lake view of a small island topped by white pines, as well as a large central island that visitors often mistake for the far shore.

The primary trail then follows the contour of the slope 200 feet above Middle Lake. Small-diameter trees choke out meaningful views, but the sparkling blue water provides a grand canvas for the leafy boughs. Slowly, the trail inches toward the lake, where a second unmarked spur ventures 200 feet to the right, reaching Middle Lake at another campsite. Here, too, a log-strewn, marshy shore greets hikers. Views feature

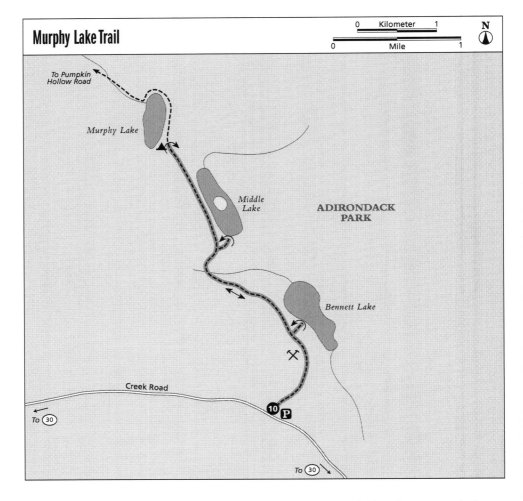

the north end of the big central island and a scenic rounded hill with western cliffs. Aquatic grasses, pickerelweed (arrowhead), and water lilies crowd the shallows.

The trail bed alternates among grass, rock, and earthen stretches as it rounds Middle Lake, with occasional open views of the water. After a woods ascent, the trail crosses a rocky drainage and curves right to meet Murphy Lake at the lean-to, where an outcrop slopes to the water. The reflecting waters of Murphy Lake and the enfolding, rounded, tree-mantled hills with their cliff outcrops hold a signature charm, dazzling in autumn attire. This is the turnaround site for the hike. Outward explorations along shore may get brushy or wet.

Miles and Directions

0.0 Start from the Creek Road trailhead and head north.
1.4 Reach the Bennett Lake spur.
2.7 Reach Middle Lake.
3.9 Reach the Murphy Lake lean-to. Turn around, backtracking to the trailhead.
7.8 End at the Creek Road trailhead.

Hike Information

Local Information

Hamilton County Department of Economic Development and Tourism, 102 County View Dr., Lake Pleasant; (518) 548-3076; www.hamiltoncounty.com

Local Events/Attractions

With a surface area of 42 square miles and 125 miles of shoreline, **Great Sacandaga Lake** offers lots of recreation opportunities: fishing, kayaking, canoeing, sailing, boating, and beaches (www.visitsacandaga.com).

Accommodations

Sacandaga (DEC) Campground & Day-Use Area, south of Wells, is open mid-May through Labor Day and has 137 sites. It was one of the first two campgrounds built in the forest preserve. 1047 Highway 30. Reservations: (800) 456-2267; www .reserveamerica.com.

Organizations

Adirondack Mountain Club, 1002 Adirondack Loj Rd., Lake Placid, NY 12946; (518) 668-4447; https://adk.org

11 Pharaoh Mountain and Lake Loop

In the Schroon Lake area of the eastern Adirondacks, this all-day or overnight hike tags the summit of Pharaoh Mountain and encircles large, deep Pharaoh Lake, touring mixed forest and wetland meadows. Summit and shore vistas, swimming and trout fishing, an expansive marsh, convenient overnight lean-tos, prized solitude, and fall color swell this Pharaoh's treasure cache.

Start: At the official Crane Pond trailhead
Distance: 18.1-mile lollipop hike
Approximate hiking time: 9.5 to 12 hours
Difficulty: Strenuous due to distance and terrain
Elevation change: The trail has a 1,500-foot elevation change, with the high point atop Pharaoh Mountain at 2,556 feet.
Trail surface: Earthen, rocky, and meadow trails; woods road; and plank walk
Seasons: Open year-round, best hiking late spring through fall
Other trail users: Hunters
Canine compatibility: Dogs permitted

Land status: New York State Department of Environmental Conservation (DEC)
Nearest town: Schroon Lake
Fees and permits: None
Schedule: No time restrictions
Maps: www.dec.ny.gov/docs/lands_forests _pdf/mappharaohlk.pdf
Trail contact: New York State DEC, Region 5, 232 Golf Course Rd., Warrensburg; (518) 623-1200; www.dec.ny.gov
Special considerations: There can be some soggy obstacles along Alder Creek; watch for bypasses and changes in bypasses.

Finding the trailhead: From the NY 74/US 9 junction (0.1 mile east of I-87), go south on US 9 for 0.6 mile and turn left (east) onto Alder Meadow Road toward Schroon Lake Airport. In 2 miles bear left on Crane Pond Road and go 1.4 miles east, reaching a parking area on the left; on the way the road changes to gravel. GPS: 43.859171, -73.688497

The Hike

Begin by hiking the retired stretch of Crane Pond Road to Pharaoh Lake Wilderness. The road narrows and changes to dirt, offering an easy, tree-shaded avenue. As you parallel Alder Creek upstream, outcrops, a dark hollow, and wetlands vary viewing. At road's end you arrive at the old Crane Pond trailhead. Cross the bridge over the watery link between Crane and Alder Ponds. Meadowy islands adorn the more-vegetated Alder Pond. Now proceed on an older woods road as it gently ascends into a hemlock-birch woods filled out by maples, firs, and 4-foot-diameter white pines.

Bear right at the loop junction to first top Pharaoh Mountain. You will skirt an elbow pond of Glidden Marsh before passing behind a low ridge, where a foot trail takes over. Slowly the climb intensifies. After an angling ascent, bedrock slabs shape a more vertical charge up Pharaoh Mountain. As the aspen and mountain ash forest thins, a view to the northwest includes Desolate Swamp, Goose Pond, and Schroon

Pharaoh Mountain lifts hikers above the treetops.

Lake. Stand atop Pharaoh Mountain near an adit, a former passage into an old graphite mine.

Before striking south, straight across the crown, mount the summit outcrops to piece together a 270-degree view—a fantastic landscape of rolling ridges, rounded peaks, and myriad lakes and marshes. The western outcrop (to your right) holds survey markers; one dates back to 1896. On descent, another outcrop lures you over for a southern view of Pharaoh Lake, big and glistening, with its rock islands, irregular shoreline, and surrounding wilderness.

Rocks and roots complicate the steep descent, which zigs and pitches south off the mountain. Areas of bedrock open views northeast to Treadway Mountain, closely followed by a plank walk over a wet meadow that leads to the lake. Bear right here, and watch for yellow markers that point the way to peninsula lean-tos in 0.25 mile. The peninsula's rocky end invites swimming, fishing, daydreaming, and stargazing.

As you continue, yellow disks also mark the lake loop. An outcrop pushes the trail up and inland, and along the shore, you see additional lean-tos or the spurs to them. Pass above the shallow, pinched outlet bay to cross a footbridge. Beaver-gnawed logs can clog the brook; in season, frogs call loudly along the bay.

From the outlet crossing, the trail pulls away from shore, traversing a corridor of spruce and reindeer lichen. Next up is an inviting lakeside lean-to, christened the "Pharaoh Hilton" by past guests. Beyond the Springhill Ponds Trail, follow along a quiet bay.

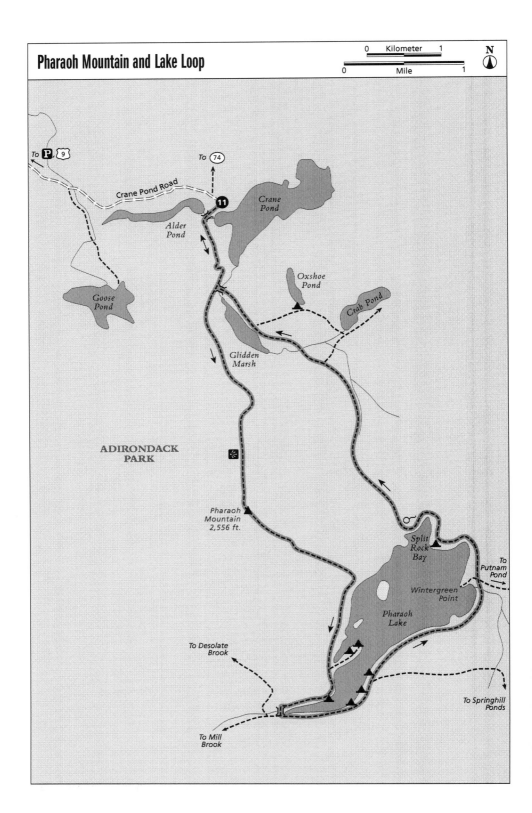

Pharaoh Mountain and Lake Loop

0   Kilometer   1

0   Mile   1

N

To **P** 9

To 74

Crane Pond Road

11

Crane
Pond

Alder
Pond

Goose
Pond

Oxshoe
Pond

Crab Pond

Glidden
Marsh

**ADIRONDACK
PARK**

Pharaoh
Mountain
2,556 ft.

Split
Rock
Bay

To
Putnam
Pond

Wintergreen
Point

Pharaoh
Lake

To Desolate
Brook

To Springhill
Ponds

To Mill
Brook

Outcrops can lure you lakeside, and views stretch to Pharaoh Mountain. Round a lily-pad bay, and from a log bridge you can admire Wintergreen Point—a long, thin, treed outcrop jut. Past the Swing Trail, heading right to Putnam Pond, a red secondary trail leads 0.1 mile to Wintergreen Point. The lake trail drifts from shore into deciduous woodland filled out by midstory hobblebush and striped maple.

Ahead is Split Rock Bay, named for a distinctive offshore feature. Views to the southwest span Pharaoh Lake to Number 8 and Little Stevens Mountains. A small ridge offers a farewell lake view before the trail turns right and ascends away. The grade is steep, the terrain rocky, and the woods deciduous; yellow remains the guiding color.

From here, the trail follows the outskirts of beaver wetlands, variously filled in with vegetation. Rock-free stretches ease the slow descent. Still on the yellow trail, you arrive at the east shore of Glidden Marsh at its snag-riddled end. Lily pads, cattails, islands of grass and rock, and open water later alter the marsh's appearance.

Round east behind a low ridge, returning to Glidden Marsh, and continue straight past a blue trail junction to return to Crane Pond. Round the west shore of a tangled meadow basin before crossing the footbridge over the dark outlet of Glidden Marsh to close the loop. A right turn returns you to the trailhead.

Miles and Directions

0.0 Start from the official Crane Pond trailhead and hike the retired road stretch east.

0.8 Pass the Goose Pond trailhead.

1.5 Take the bypass trail left to skirt a flooded site.

1.8 Reach the old Crane Pond trailhead (at road's end). Follow red markers, crossing the split-level bridge over the outlet linking Crane and Alder Ponds.

2.4 Reach the loop junction and head right.

4.7 Reach Pharaoh Mountain summit. Head south straight across the crown.

6.3 Reach Pharaoh Lake. You'll encircle it counterclockwise.

7.2 Reach the peninsula spur. Detour left to the peninsula and its lean-tos.

8.7 Cross the outlet bridge, coming to a junction. Follow the yellow markers uphill to the left, soon hiking on a soft woods road.

9.3 Bypass the "Pharaoh Hilton" lean-to and keep left where the Springhill Ponds Trail heads right.

10.5 Reach a camp flat. Turn right, ascending to round the steep rocky slope above a lily-pad bay.

11.0 Bypass the Swing Trail, which heads right to Putnam Pond, reaching the Wintergreen Point spur. Continue on the lake trail. **Option:** A 0.1-mile detour leads to Wintergreen Point.

12.0 Round Split Rock Bay.

14.7 Reach a junction. Continue straight on the yellow trail to Glidden Marsh.

15.3 Reach a blue trail junction. Continue straight for Crane Pond.

15.7 Close the loop. Turn right to return to the old trailhead.

16.3 Reach the old Crane Pond trailhead and backtrack to the official trailhead.

18.1 End at the official trailhead.

Options

An alternative start to the **Pharaoh Mountain and Lake Loop** would be to take the 2.8-mile blue Long Swing Trail, which heads south from NY 74 just west of the Paradox Lake Campground road. It comes out on the retired stretch of Crane Pond Road 0.1 mile northwest of the old trailhead. This would make it a 20.3-mile round-trip hike. GPS: 43.879545, -73.678469

Hike Information

Local Information

Lake Champlain Region, 814 Bridge Rd., Crown Point; (518) 523-2445; www.lake champlainregion.com

Local Events/Attractions

Fort Ticonderoga National Historic Landmark offers costumed interpreters, guided tours, historical collections, and musket firing demonstrations at the restored military fortress, a critical Lake Champlain/Lake George defense during the French and Indian and Revolutionary Wars. The fee site is open from 10 a.m. to 5 p.m. Tuesday through Sunday from early May to the end of October. Fort Ticonderoga, 102 Fort Ti Rd., Ticonderoga; (518) 585-2821; www.fortticonderoga.org.

Accommodations

Paradox Lake (DEC) Campground, about 4 miles east of the US 9/ NY 74 junction, is open mid-May through Labor Day and has fifty-eight sites. www.dec.ny.gov/outdoor/24488.html. Reservations: (800) 456-2267; www.reserveamerica.com.

Organizations

Adirondack Mountain Club, 1002 Adirondack Loj Rd., Lake Placid, NY 12946; (518) 668-4447; https://adk.org

12 Stony Pond Trail

This Adirondack Park trail north of Irishtown and Minerva traverses varied terrain to visit Stony Pond along with its neighbors Little and Big Sherman Ponds to the south and Center Pond to the north. A hardwood and conifer forest, beaver sites, and fall foliage complement the serenity of the blue ponds.

Start: At the NY 28N trailhead
Distance: 8.8 miles out-and-back
Approximate hiking time: 4.5 to 6 hours
Difficulty: Moderate
Elevation change: The trail has a 100-foot elevation change.
Trail surface: Earthen path, woods road
Seasons: Open year-round, best hiking spring through fall
Other trail users: Hunters, snowmobilers, snowshoers, cross-country skiers
Canine compatibility: Dogs permitted

Land status: New York State Department of Environmental Conservation (DEC)
Nearest town: Chestertown
Fees and permits: None
Schedule: No time restrictions
Maps: www.dec.ny.gov/docs/lands_forests _pdf/2022vanderwhackernorthgeoref.pdf
Trail contact: New York State DEC, Region 5, 232 Golf Course Rd., Warrensburg; (518) 623-1200; www.dec.ny.gov
Special considerations: Beaver activity can muddle, muddy, or rewrite the trail.

Finding the trailhead: Find the trailhead east off NY 28N, 3.9 miles north of its intersection with Olmstedville Road in Minerva and 2.8 miles south of Hewitt Lake Club Road in Aiden Lair. Parking is roadside; a DEC sign indicates the trail. GPS: 43.832782, -74.016047

The Hike

The trail wears a single track down the middle of the woods road that leads east, away from NY 28N. Yellow snowmobile and red-disk markers help indicate this route, which slowly ascends. Fir, spruce, tamarack, birch, maple, beech, and hobblebush frame the travel aisle. Beyond a site that appears to have been quarried, you'll proceed forward, passing first a private trail to a small pond and then a closed woods road, both on the right.

The trail tops out and slowly descends, passing an area of rocks like tumbled dominoes. Cross Deer Creek headwaters just below a beaver dam, and take a moment to see if you can spot the structure's engineer. Here you have the uncommon experience of being at eye level with the resulting pond. Cross via the dam or on a makeshift array of limbs, or simply give in and wade.

Another slow ascent follows, through low spruce and hemlock trees growing roadside. In half a mile follow the beaver bypass, heading right for drier footing. Where the bypass returns to the snowmobile trail, follow Stony Pond Brook upstream to Stony Pond, a quiet enchantress with a wooded rim, a flat island, and near-shore rocks. Green Mountain rises to the east. The lean-to looks out at the pond, so if you're camping here, you can enjoy this image until shut-eye.

Woods travel leads to Stony and Sherman Ponds.

From the lean-to, trails head around the pond in both directions. To the left, a stone-and-log crossing of the Stony Pond outlet leads to Center Pond, with Barnes and Hewitt Ponds beyond—but first, head right for Sherman Ponds. Follow the orange or red disks, tracing a line where the hardwood slope and conifer shore meet. The trail takes you below some noteworthy 100-foot-tall gray cliffs, where you can see block fracturing, mossy ledges, and a whitewash of lichen.

Eventually the trail climbs away to the right to follow the snowmobile branch that heads toward Sherman Ponds. Another snowmobile route heads left. Before long, the trail descends to Little Sherman Pond, enlarged by beaver-elevated waters. A left spur leads to the marshy shore, while the primary trail bears right, rimming the lake through woods. Green Mountain adds to skyline views. Keep following the snowmobile and red-disk markers.

Skirt the shallow neck joining Little and Big Sherman Ponds. Snags rim the main lake body, but you'll gain views of a wooded peninsula as the trail progresses, skirting a campsite before veering away from the pond. Although the trail continues along Big Sherman Pond, for this hike turn back at the outlet, returning to the Stony Pond lean-to.

To visit Center Pond, cross the Stony Pond outlet and follow the trail as it drifts above and away from shore to round the wooded slope. You'll overlook the gorge-like channel of an inlet brook before hopping across the inlet. Here the trail becomes wetter for a bit, with sphagnum moss growing beneath the fir and spruce branches. Trail markers are sporadic.

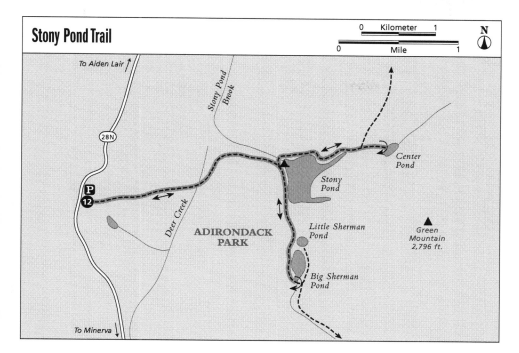

Stony Pond Trail

At the next small brook, look for the trail to jog downstream to an easy crossing point. Stony Pond is just a 100-foot spur away. The trail returns upstream and follows the contour of the slope above a beaver pond, and later a larger pond with reflections of the near-shore snags and trees. At the upcoming junction, follow the yellow trail right to Center Pond.

A steep climb and descent through a similar forest leads to Center Pond. Arrive at a narrow opening in the shrubby shoreline ring that otherwise limits access. This pond is about a quarter of the size of Stony Pond but offers nice solitude. Hooded mergansers or mallards may scatter as you approach. Return to Stony Pond, and then backtrack to NY 28N.

Miles and Directions

0.0 Start from the NY 28N trailhead and head east.

1.1 Cross Deer Creek headwaters.

2.0 Reach the Stony Pond lean-to. Round the lake to the right to continue to Sherman Ponds.

3.2 Reach Big Sherman Pond's outlet and backtrack to the Stony Pond lean-to.

4.4 Reach the lean-to again and cross Stony Pond's outlet.

5.3 Reach a junction. Head right on the yellow trail to Center Pond. *Note:* Straight on the red trail leads to Barnes and Hewitt Ponds.

5.6 Reach Center Pond. Return to Stony Pond and the NY 28N trailhead.

8.8 End at the NY 28N trailhead.

Hike Information

Local Information

Lake Placid Convention and Visitors Bureau/Regional Office of Sustainable Tourism, 2608 Main St., Lake Placid; (518) 523-2445; www.lakeplacid.com

Local Events/Attractions

Stock up for your Adirondack weekend at the **Chestertown Farmers Market,** open from mid-June to mid-September. There's no better place to find locally grown produce and other food items, as well as craft items from wood products to candles. The market runs on Wednesday mornings from 10 a.m. to 2 p.m. in season, on the lawn of the Chester Town Hall, 6307 State Route 9 (chestertownfarmersmarket.com).

Organizations

Adirondack Mountain Club, 1002 Adirondack Loj Rd., Lake Placid, NY 12946; (518) 668-4447; https://adk.org

13 Middle Settlement Lake Hike

Southwest of Old Forge, this all-day or overnight rolling meander through the forests and meadows of Ha-De-Ron-Dah Wilderness visits prized lakes. Wildlife sightings, wilderness quiet, and a complete escape from the trappings of civilization make this a special outing. Beaver activity and the trail's sometimes-sparse markings can compound the challenge, so you'll need to keep your wilderness skills sharp.

Start: At the southern (conservation easement) Middle Settlement Lake trailhead

Distance: 15.2-mile lasso-shaped hike, including spurs to Middle Branch Lake and Grass Pond

Approximate hiking time: 8 to 10 hours

Difficulty: Strenuous because of areas of awkward footing and lack of markers

Elevation change: The trail passes from a low point of 1,650 feet at Stony Creek to a high point of 1,800 feet.

Trail surface: Time-reclaimed earthen and grassy logging roads, foot trail, and boardwalk

Seasons: Best for hiking late spring through fall

Other trail users: Hunters, snowshoers, cross-country skiers

Canine compatibility: Dogs permitted but must be controlled at owner's side by leash or voice command

Land status: New York State Department of Environmental Conservation (DEC) land and private land (at trail's start)

Nearest town: Old Forge

Fees and permits: None

Schedule: No time restrictions

Maps: www.dec.ny.gov/docs/lands_forests _pdf/maphaderondah.pdf

Trail contact: New York State DEC, Region 6, Herkimer Office, 225 North Main St., Herkimer 13350; (315) 866-6330; www.dec.ny.gov

Special considerations: You will need good map and trail detective skills. Be aware that in places the trail markers can grow scarce or disappear altogether or may not adhere to color scheme. Beaver-caused wet passages may require ingenuity. Keep to the initial trail easement, and respect private property.

Finding the trailhead: From Old Forge, go 6.4 miles southwest on NY 28 and turn right at the signed easement for the trails to Ha-De-Ron-Dah Wilderness and Middle Settlement Lake. Go 0.5 mile north on the gravel road to find parking on the right; the brown sign for the trail is just beyond it on the left. GPS: 43.655512, -75.083241

The Hike

A forest of maple, birch, beech, and viburnum engages the eye as you travel the conservation easement trail and Copper Lake Road, following yellow markers weaving into the wilderness. Posted signs occasionally indicate that you are in the wild forest preserve.

Cross small, braided Stony Creek and ascend to the loop junction. Follow the trail to the left, now passing beneath big black-cherry trees. The trail continues its rolling meander, crossing small brooks and soggy bottoms of sphagnum moss. Watch your footing, and keep an eye out for sparse markers.

Beavers are active in many areas of New York, including along Middle Settlement Loop.

After a couple of miles, descend to round the southwestern arm of Middle Settlement Lake, where cross-lake views can include a large beaver lodge, lily-pad clusters, evergreen points, islands, and the large open-water lake. Ruffed grouse, owl, deer, beaver, mink, toad, frog, and eastern newt may contribute lively interludes.

Cross the inlet on either of two beaver dams within easy reach; the trail stays low to the water before pulling away from shore and coming to a trail junction. Bear right, following yellow disks to the Middle Settlement lean-to. After crossing the outlet on rocks and boot-polished logs, reach the shelter atop a 10-foot-high outcrop overlooking the main body of Middle Settlement Lake. The lake's shimmery depths may suggest a swim.

The loop resumes north, rounding the wooded shore with the hummocky floor on a well-traveled path. Among the gargantuan boulders at the end of the lake, come to a junction with a blue trail and pass it, bearing left on the trail you've been following and staying along the drainage. A soggy meadow passage precedes the stone-stepping crossing (or high-water wading) of the outlet of Cedar Pond. Ahead you will glimpse Cedar Pond, a mosaic of open water and soggy shrub islands. Spruce, maple, and birch compose the forest.

Where red disks take over as the loop markers, detour left on the yellow trail if you like, to add a visit to Middle Branch Lake. This detour shows marked climbs and pitches. Go about a mile and turn left to reach the shelter, which occupies a small point overlooking the long water body of Middle Branch Lake. During rainstorms you can pass time reading sagas penned in the lean-to's journal.

Boardwalk eases travel along wet woods segments.

Back on the clockwise loop, the trail, sometimes marshy or rocky, rolls through open woods. Stones ease your crossing of the Grass Pond outlet's dark-ale water. In another half mile, look for the yellow trail angling left to the pond. On your way to Grass Pond, close-growing beech and striped maples may crowd the trail. You'll arrive at a camp flat between the spruce woods and meadow shore, but the pond requires a bushwhacking approach.

Back on the loop, a tranquil woods stroll unrolls before you. Where yellow markers again show the way, travel on the boardwalk through a wet bottomland near the state lands boundary. Keep to the yellow trail, now wide, flat, and easy, bypassing the trail to the popular Scusa Access and a later one to Middle Settlement Lake. The route grows less broad and less refined. As you near a beaver pond, turn left, cross atop the earthen dam, and again turn left to travel along the wooded edge of the floodplain meadow.

Before long, turn right onto an overgrown woods road; the tracked trail usually remains visible beneath the masking ferns. This part of the hike requires greater attention to avoid straying off trail. Bottom areas can be soggy, even in August.

The overgrown roadbed then curves away from the Middle Settlement Creek floodplain. Where hardwoods prevail, rocks and leaves replace the fern wade. Now keep watch for the path on the right, where you'll veer off the woods road to quickly close the loop. From the loop junction, proceed straight toward Copper Lake Road, retracing your steps to the trailhead.

WHAT'S IN A NAME?

Middle Settlement Lake takes its name from an early colony of John Brown—not the famed abolitionist, but a land speculator in the Old Forge area. He attempted to subdivide his lands to attract farmers to the region, but the stern climate and poor soils thwarted his plans and led to the abandonment of his settlements.

The wilderness's name, Ha-De-Ron-Dah, attempts to more accurately reflect the Iroquois term for "bark-eater," previously interpreted as "Adirondack." The Iroquois gave the disparaging name Ha-De-Ron-Dah to their Algonquin neighbors because they would eat the inside of the bark of white pines during times of food scarcity, a practice the Iroquois considered distasteful.

Miles and Directions

0.0   Start from the southern Middle Settlement Lake trailhead. Follow the arrow and yellow markers around a metal gate and along the conservation easement across paper company land.

0.7   Meet narrow dirt Copper Lake Road and follow it left.

1.1   Reach a junction. Turn right off Copper Lake Road onto an established footpath.

1.3   Reach the loop junction and head left. *Note:* Before continuing, observe how and from where the return leg of the loop arrives. It may help when navigating the end of the trail.

2.7   Descend to round the southwestern arm of Middle Settlement Lake.

3.1   Reach a junction and bear right, still following yellow disks. *Note:* A left leads to Lost and Pine Lakes.

3.5   Reach the Middle Settlement Lake lean-to.

3.8   Reach a junction with the blue trail. Pass it and bear left, staying along the drainage. *Note:* The blue trail leads to the right and back to NY 28 (a more established access), if you need to head back to the parking area sooner than planned.

4.8   Reach a junction. Detour left on the yellow trail to Middle Branch Lake before continuing the loop on the red trail straight ahead.

6.0   Follow the left spur to the shelter.

6.3   Reach the Middle Branch Lake shelter. Backtrack to the loop at the 4.8-mile junction.

7.8   Resume the clockwise loop, now following red markers. **Ballout:** Backtrack to the trailhead, forgoing the remainder of the loop, for a 12.6-mile out-and-back hike.

9.1   Cross the Grass Pond outlet.

9.5   Detour left to Grass Pond.

10.0   Reach Grass Pond. Backtrack to the loop.

10.5   Resume the clockwise loop, turning left. **Ballout:** Because the loop ahead becomes trickier to follow, you may choose instead to backtrack from here to the trailhead for a 17-mile out-and-back trek.

Middle Settlement Lake Hike

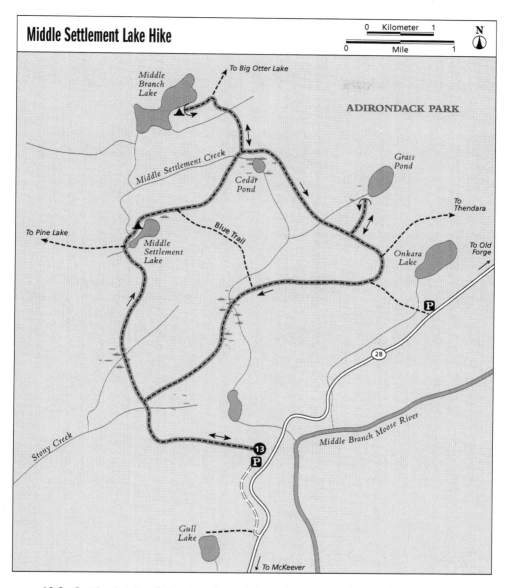

10.8 Reach a junction. Follow the yellow trail forward to traverse a boardwalk.

11.0 Reach a junction. Proceed forward on the yellow trail. *Note:* A left here finds NY 28 and the popular Scusa Access.

11.9 Reach a junction. Follow the yellow markers ahead. *Note:* The blue trail heading right leads to Middle Settlement Lake.

12.3 Cross a beaver dam. Turn left to travel at the wooded edge of the floodplain meadow.

12.6 Turn right, following an overgrown woods road.

13.9 Veer right, returning to the loop junction. Continue straight for Copper Lake Road.

14.1 Turn left onto Copper Lake Road.

14.5 Turn right off Copper Lake Road, retracing the easement to the trailhead.

15.2 End back at the southern trailhead.

Hike Information

Local Information

Adirondack Base Camp, Town of Webb Visitor Information Center, 3140 State Route 28, Old Forge; (315) 369-6983; (877) OLD-FORGE, www.oldforgeny.com

Local Events/Attractions

Just outside Old Forge, **McCauley Mountain Scenic Chairlift Rides** carry you to the mountaintop for scenic viewing of the surrounding lakes and peaks. The fee lift is open June 24 through Indigenous Peoples' Day Wednesday through Monday from 9 a.m. to 4:15 p.m. (315) 369-3225; www.mccauleyny.com/chair_lift.html.

Moose River whitewater rafting is another popular Old Forge draw, with easy trips on the Middle Moose River (May–Sept) and challenging Class V trips on the Lower Moose (Apr only). For information contact the Old Forge visitor center (listed above) or visit www.aroadventures.com/white-water-rafting/moose-river/.

Accommodations

Nicks Lake (DEC) Campground, 278 Bisby Rd., Old Forge, is open mid-May through Indigenous Peoples' Day and has 112 sites. Reservations: (800) 456-2267; www.reserveamerica.com.

Organizations

Adirondack Mountain Club, 1002 Adirondack Loj Rd., Lake Placid, NY 12946; (518) 668-4447; https://adk.org

14 West Canada Lakes Wilderness Hike

In the Moose River Recreation Area in the west-central Adirondacks, this designated wilderness encompasses one of the last regional wilds to be opened to foot travel and human visitation. This overnight outing or demanding all-day hike travels to the core of the West Canada Lakes Wilderness, passing through conifer-hardwood forest and meadow breaks to visit three pristine lakes: Falls Pond, Brooktrout Lake, and West Lake. From the trail, you can access the trans-Adirondack Northville-Placid Trail or visit such other celebrated features as Spruce Lake and Cedar Lakes.

Start: At the Brooktrout Lake trailhead
Distance: 18.2 miles out-and-back, including the Falls Pond detour
Approximate hiking time: 9 to 11.5 hours
Difficulty: Strenuous
Elevation change: The trail has a 550-foot elevation change.
Trail surface: Earthen or grassy foot trail, retired logging roads, and outcrop
Seasons: Open year-round; Memorial Day weekend through fall are best for hiking
Other trail users: Hunters
Canine compatibility: Dogs permitted (leash recommended)

Land status: New York State Department of Environmental Conservation (DEC)
Nearest town: Inlet
Fees and permits: None, but drivers entering Moose River Recreation Area must register upon entering
Schedule: No time restrictions
Maps: www.dec.ny.gov/docs/lands_forests _pdf/mapwcanada.pdf
Trail contact: New York State DEC, Region 5, 701 South Main St., Northville; (518) 863-4545; www.dec.ny.gov

Finding the trailhead: From central Inlet, go southeast on NY 28 for 0.8 mile, and turn south onto Limekiln Road for the Moose River Recreation Area. Go 1.8 miles, turn left, and register for the recreation area. Continue east on the wide improved dirt road (15 mph), following signs to Otter Brook. In 11.4 miles cross the Otter Brook bridge and follow the signs to Brooktrout Lake (right). Find the trailhead on the left in 0.9 mile and parking for a dozen vehicles. GPS: 43.645580, -74.689505

The Hike

The trail ascends steadily, overlooking a series of beaver ponds. Boughs of maple, spruce, birch, and beech interlace overhead; sarsaparilla, ferns, whorled aster, and brambles edge the lane.

Detour right on the yellow-marked trail to Falls Pond. Pass through scenic fir-spruce woods, edge the outlet meadow, and cross the outcrop at the head of the meadow before reaching the lake outlet, a campsite, and an outcrop view. Falls Pond, a mountain beauty with an irregular shoreline, enchants with outcrop points and islands, an evergreen rim, and enfolding leafy hillsides.

Fog lends atmosphere to lakes in West Canada Lakes Wilderness.

On the main trail, outcrops open up the trail corridor, while dense, low-growing spruce and fir squeeze it. By August's last days, the leaves show the onset of change, with orange, yellow, red, and maroon hues. The trail rolls to cross the bridge over the Wolf Lake outlet, coming to a junction. You may opt to explore the path on the left, which takes you to two additional lakes: Deep and Wolf, each within a mile of the trail. For this hike alone, though, continue forward.

The main trail passes over exposed bedrock (slippery when wet) and among young deciduous trees. A cairn points you onto the lower edge of the outcrop, which then leads to trail. Paired planks cross wet spots and meadow habitats. Blue gentian and sunlit nodding cotton grass adorn meadow swaths in late summer. At a beaver pond, you might spy the industrious furball.

Later you lose all trace of the old road, as well as such niceties as the wetland foot planks, but more yellow disks show the way. Cross the Deep Lake outlet atop stones. Past a scenic cluster of mossy boulders and logs, keep left, traversing a spruce bog. Here the trail becomes muddied both literally and figuratively; beware of impostor paths. At a rise, hobblebush and young beech frisk passersby.

The trail then contours the wooded slope above Brooktrout Lake—a gleam in the basin. Because the wilderness trail is removed from the lakes, take advantage of all the side trails to camp flats and lean-tos to get satisfying looks at the lake. At the Brooktrout Lake lean-to, side trails venture to the lake and a boulder-and-marsh shore. Although the legacy of acid rain still silences these remote lakes, their beauty is uncompromised.

WATER

Even in frigid conditions, you need at least two quarts of water a day to function efficiently. Add heat and taxing terrain, and bump that figure up to one gallon. That's simply a base to work from—your metabolism and your level of conditioning can raise or lower that amount. Unless you know your level, assume that you need one gallon of water a day. But where do you plan on getting the water?

The easiest solution is to bring water with you. Natural water sources can be loaded with parasites, bacteria, viruses, and fertilizers. *Giardia lamblia,* the most common of these, is a protozoan parasite that lives part of its life cycle as a cyst in water sources. The parasite spreads when mammals defecate in these water sources. Once ingested, *Giardia* can induce cramping, diarrhea, vomiting, and fatigue within two days to two weeks after ingestion. If you believe you've contracted giardiasis, see a doctor immediately, as it is treatable with prescription drugs.

Past the lean-to, bear left, rounding away from the lake. You'll cross over a rise to tour above the meadow basin at the upper extent of West Lake. At a trail sign near a split boulder, a spur leads to a lakeside camp, where views span the lake to Pillsbury Peak. The rolling trail now contours the forested slope above West Lake. Beyond piped spring water, you'll reach the first of two West Lake lean-tos. Spurs branch to the boulder-strewn lakeshore.

Continue rounding the lake to the southeast, crossing in wet meadow. Where the trail returns to woods, beautiful carpets of oxalis complement the curvature of the trail. Cross the outlet bridge, bypass the historic dump from the former rangers' cabin, and look for a junction post in the meadow.

Here you meet the blue Northville-Placid Trail, leading left to Cedar Lakes. Go right for the second West Lake lean-to, this hike's turnaround point. A cross and an old rock foundation sit near the junction. The cross commemorates the rangers' cabin that stood here, but the ruin isn't part of that—it's what is left of the fireplace from the legendary French Louie's cabin, which preceded the rangers' cabin. Canadian-born French Louie Seymour, a circus worker, trapper, lumber worker, and woodsman, lived as a hermit in cabins he built himself in the Adirondack backcountry until his death in 1915. If you pick up nearly any book about the history of the Adirondacks, you'll find some mention of French Louie and his love of the north country woodlands.

The West Lake lean-to looks out at West Lake, its boulder-strewn shore, a string of rocks concluding at a small rock island, and an attractive rolling wooded terrain. Return as you came, or check out some of the other lakes in this area.

West Canada Lakes Wilderness Hike

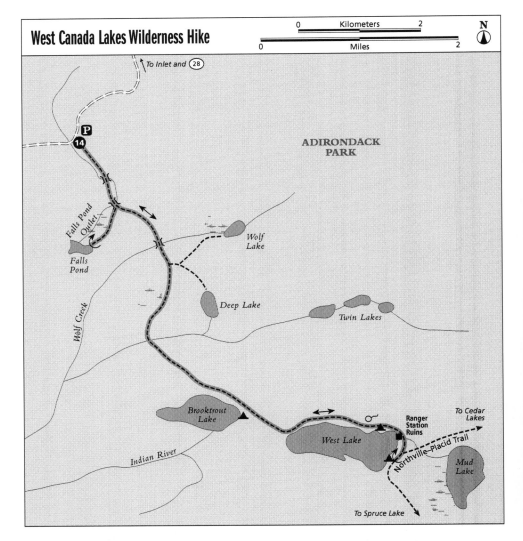

Miles and Directions

0.0   Start from the Brooktrout Lake trailhead. Round the barrier to follow a retired logging road.

1.2   Cross a small logging bridge.

1.5   Reach a junction. Detour right to Falls Pond.

2.0   Reach Falls Pond and return to the main trail.

2.5   Reach the main trail and turn right.

3.2   Cross the bridge over the Wolf Lake outlet. In 200 yards reach a junction and proceed forward. **Option:** The trail on the left leads to Deep and Wolf Lakes, reaching Deep Lake in 0.9 mile or Wolf Lake in 1 mile. Wetlands and beaver dam flooding can create a soggy trek to the latter.

5.5	Pass a scenic cluster of mossy boulders and logs. Keep left, traversing a spruce bog.
6.5	Reach the Brooktrout Lake lean-to. Hike past the lean-to and bear left away from the lake, following red and yellow disks.
8.9	Reach the first West Lake lean-to.
9.4	Meet the Northville-Placid Trail, head right, and then bear right at the next junction.
9.6	Reach the second West Lake lean-to. Return to the trailhead.
18.2	End at the Brooktrout Lake trailhead.

Hike Information

Local Information

Adirondack Base Camp, Town of Webb Visitor Information Center, 3140 State Route 28, Old Forge; (315) 369-6983; (877) OLD-FORGE; www.oldforgeny .com

Local Events/Attractions

The Old Forge Mountain Bike Trail System between Old Forge and Eagle Bay in the Adirondack Forest Preserve incorporates 100 miles of interlocking mountain bike trails, fun rides for the entire family. Contact the Old Forge visitor information center (https://rideoldforgemtb.com).

Accommodations

Limekiln Lake (DEC) Campground, off Limekiln Road on the way to the trail-head, is open mid-May through Labor Day and has 271 sites. Reservations: (800) 456-2267; www.reserveamerica.com.

Organizations

Adirondack Mountain Club, 1002 Adirondack Loj Rd., Lake Placid, NY 12946; (518) 668-4447; https://adk.org

15 Siamese Ponds Hike

This all-day or backpack hike travels a scenic low-elevation central Adirondack forest, parallels the East Branch Sacandaga River, and visits a large wilderness pond. The hike follows the historic 1800s Bakers Mills–North River Stagecoach Route and travels a wild area suitable for beaver, bear, mink, otter, grouse, and other woodland creatures. Autumn brings rustling bursts of vibrant color.

Start: At the Siamese Ponds Highway 8 trailhead
Distance: 12.0 miles out-and-back
Approximate hiking time: 6 to 8 hours
Difficulty: Moderate
Elevation change: This trail has a 500-foot elevation change. From a trailhead elevation of 1,800 feet, the trail ascends 200 feet before descending to a river elevation of 1,600 feet and ultimately climbing to Siamese Ponds at 2,118 feet.
Trail surface: Earthen path, stage route, old road

Seasons: Open year-round, spring through fall are best for hiking
Other trail users: Hunters
Canine compatibility: Dogs permitted
Land status: New York State Department of Environmental Conservation (DEC)
Nearest town: Wells
Fees and permits: None
Schedule: No time restrictions
Maps: www.dec.ny.gov/docs/lands_forests _pdf/mapsiameseponds.pdf
Trail contact: New York State DEC, Region 5, 232 Golf Course Rd., Warrensburg; (518) 623-1200; www.dec.ny.gov

Finding the trailhead: From Bakers Mills (south of Wevertown), go 3.8 miles south on NY 8. A small DEC sign marks the trail's large gravel parking lot on the west side of the highway. GPS: 43.590367, -74.090316

The Hike

Ideal for a family backpack or your very first backpack outing, this trail journeys west into Siamese Ponds Wilderness, initially ascending on a former roadbed through an arbor of young birch, aspen, and maple. The blue-disk trail markers are few in number, but you won't need many to stay on this trail. Ferns, hobblebush, and sarsaparilla contribute to the woodland understory; jewelweed fills the moist drainages in late summer.

The grade eases as the trail parallels a small drainage upstream, crossing over the low shoulder of Eleventh Mountain. From here, the route follows a historic stagecoach route, and the trail descends. The forest's spatial order and changing mix of trees lend visual diversity. After a mile firs and spruce fill out the complex, and black-cherry trees make an appearance. In meadow clearings you may discover milkweed in spring and early summer, and Joe Pye weed and aster as fall approaches.

The stage route levels off along the riparian corridor of the East Branch Sacandaga River. At the Diamond Brook bridge crossing, budding biologists often kneel

East Branch Sacandaga River suggests a lingering stop en route to Siamese Ponds.

on the bank in search of tiny fry, crayfish, and mud puppies. Brambles, low alders, and goldenrod in late summer contribute to the riparian meadow bordering the trail. At the plank bridge ahead, look for Diamond Mountain to the right. Woodland travel resumes within 100 feet of the river.

The trail briefly tags the herb-and-forb riverbank for an open look at the shallow, 50-foot-wide river, interrupted by occasional riffles, rocks, and bedrock, varying widely with the ebb and flow of seasonal currents. The mild-grade earthen trail frees eyes to enjoy the setting, perhaps even to spy a bear slogging across the river—something we were fortunate enough to do.

After the trail draws farther from the river, it becomes more rolling. Abandoned apple trees and a younger, more open woods hint at a former farm. Afterward, the trail drifts back toward the river.

At the fork, bear left for Siamese Ponds. Follow a former road grade as it dips to a drainage crossing and returns to the wooded riverbank for occasional views. When you reach the suspension bridge over the East Branch Sacandaga, a lean-to overlooks the water, a rain-tight lodging complete with table, fireplace, and functional privy. A connecting spur to the Old Farm Trail passes in front of the lean-to; don't take it—instead, cross to continue toward the ponds.

The suspension bridge affords fine views of the East Branch Sacandaga River. As you step off the bridge, continue straight ahead, passing side spurs that branch to camp flats and shore. The trail rolls and then dips, coming to a small runoff meadow where a pair of hewn logs aid crossing. A rock-riddled ascent follows, but easy travel resumes with an earthen bed, and nothing more strenuous than a moderate grade.

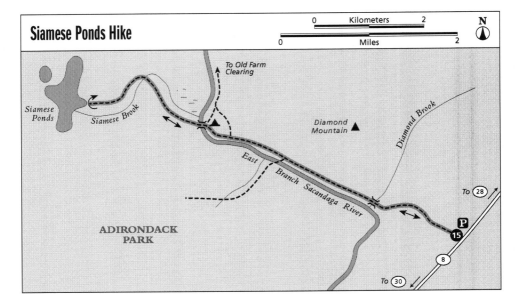

Siamese Ponds Hike

Fir, spruce, birch, hemlock, and striped and sugar maples shade the way, with a fickle showing of ground cover.

After crossing Siamese Brook, you assume a more continuous rocky ascent. Where a few boulders dot the slope, the trees can exceed 18 inches in diameter, and the trail becomes more rolling. One of the Adirondacks' five species of woodpecker, ruffed grouse, or eastern newt may divert your eyes. The trail then passes campsites, descending to Siamese Ponds.

Shaped like an amoeba, the primary pond has a beach of boulders and sand at its point of access. Humpbacked conifer-deciduous hills, including Hayden Mountain to the north, overlook the pond. Aquatic vegetation spots its shallow edge. To round the shore for more views or to reach Upper Siamese Pond, you'll need to do some bushwhacking—which may be miserable during blackfly season. When you're ready, return as you came.

Miles and Directions

0.0   Start from the Siamese Ponds Highway 8 trailhead and head west.

0.4   Cross the shoulder of Eleventh Mountain.

1.5   Cross Diamond Brook bridge.

3.5   Reach a fork. Bear left on a former road grade for Siamese Ponds. *Note:* The old stagecoach route continues to the right toward the Old Farm trailhead.

3.9   Cross the East Branch Sacandaga River suspension bridge.

4.9   Cross Siamese Brook atop rocks.

6.0   Reach Siamese Ponds, then return to the trailhead.

12.0   End back at the Highway 8 trailhead.

Hike Information

Local Information

Adirondacks Speculator Region Chamber of Commerce, 2960 NY 30, Speculator; (518) 548-4521; www.speculatorchamber.com

Local Events/Attractions

The Speculator Region (southwest of Siamese Ponds) is noted for its fishing. Lakes, ponds, and rivers produce catches of smallmouth bass, trout, salmon, and walleye. Contact the chamber (see above) for details and for outlets where fishing licenses are sold.

Organizations

Adirondack Mountain Club, 1002 Adirondack Loj Rd., Lake Placid, NY 12946; (518) 668-4447; https://adk.org

16 Tongue Mountain Range Loop

Northeast of Bolton Landing, this demanding loop tags five summits of the peninsular Tongue Mountain Range for unsurpassed looks at the Lake George countryside. It then dips to lake level and visits Point of Tongue before returning along Northwest Bay. Although the trail's signature offerings are its spectacular lake, island, and ridge views, diverse woods, colorful fall foliage, marsh, cliffs, vernal pools, and wildlife sightings will further reward your breaking a sweat.

Start: At the Clay Meadow trailhead
Distance: 14.0-mile lasso-shaped hike
Approximate hiking time: 8 to 10 hours
Difficulty: Strenuous due to terrain and elevation gains and losses
Elevation change: This peak-tagging trail has a 1,500-foot elevation change, with the low point at Montcalm Point (Point of Tongue), and the high point at the Fifth Peak lean-to (1,813 feet).
Trail surface: Woods road, rocky and earthen path
Seasons: Best for hiking spring through fall
Other trail users: Hunters
Canine compatibility: Dogs permitted

Land status: New York State Department of Environmental Conservation (DEC)
Nearest town: Bolton Landing
Fees and permits: None
Schedule: No time restrictions
Map: www.protectadks.org/hike-tongue-mountain/
Trail contact: New York State DEC, Region 5, 232 Golf Course Rd., Warrensburg; (518) 623-1200; www.dec.ny.gov
Special considerations: The trail has steep pitches that may require hand assists. Markers may be few and faint in places, so keep a careful watch for them. Carry adequate drinking water, and beware: Rattlesnakes live in this rugged terrain.

Finding the trailhead: From I-87, take exit 24 and head east toward Bolton Landing. In 5 miles turn north on NY 9N and go 4.4 miles to find head-in parking on the east side of the highway at the old quarry pond. You'll find the Clay Meadow trailhead just south of the parking lot; the trail heads east. GPS: 43.629255, -73.608269

The Hike

Travel a time-softened woods road through a conifer plantation and across a wetland boardwalk to reach the loop junction. Common wetland sightings include white-tailed deer, frogs, and great blue herons. For the clockwise loop, bear left toward the Fifth Peak lean-to on a steadily ascending, sometimes rocky and rootbound woods road. Hikers enjoy views of Lake George from shore and ridgetop.

A severe windstorm in 1995 razed some of the bigger framing hemlock, beech, and maple along this route. Where the trail grows steeper, look for it to switchback to the left, where it rounds below mossy outcrop cliffs on a scenic hemlock-birch plateau.

Hikers enjoy views of Lake George from shore and ridgetop.

The ascent resumes to the saddle junction. Turn right for the loop, continuing toward the Fifth Peak lean-to, and stay right for a pleasant rolling hike to the shelter junction. A half-mile out-and-back detour with yellow markers leads left to the Fifth Peak lean-to, with its dry overnight wayside, privy, and an open outcrop delivering a southern Lake George vantage.

The primary trail journeys south along a narrow, less-used foot trail, descending a hemlock-pine slope to reach a moist deciduous bottom. On Fourth Peak, cross outcrops within an old fire zone, hinted at by silver snags. Views stretch south and west.

At the base of an outcrop, a trail marker points left. Briefly follow the contour of the slope, then sharply descend right, easing over rocks and coming to a notch. Once again, climb from maple-hemlock woods to a piney crest, with overlooks of Lake George and the forested islands from Saint Sacrament to Floating Battery Island, and with cross-lake views of Black and Erebus Mountains.

Atop Third Peak you'll find a steep pitch before climbing to another open view. The trail then pitches, rolls, and streaks up French Point Mountain for the best views of the hike. Open outcrop vantages encompass French Point (a peninsula extending into Lake George), the many treed islands of The Narrows, the chain of islands stretching north, and the ridges and mountains rolling east.

Round a small cairn and descend past a vernal pool to an outcrop view of Northwest Bay and First Peak—the final summit conquest, separated by a 400-foot elevation drop and a matching gain. The trail shows a similar pitch-and-climb character, passing through an oak-and-grass habitat. Where the path again overlooks the steep eastern flank, views feature the narrow lake, the dark humpbacked ridges, and the jigsaw puzzle of islands.

Atop First Peak awaits a 180-degree Lake George vista. The trail now hugs the east side of the ridge, passing among oak, hickory, and ash. Shortly, two small bumps add views toward Bolton Landing. The trail opens up ahead, descending and offering views of Montcalm Point.

After the trail curves west into hemlock and deciduous woods, arrive at a junction. Here the loop bears right; a detour left follows blue markers to Montcalm Point (Point of Tongue). This travels the forested peninsula to the point, which extends views to Lake George and Northwest Bay, as well as an outcrop that beckons swimmers and sunbathers.

Resume the loop north, passing through moist woodland along Northwest Bay, heading toward Clay Meadow. The trail rolls to and from shore, rounding shallow coves and cutting across points. Cross an ash swale (formerly a beaver pond) before the trail drifts away into mixed woods. A spur branches to a viewpoint of the marshy head of Northwest Bay. Passing looks at the marsh grass, lily pads, and stands of red maple and cedar lay ahead.

At a footbridge the trail heads inland for a steady half-mile ascent. You'll return once more to the marsh's edge before crossing another footbridge to close the loop. Backtrack the short distance to the trailhead.

Miles and Directions

0.0 Start from the Clay Meadow trailhead and follow blue disks along a woods road.

0.4 Reach the loop junction. Bear left, following red disks uphill.

1.3 Look for the trail to switchback left.

1.9 Reach the saddle junction. Turn right and keep right, heading toward the Fifth Peak lean-to.

2.4 Reach the Shelter junction; turn left.

2.6 Reach the Fifth Peak lean-to and vantage. Return to the loop and turn left.

3.5 Look at the base of an outcrop for the trail marker, pointing you left.

3.9 Reach Third Peak.

4.9 Reach French Point Mountain.

6.0 Reach First Peak.

7.6 Follow the trail as it curves west into hemlock-deciduous woods.

8.0 Reach a junction. Detour left to Montcalm Point (Point of Tongue) before resuming the loop, which heads right here.

8.4 Reach Montcalm Point. Return to the loop and bear left.

10.4 Cross an ash swale (formerly a beaver pond).

11.8 Pass a spur to the marshy upper bay.

12.0 Cross a drainage footbridge. Ascend inland on trail.

13.6 Close the loop and backtrack left to the trailhead.

14.0 End at the Clay Meadow trailhead.

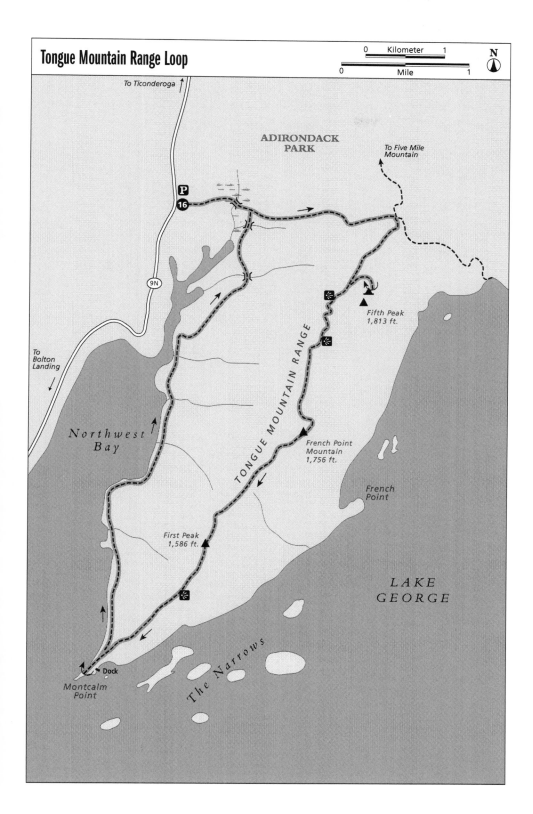

Tongue Mountain Range Loop

0   Kilometer   1

0   Mile   1

N

To Ticonderoga

ADIRONDACK
PARK

To Five Mile
Mountain

P
16

9N

Fifth Peak
1,813 ft.

TONGUE MOUNTAIN RANGE

To
Bolton
Landing

French Point
Mountain
1,756 ft.

French
Point

Northwest
Bay

First Peak
1,586 ft.

LAKE
GEORGE

The Narrows

Dock

Montcalm
Point

Hike Information

Local Information
Warren County Tourism Department, 1340 State Route 9, Municipal Center, Lake George; (800) 95-VISIT; www.visitlakegeorge.com

Local Events/Attractions
Lake George is noted for its fishing and boating. Charter cruises and steamboat tours are popular, offering leisurely introductions to the lake. Contact the county tourism department (see above) for names of operators.

Accommodations
Rogers Rock (DEC) Campground, about 20 miles north on NY 9N, is open early May through Labor Day and has 332 sites. Reservations: (800) 456-2267; www .reserveamerica.com.

Organizations
Adirondack Mountain Club, 1002 Adirondack Loj Rd., Lake Placid, NY 12946; (518) 668-4447; https://adk.org

17 Jockeybush Lake Trail

This easy climb through rich mixed forest follows the outlet drainage to Jockeybush Lake—attractive, cold, and deep. Although the hike is short and the lake is small, the offering is big with its fishing, woods flora, and sense of calm. This trail is ideal to cap off the day or to tuck into a busy travel schedule.

Start: At the Jockeybush Lake Trailhead
Distance: 2.2 miles out-and-back
Approximate hiking time: 1.5 to 2 hours
Difficulty: Easy
Elevation change: The trail has a 250-foot elevation change.
Trail surface: Earthen path, sometimes muddy or rocky
Seasons: Open year-round, spring through fall are best for hiking
Other trail users: Hunters, snowmobilers, snowshoers, cross-country skiers
Canine compatibility: Dogs permitted (leashing recommended)

Land status: New York State Department of Environmental Conservation (DEC)
Nearest town: Gloversville
Fees and permits: None
Schedule: No time restrictions
Map: https://cnyhiking.com/JockeybushLake .htm
Trail contact: New York State DEC, Region 5, 701 South Main St., Northville; (518) 863-4545; www.dec.ny.gov
Special considerations: Expect some soggy reaches. Because the lake access is limited, this trail is best hiked when there are few or no other vehicles at the trailhead.

Finding the trailhead: From the junction of NY 29A and NY 10 in the village of Caroga Lake, go north on NY 10 for 14.6 miles, passing through the village of Canada Lake and the small hamlet of Arietta. Find the marked trailhead and paved parking area on the left side of NY 10, across from a lily pond. A register is on the left at the hike's start. GPS: 43.300874, -74.564941

The Hike

Head west, ascending into woods and following the orange snowmobile markers. The mixed-age, multistory forest of white pine, hemlock, birch, black cherry, maple, and beech, along with hobblebush and ferns, weaves an enchanting study. Sunlight filters through the branches, and a breeze often lilts through the woods. Soon a pair of grand hemlocks stand sentinel.

At a mudhole crossing a disorganized scatter of logs left over from an old corduroy road helps keep your feet dry. The trail now travels the north shore above the outlet brook. Early in the hiking season, side drainages also can complicate travel. Most times, though, the foot trail presents a pleasant, meandering tour.

Next make a stone-stepping crossing over the 10-foot-wide, clear-flowing outlet brook. (High water may require you to wade.) A mossy cascade accentuates the outlet where the brook washes over the outcrop. As the trail grows rockier with muddy pockets, evasive paths may disguise the true trail. In this stretch, just keep the outlet brook to your right, and before long the trail and brook will become more closely paired.

As you ascend the ridge to the lake basin, you again find a good earthen path. Arriving at the lake, cross the beaver dam at the outlet, now crowded with silver logs, to reach a shoreline outcrop. This presents an open view spanning the length of this long, deep lake, taking in the shrub banks and enfolding conifer-deciduous rims. You may see people fishing here. Regularly stocked with fish, Jockeybush Lake offers anglers a challenge, if not always success. Local anglers typically

Forest critters like this American toad lend interest and surprise to hikes.

carry in a fishing tube or small raft to escape the shrubby entanglements of shore.

To round the shore to the main body of the lake requires some determination and a bit of bushwhacking through thick spruce and hobblebush. Frogs and toads dwell lakeside, while insect hatches rise from the lake surface. You'll likely choose to linger awhile before breaking away from the lake view. The return is back the way you came.

Miles and Directions

0.0 Start from the Jockeybush Lake Trailhead and ascend west.

0.4 Cross the outlet brook.

1.1 Reach Jockeybush Lake. Return by the same route.

2.2 End at the Jockeybush Lake Trailhead.

Hike Information

Local Information

Hamilton County Department of Economic Development and Tourism, 102 County View Dr., Lake Pleasant; (518) 548-3076; www.hamiltoncounty.com

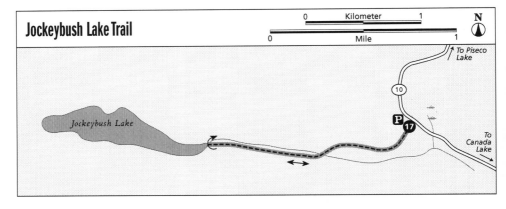

Jockeybush Lake Trail

INCREDIBLE ADIRONDACK PARK

Adirondack Park is the outcome of one of the oldest conservation efforts in the nation. Verplanck Colvin's early survey work and reports to the legislature on the Adirondacks laid the groundwork for this wild area to receive permanent protection. In 1885 the New York State legislature passed the act that created both the Adirondack and Catskill Forest Preserves, declaring that the state-owned lands in eight Adirondack and three Catskill counties should "be forever kept as wild forest lands." Legislators went even further in 1892, stretching the boundaries of these special places to include neighboring private lands, forming Adirondack and Catskill Parks. The forward-thinking conservation movement culminated in 1895 when the "Forever Wild" Amendment was written into the New York State Constitution, bolstering up and sealing the protection.

Today, at 6 million acres, Adirondack Park is the largest intact publicly protected landmass in the contiguous United States. To grasp its size, Adirondack Park exceeds the combined land areas of the biggest national parks: Yellowstone, Yosemite, Everglades, and Grand Canyon. Although the protective legislation for the Adirondacks has faced challenges over the past hundred years, residents and their legislators remain committed to keeping these regulations in place.

Besides pristine forests, Adirondack Park contains more than 8,000 square miles of mountains, including forty high peaks topping 4,000 feet in elevation; more than 2,000 lakes and ponds; and more than 1,500 miles of river. Taking us to and through this bonanza, more than 2,000 miles of hiking trails crisscross Adirondack Park.

Local Events/Attractions

Piseco Lake, to the north of Jockeybush Lake, is a popular center for fishing and camping.

Accommodations

Little Sand Point and Point Comfort (DEC) Campgrounds on the north side of Piseco Lake, 8 miles north on NY 10, are open early May through Labor Day and have a total of 154 sites. Reservations: (800) 456-2267; www.reserveamerica.com.

Organizations

Adirondack Mountain Club, 1002 Adirondack Loj Rd., Lake Placid, NY 12946; (518) 668-4447; https://adk.org

Honorable Mentions

○ Grass River Wild Forest Hike

About 15 miles south of Canton, Grass River Wild Forest offers a 2,900-foot-long all-ability trail leading to the nearly 100-foot plunge of Lampson Falls and gathering views of rapids, deep pools, and cascades. Mixed forest, meadow shores, wildlife, and solitude help the river wash away stress. For a longer exploration, you can take a 3-mile out-and-back hike following the trail downstream along the east shore of the river from the falls to a former bridge site, where an island still divides the Grass River flow (1.5 miles). From there, a more informal trail continues north (downstream) along the east bank. There are plans to develop the river trail all the way from Lampson Falls north to Harper's Falls on the North Branch Grass River.

From Cranberry Lake Village, go west on NY 3 for 19.9 miles. Turn north toward DeGrasse on NY 27 (DeGrasse Fine Road). Bear right in 0.8 mile, and go another 7.6 miles and turn right at a T junction in DeGrasse, remaining on CR 27. Go 4.3 miles from DeGrasse to find the DEC sign for Grass River Wild Forest on the left. GPS: 44.405038, -75.061719. Contact New York State Department of Environmental Conservation (DEC), Region 6, 190 Outer Main St., Potsdam; (315) 265-3090; www.dec.ny.gov.

Sheeting waters shade the head of Lampson Falls.

D Indian Pass-Lake Colden Loop

In the MacIntyre Mountain Range of Adirondack Park, this grueling boulder-and-mud obstacle course passes through typical Adirondack splendor: mixed forests, shining waters, meadows, and great views. Beware, though: The loop includes the notoriously difficult Cold Brook Pass, and the missing trail markers sometimes leave you on your own. But sterling views of Wallface Cliff and the Adirondack High Peaks, chill-blue lakes, and crystalline brooks counter the physical and mental challenges and, sometimes, torment of the trail.

So muster up some steely determination, and gather maps and your best backcountry travel skills and aids, if you plan to hit this 15.9-mile loop. Starting at the Upper Works trailhead, the loop swings clockwise past Henderson Lake, along Indian Pass Brook past Wallface Peak, and then up and over the MacIntyre Mountains at Cold Brook Pass. The route then curls back, visiting Colden Lake, Flowed Ponds, and Calamity Brook. The loop is best hiked in summer and fall. Avoid during high water because of the boulder-hopping passage along and across Indian Pass Brook and the many side brook crossings. Even under the best conditions, this stretch threatens a cracked tailbone if you lose your footing. For a map, use the National Geographic Adirondack Park Lake Placid/High Peaks map.

From the NY 30–NY 28N junction in Long Lake, go east on NY 28N for 18 miles. Turn left on NY 2 (seasonally maintained), bearing left at the intersection in 0.4 mile. In another 0.8 mile turn left on NY 25 toward Tahawus, following the road to where it dead-ends at the Upper Works trailhead (another 9.5 miles). Trailhead parking and the trail's start and end are all state easements on private land. GPS: 44.089119, -74.056297. Contact the New York State Department of Environmental Conservation, Region 5, PO Box 296, 1115 NY 86, Ray Brook 12977; (518) 897-1200; www.dec.ny.gov.

E Camp Santanoni Trail

In the Newcomb Area, this trail journeys 5 miles (10 miles out-and-back) along a carriage road to a classic Adirondack Great Camp, a National Historic Landmark. In the late nineteenth and early twentieth centuries, these camps offered luxury vacation getaways to the elite of the city. Camp Santanoni belonged to the Pruyn family of Albany. It included a working farm that provided meat, fruit, and dairy for the vacationers and the large, woodsy lakeside mansion on Newcomb Lake.

The main lodge dates to 1893, designed by noted architect Robert H. Robertson. A common roof and extensive porches adjoin the sleeping and common living areas of this large, dark log complex. Stone fireplaces and rustic limb-fashioned doors add to its charm. The Great Camp came into the state's hands in 1972, and much of it is still undisturbed, with restoration and preservation ongoing to keep this emblem of the past for generations to come. The carriageway trail extends an enjoyable and comfortable woods stroll to the camp. The leafy boughs of mixed hardwoods decorate

Rustic historic structures recall the glory days of the Great Camps.

the roadside and weave a picturesque cathedral. In summer horse-drawn wagon rides (a private tour) may share the way, harkening back to the era of the Great Camp.

The trail's marked turnoff is north off NY 28N at the west end of Newcomb, east of the Newcomb Visitor Interpretive Center (VIC). The NYSDEC trailhead and parking are just up the road near the camp's Gateway Arch. GPS: 43.972588, -74.164099. You can obtain brochures and trail information at the Newcomb VIC or contact New York State DEC, Region 5, 232 Golf Course Rd., Warrensburg 12885; (518) 623-1200; www.dec.ny.gov.

F Goodnow Mountain Trail

Also in the Newcomb area, this self-guided hiking trail in the Huntington Wildlife Forest, privately owned by the College of Environmental Science and Forestry (ESF) in Syracuse, offers one of the most manageable and popular climbs in the Adirondacks. Beech, birch, and maple, along with a few hemlocks and white pines, shape the woodland setting. The trail leads to the nine-story restored 1922 lookout tower and partially open summit that extend grand forest, basin, and High Peaks–Hudson River views. You can enjoy Adirondack wilds as far as the eye can see, but use the tower at your own risk, and beware of high winds. Historic structures remain from the Archer and Anna Huntington estate: foundations, a well, and an old horse barn add to discovery. The 3.8-mile out-and-back hike has a moderate gradient. Arrows and interpretive posts keyed to the ESF trail brochure keep you on track. Obey all ESF rules.

Locate the marked trail and its parking south off NY 28N, 1.5 miles west of the Newcomb Visitor Interpretive Center and about 12 miles east of Long Lake. GPS: 43.969660, -74.214388. Contact the State University of New York (SUNY) College of Environmental Science and Forestry, 1 Forestry Dr., Syracuse; (315) 470-6500; www.esf.edu.

G Whetstone Gulf State Park

South of Lowville, Whetstone Creek cuts a 380-foot-deep, 3-mile-long gash into this 2,100-acre park on the eastern edge of the Tug Hill Plateau. The park's North and South Trails shape a 6-mile rim loop, overlooking the gulf. Picturesque Whetstone Creek, dramatic sandstone-shale cliffs, fossils, a waterfall, and wildflowers nudge you forward. Pass through either pine woods intermixed with oak, maple, beech, and birch, or a pine plantation. Whetstone Creek makes a hairpin turn in a sheer cliff bowl, and in a squeezed gorge at the head of the gulf, the creek tumbles furiously in serial cascades that grade from 2 feet high at the top to 40 feet high at the bottom. You must be off the trail by 6 p.m., and no one may start a hike after 3 p.m. Leashed dogs are allowed, but owners must present proof of each animal's rabies shot.

Tannin-colored waters spill between the cliffs of Whetstone Gulf.

From central Lowville, go south on NY 26 for 6.1 miles and turn right (northwest) onto West Road (NY 29). Go 0.2 mile and turn left, entering the state park. Find the trailhead near the beach house/swimming area. GPS: 43.702541, -75.465013. Contact Whetstone Gulf State Park, 6065 West Rd., Lowville; (315) 376-6630; https://parks.ny.gov/parks/whetstonegulf/details.aspx.

H Gleasmans Falls Trail

East of Lowville, find this relaxing stroll through magnificent woods and meadow clearings that leads to an outcrop overlooking the picturesque stepped falls on the Independence River. The 6.5-mile out-and-back trail journeys past the stone ruins of a sawmill and a beaver pond and welcomes nature study. At the first rocky access to the Independence River, the river pulses through a gorge shaped by outcrops, cliffs, and boulders—an exciting union of cascades, deep pools, dark water, and gneiss (metamorphic rock). Pockets of ferns adorn the gorge. The view at the end of the trail overlooks the upper cascade of Gleasmans Falls, which shows the greatest drop of 12 feet. Overall, the waterfall plunges 50 to 60 feet over a 0.2-mile distance. Flat stretches interrupt the half dozen stepped cascades.

Cascading waters characterize Gleasmans Falls.

From NY 12/NY 26 in Lowville, turn east on River Street, which becomes Number Four Road (NY 26) upon leaving town. In 4.1 miles turn left, staying on Number Four Road for another 4.8 miles. Turn right onto Erie Canal Road, go 2.5 miles, and turn left onto McPhilmy Road, a single-lane dirt road. In 0.2 mile turn left onto Beach Mill Road, a narrower dirt road with limited shoulder for turnouts; reduce speed. Where this road forks in 0.9 mile, stay left and go another 2 miles to reach the trailhead at road's end. GPS: 43.808432, -75.276210. Contact New York State Department of Environmental Conservation, Region 6, 7327 State Route 812, Lowville; (315) 376-3521; www.dec.ny.gov.

| Peaked Mountain Trail

In Siamese Ponds Wilderness, this split-personality trail joins an easy hike to Peaked Mountain Pond with a rugged summit ascent of Peaked Mountain. The final 0.3 mile to the summit laughs at gravity, uniting boot-skidding, steep dirt surfaces and severe bare-rock inclines—all the more tricky on descent. For anyone uninitiated with the rugged nature of the Adirondacks, this summit approach shouts a loud, clear "Howdy!" Exposed summit outcrops among the low-growing spruce unfold a 270-degree view; obtaining northern views requires more effort. The best views sweep the immediate neighborhood with Peaked Mountain Pond, the meadows, Big and Little Thirteenth Lakes, and Slide and Hour Pond Mountains. Far-reaching views round up the Adirondack High Peaks and Vermont Green Mountains. Ravens offer noisy commentary while vultures drift on thermals. Lake, brook, pond, forest, and meadow habitats surround the trail, which travels 6 miles out-and-back. The best time to hike the trail is summer and fall; wet weather increases the summit challenge.

At the hamlet of North River on NY 28 (12 miles east of Indian Lake), turn south on Thirteenth Lake Road for Siamese Ponds Wilderness/Thirteenth Lake. Go 3.3

Peaked Mountain Pond shines from its wooded basin.

miles and turn right onto improved-dirt Beach Road to reach the wilderness entry and trailhead parking in another 0.5 mile. GPS: 43.718754, -74.118636. Contact New York State Department of Environmental Conservation, Region 5, 232 Golf Course Rd., Warrensburg; (518) 623-1200; www.dec.ny.gov.

⌡ Black Mountain Loop

This 7-mile lasso-shaped trail tops Black Mountain, the tallest mountain above Lake George, for a superb panorama of the lake region, with its open water, islands, and bumpy ridges; eastern looks extend to Vermont. Counterclockwise, the hike pairs a fairly steep assault on the mountain with a tempered, switchbacking descent. Mountaintop views unite Lake George; Elephant and Sugarloaf Mountains; Main, Harbor, and Vicars Islands; Five Mile Mountain; and the northern Tongue Mountain Range. You'll find superb viewing from the outcrop nose at the abandoned fire tower. The hike's descent builds on these views. Stay alert for where this trail loops back east at the base of the mountain. Rangers report this is a trouble spot for many hikers.

Ponds and beaver marshes put a stamp on the tour. At the base of the mountain, you'll travel the north shore of Black Mountain Pond, an open water with a broad meadow shore of leatherleaf and other marsh shrubs. Fish tap the surface, leaving ever-widening rings. Next up is Round Pond, which resembles the first pond but with a broader marsh shore and small silvered snags. Lapland Pond completes the roll call. Meadow, beaver marsh, and woods carry the hike home.

From the junction of NY 74 and NY 22 at Ticonderoga, go 17 miles south on NY 22, turning west on County Road 6 for Huletts Landing. In 2.5 miles turn south on Pike Brook Road, finding the gravel parking lot for the trailhead on the right in 0.8 mile. GPS: 43.611546, -73.493189. Contact New York State Department of Environmental Conservation, Region 5, 232 Golf Course Rd., Warrensburg; (518) 623-1200; www.dec.ny.gov.

Niagara Frontier

At the western extreme of New York State, the Niagara Frontier follows the rocky escarpment that shares its name, linking two Great Lakes: Erie to the west and Ontario to the north and east. The Allegheny Mountains nudge the region from the south, while the westernmost Finger Lakes—Conesus and Hemlock—shape the frontier's eastern border. The nation's three most famous waterfalls—American, Horseshoe, and Bridal Veil— form the torrents known collectively as Niagara, tumbling over the border between the United States and Canada. It's fitting that the people of the Seneca Nation, who long stood guard here, were known as "Keepers of the Western Door."

Father Hennepin, a French Recollect priest who was among the first to explore the area, popularized Niagara Falls in his 1683 published travel account, and the curiosity and wonder associated with Niagara Falls have never ceased. The isolation and protection afforded by the Great Lakes and the Niagara River shaped this region's history: one conflict after another focused on taking this land, first among the Indigenous people and later through wars between the French, the British, and the newly independent Americans. The French and Indian War of the 1750s and the War of 1812 saw some of their most dramatic battles here. Once the Americans finally sealed their ownership, wars ended and development began—and within two decades, the Erie Canal linked the Hudson River to the Great Lakes, pushing commerce westward and opening a water route through the Great Lakes and into the Louisiana Purchase. In the years leading up to the Civil War, the Underground Railroad, firmly established in the Niagara Frontier, helped fleeing slaves as they tackled the final leg north to Canada. By the turn of the twentieth century, clever engineers and inventors found ways to harness the power of Niagara Falls to make Buffalo the first city in America to bring electricity to every home.

Agriculture, industry, and tourism are the big callings for this area. Less flashy landscapes of lowland forest, plains, and swamp hold their own appeal and discovery. The deep incision of the Genesee River Gorge, centerpiece to Letchworth State Park, is an undeniable star. Glacial activity gouged out this attraction.

18 Erie Canal Heritage Trail

Between Lockport and Albany, the former towpath of the Erie Canal, now a National Recreation Trail, traces the past and provides an attractive off-road avenue for hiking, cycling, jogging, and exercise walking. Working features of the historic and present-day canal, canal-side museums, lowland forest, rural landscapes, greenway parks, and the communities that emerged and blossomed with the canal bring to life the era's exciting story. This Section of the 300-mile trail stretches from Lockport to Rochester.

Start: At the Lockport trailhead
Distance: 55.0 miles point-to-point between Lockport and Henpeck Park in Greece, west of Rochester
Approximate hiking time: Dependent on distance traveled, anywhere from 1 hour to 4 or 5 days
Difficulty: Easy
Elevation change: The trail is flat, at about 550 feet above sea level.
Trail surface: Paved, crushed limestone, stone dust, or natural surface
Seasons: Open year-round, but only a few segments are plowed in winter. Hiking is best spring through fall.
Other trail users: Cyclists, joggers, snowshoers, cross-country skiers
Canine compatibility: Leashed dogs permitted
Land status: New York State Canal Corporation public lands

Nearest towns: Lockport, Gasport, Middleport, Medina, Albion, Hulberton, Holley, Brockport, Spencerport, Greece
Fees and permits: None
Schedule: Dawn to dusk
Map: www.canals.ny.gov/maps/index.html ?layer=trail
Trail contact: New York State Canal Corporation, Buffalo Division, 4950 Genesee St., Suite 190, Cheektowaga; (716) 686-4400, www.canals.ny.gov
Special considerations: Because the sun can be harsh and there is little or no drinking water available along the trail, carry plenty of drinking water for both you and your pets. Several greenways have picnic tables, serving boaters and trail users. A few have chemical toilets. Facilities are available in towns, often just a short walk from the trail. Beware of poison ivy growing along the trail's sides.

Finding the trailhead: Find the western terminus at Locks 34 and 35 in downtown Lockport at the corner of Cottage and Main Streets, opposite the Lockport Municipal Building and Visitor Center, where brochures are available. GPS: 43.171442, -78.692430

Multiple north–south roadways cross the canal trail, providing convenient access to or egress from the route. For the trail segment discussed here, the eastern terminus is at Henpeck Park on NY 386 in the town of Greece. GPS: 43.188271, -77.730976

The Hike

In the nineteenth century, the Erie Canal brought New York State an efficient means of transporting weighty goods from New York City's ports, the mills and mines in the Adirondacks, and the state's farms and industries to developing lands west of Buffalo.

Locks level passage along the Erie Canal.

No longer did it take weeks to transport the products of forests and mines by horse-drawn wagon, making it possible to sell raw materials like bluestone, coal, garnets, lumber, and much more to builders in the newly acquired lands around the western Great Lakes. Railroads eventually ended the need for the canal as a commercial route, but it continues to serve recreational boaters, naturalists, and hikers, offering a gentle escape from the industrial world it fostered. The communities that sprang up along the canal continue to provide services to canal travelers.

Making a west-to-east journey along the northern towpath, descend along Locks 34 and 35, where impressive gates of wood and steel close at an angle, sealed by the force of the water. Here the lock's chambers fill and empty in 15 minutes, raising boats heading west, or lowering them to head east. Where the trail crosses the grate of a thundering spillway, interpretive signs explain the operation and history of the canal. The Canal Museum, also located here, deepens the story with historic photographs, artifacts, and personal accounts of this great engineering feat.

Dubbed the "Long Level," the canal tour from here to Rochester is lock-free. Pass through tree-shaded Upson Park and skirt the New York State Canal Corporation maintenance yard before towpath travel begins in earnest. A border of locust, mulberry (recalling an early venture into the silk industry), box elder, willow, and cottonwood shades travelers. Queen Anne's lace, chicory, daisy, black-eyed Susan, tiger lily, and a dozen other wildflowers fill the trailside with color. Long open stretches occur later.

Orchards, cornfields, and cropland; farmhouses and silos; and historic homes complete the canal surroundings. In this flat terrain, the height of the towpath levee is adequate to provide an overview. A marina and a few primitive boat docks access the 60-foot-wide canal. Ring-billed gulls, belted kingfishers, barn and tree swallows, and great blue and green herons share the corridor.

Small towns mark off travel: Gasport (5 miles), Middleport (11 miles), Medina (15 miles), Albion (25 miles), Holley (36 miles), Brockport (42 miles), and Spencerport (50 miles). Typically, the heart of each town sits on the south side of the canal. Recent renovations in anticipation of the canal's bicentennial in 2025 gave these towns freshly painted lift bridges, which facilitate boat traffic and link the canal towpath to town. Attractive brick buildings with their original nineteenth-century architecture, some with side murals depicting the canal era, help emphasize the link between the canal and its central role in the history of these towns.

Outside of the towns, single-lane bridges span the canal and towpath; all date back to the 1910s. East of Medina the trail passes over Culvert Road. Ripley's Believe It or Not! recognizes Culvert Road as the only road that passes under the Erie Canal. This 1823-built road shows a stone block construction and dripping archway.

East of Gallop Road Bridge, the towpath halts, detouring onto Canal Road for 0.2 mile. It returns quickly to the northern towpath, where a canal breach feeds a lake on the south shore.

Past Brockport and Adams Basin, the tree border fills out, casting shadows and closing out views. The trail landscape blinks from rural to rural-suburban. At Canal and Union Streets in Spencerport, Towpath Park offers another likely stopping point.

The selected hike ends on the east side of NY 386 at the town of Greece's Henpeck Park. In the 1800s Henpeck (the port of South Greece) boasted a grocery, post office, school, apple dryhouse, two doctors, and a community of twenty-five homes. Today Greece is one of the largest suburbs of Rochester, with 14,500 residents.

Erie Canal Heritage Trail

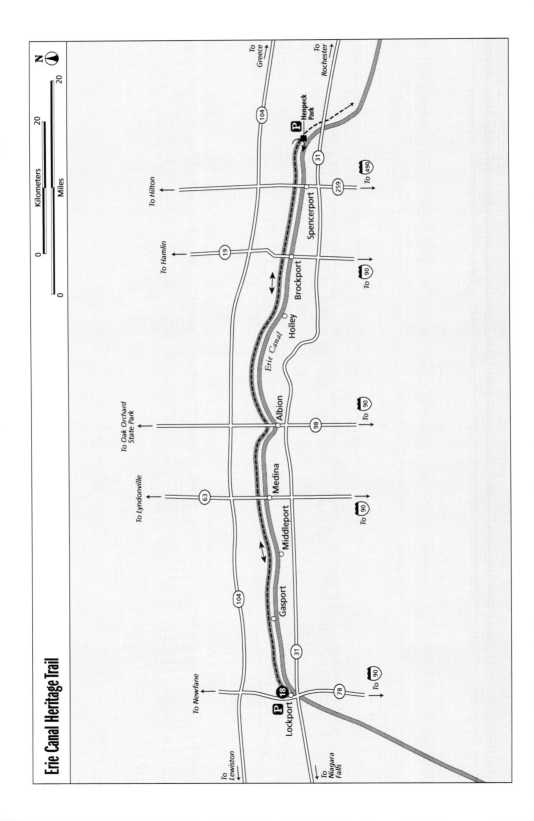

Miles and Directions

0.0 Start from the western (Lockport) trailhead and follow the northern towpath east. **Option:** To set the stage, detour to the Canal Museum for a bit of history.

5.0 Reach Gasport.

11.0 Reach Middleport.

15.0 Reach Medina.

17.0 Cross over Culvert Road.

25.0 Reach Albion.

36.0 Reach Holley.

42.0 Reach Brockport.

50.0 Reach Spencerport. **Bailout:** At Canal and Union Streets, you may end at Towpath Park.

55.0 End at Henpeck Park in the town of Greece.

Hike Information

Local Information

Destination Niagara USA, 10 Rainbow Blvd., Niagara Falls; (877) FALLS-US (325-5787); www.niagarafallsusa.com

Local Events/Attractions

One block from the Lockport Lock, the **Erie Canal Discovery Center,** open daily May through October, celebrates the great endeavor of the Erie Canal and Lockport's own supporting role through video, exhibits, and a mural. The Erie Canal Discovery Center, 24 Church St., Lockport; (716) 439-0431; https://niagarahistory.org/ECDC.html.

In Medina the **Medina Railroad Museum** in the old New York Central freight depot holds exhibits, models, and dioramas devoted to railroading history. An excursion train departs the depot and travels through canal country. Museum hours are Wednesday through Sunday from 10 a.m. to 5 p.m.; call for train schedules. Medina Railroad Museum, 530 West Ave., Medina; (585) 798-6106; www.medinarailroadmuseum.org.

Accommodations

Nearly two dozen B&Bs or quaint inns sit in the historic towns along this section of the canal. Contact Destination Niagara USA (see above for phone and website).

Organizations

New York State Canal Corporation provides oversight, maintenance, and interpretation of the 300-mile Erie Canal path. Buffalo Division, 4950 Genesee St., Suite 190, Cheektowaga; (716) 686-4400; www.canals.ny.gov.

Parks & Trails New York helps promote, expand, and protect trails, parks, and open spaces statewide and prints and sells a cycling guide to the Erie Canal. Parks & Trails New York, 33 Elk St., Albany; (518) 434-1583; www.ptny.org.

19 Letchworth State Park

South of Rochester, the 17-mile-long Genesee River Gorge of Letchworth State Park contains three major waterfalls, elegant side-creek falls, and 400- to 600-foot-tall sheer sandstone-shale cliffs. Trails explore the developed park of the western rim. The park's celebrated Gorge Trail provides stunning views of the canyon rim and waterfall features, while the Mary Jemison Trail opens a chapter of early Seneca Nation history. The historic Glen Iris Inn holds a place of honor at the edge of the falls area.

Start: At the Gorge Trail's upper trailhead
Distance: 7.8 miles one-way
Approximate hiking time: 4 to 5.5 hours
Difficulty: Moderate, due to stairs and some uneven footing
Elevation change: The rolling trail has a 300-foot elevation change.
Trail surface: Earthen forest path
Seasons: Open year-round, hiking is best spring through fall.
Other trail users: None
Canine compatibility: Leashed dogs (with proof of rabies shot) permitted on short lead. Because this is a busy trail, it is best to leave high-strung and rambunctious dogs at home.
Land status: New York State Park

Nearest town: Mount Morris
Fees and permits: Park admission fee
Schedule: Daylight hours for trails
Map: https://parks.ny.gov/documents/parks/LetchworthTrailMapSouth.pdf
Trail contact: Letchworth State Park, 1 Letchworth State Park, Castille; (585) 493-3600; https://parks.ny.gov/parks/letchworth/
Special considerations: The park allows spring turkey hunting and deer hunting in season (Oct–Dec); wearing blaze orange is recommended for hiker safety during deer season. Keep to the trails and keep well back from the cliffs due to undermining and unstable, crumbling edges.

Finding the trailhead: From the NY 36–NY 408 junction in the village of Mount Morris, go north on NY 36 for 1.1 miles and turn left, reaching the Mount Morris entrance to the state park in 0.4 mile. From this entrance, proceed 15.8 miles south to the Gorge Trail upper trailhead; it is 0.4 mile north of the park's southern entrance. GPS: 42.577868, -78.050878

The Hike

The popular Gorge Trail (Trail 1) represents the premier hiking trail within the developed park. This downstream stroll begins at the upper trailhead, passing under the railroad bridge. The first rim vista overlooks the 70-foot horseshoe drop of Upper Falls. A plume of mist shoots up and out from the white rushing fury, nurturing the green cloak of the eastern wall.

As the well-groomed trail continues, it presents new perspectives. Basswood, maple, oak, and spruce overhang the route. As the trail skirts a landscaped day-use area, it offers downstream looks at the delicate streamers of a side-creek falls and the bulging west cliff.

Upper Falls is the first of three major falls on the Genesee River.

Soon a side perspective of a waterfall of Niagara proportion comes into view. This is Middle Falls, the most spectacular of the three falls in this section of the park. A viewing deck below the Glen Iris Inn serves up a grand look at this 107-foot-high, 285-foot-wide waterfall as it thunders over an abrupt river ledge. Follow the yellow blazes up and away from the inn, where the trail frequently travels the thin woods-and-grass buffer between the rim and the park road. After passing through a mixed evergreen stand planted in 1917, look for an obelisk dedicated to New York's First Dragoons of the Civil War on a roadway island.

At the roadside vista dubbed Inspiration Point, an upstream view opens before you of Middle and Upper Falls and the railroad bridge. Interpretive signs now mark the tour as the trail descends the rim's tiers. In another mile come to a side trail that descends 127 steps to Lower Falls. A broad vista deck, a river bridge, and a 0.1-mile upstream spur present this 50- to 60-foot waterfall, a curving crescent with a tumble of cascades. At the bridge the platy shale and sandstone seams of the cliff become clearly visible.

Retrace your steps uphill to resume the downstream hike, skirting below the Lower Falls day-use area. Hemlock and beech offer rich shade. After the Gorge Trail turns away from the rim, bear right to pass a restaurant and again travel near the park road, where you share roadside vistas with motorists, now overlooking Great Bend. Copper-gilded turkey vultures soar on the thermals.

The designated Great Bend Overlook Viewing Area provides the best view in the park of the dizzying 550-foot cliffs, scoured bowl, and raging Genesee River.

Afterward, the trail descends fairly steeply, crossing a footbridge over a charming side water. The trail flip-flops from rim to road until it joins with Wolf Creek. Here you can admire the eroded and fluted river cliffs, the broad Genesee River, and twisting Wolf Creek Falls in its own narrow canyon.

Skirt the picnic areas of Wolf Creek, Tea Table, and Saint Helena, with their rustic stone-and-slab tables. The Gorge Trail stops at the lower Saint Helena Picnic Area, where it meets the Saint Helena Trail (Trail 13), the end of this hike.

Miles and Directions

0.0 Start from the Gorge Trail upper trailhead. Cross the park road from the upper trailhead parking lot, pass under the railroad bridge, and follow rockwork steps downhill to the gorge rim. Turn left (downstream).

0.2 Reach the Upper Falls view.

0.7 Reach the Middle Falls viewing deck.

1.4 Reach Inspiration Point.

2.4 Take the spur to the right to the Lower Falls area.

2.8 Reach the Lower Falls vantages. Return to rim trail travel.

3.2 Resume downstream rim travel, skirting the Lower Falls picnic area.

3.5 After the Gorge Trail turns away from the rim, reach a junction and bear right, skirting a restaurant to again travel near the park road.

4.2 Reach a roadside vantage.

4.7 Reach another roadside vantage.

5.6 Reach Great Bend Viewing Area.

6.6 Cross Wolf Creek.

7.8 End at the Saint Helena Trail (Trail 13) in the lower Saint Helena Picnic Area. **Option:** You may continue on the Saint Helena Trail, which forks in 0.1 mile. Each branch then leads 0.2 mile to the river shore and an interior view of the Gorge.

Options

While at the park, here are a couple of other trails to investigate:

The 2.8-mile knot-shaped **Kisil Point Trail** (Trail 18) travels a canyon jut, Kisil Point Ridge, to overlook Silver Lake Outlet and the Genesee River farther downstream from the Gorge Trail. The hike begins from a roadside trailhead near the Highbanks Campground entrance or near Campground Loop 100, if you are camped. Where the trails merge, travel the piney outskirts of the camp past an old picnic shelter to arrive at a loop junction (0.4 mile). The right fork travels the Genesee River side of Kisil Point Ridge; the left fork overlooks Silver Lake Outlet. At 0.9 mile the arms of the loop reunite and a spur branches to the end of Kisil Point (1.4 miles). The point view includes the tinsel stream of Silver Lake Outlet as it parts a thick green swath of forest, and the Genesee River Canyon, with its steep gray cliffs, eroded silt skirts, and broad

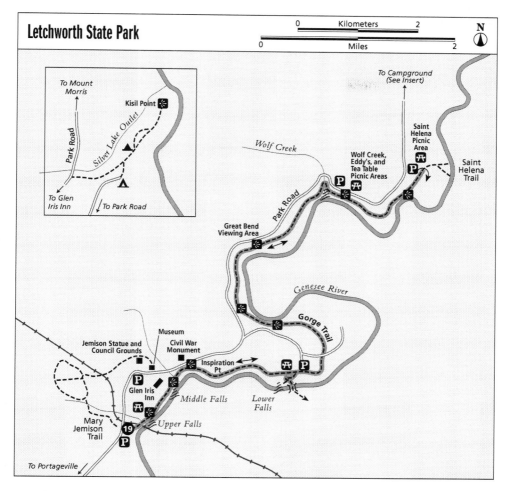

0   Kilometers   2

0   Miles   2

N

To Campground
(See Insert)

To Mount
Morris

Kisil Point

Silver Lake Outlet

Park Road

To Glen
Iris Inn

To Park Road

Wolf Creek

Wolf Creek,
Eddy's, and
Tea Table
Picnic Areas

Saint
Helena
Picnic
Area

Saint
Helena
Trail

Great Bend
Viewing Area

Park Road

Genesee River

Gorge Trail

Museum

Jemison Statue and
Council Grounds

Civil War
Monument

Inspiration
Pt.

Glen Iris
Inn

Middle Falls

Lower
Falls

Mary
Jemison
Trail

19

Upper Falls

To Portageville

floodplain. Return to the loop, taking the arm not traveled, and return to camp or car. Kisil Point Trail starts 4 miles south of the Mount Morris park entrance.

The 2.5-mile loop of the **Mary Jemison Trail** (Trail 2) unveils area history. The trail's name honors the white-woman captive who came to revere the Seneca people with whom she lived. The trail begins at the museum and travels to Council Grounds, where a statue of Mary Jemison, an 1800s pioneer cabin, and a tribal Council House predating the American Revolution become a satisfying detour. The trail then heads west, negotiating a series of confusing junctions. Follow the number "2" through mixed woods, hemlock stands, and a pine plantation to visit a couple of linear reservoirs. Evidence of beaver activity surrounds the ponds; in the woods, deer may cross your path. Reach the Mary Jemison Trail and Council Grounds 14.9 miles south of the Mount Morris entrance to the park.

Hike Information

Local Information

Wyoming County Chamber & Tourism, 36 Center St., Suite A, Warsaw; (800) 839-3919; www.gowyomingcountyny.com

Local Events/Attractions

April through October, **Balloons Over Letchworth,** a private hot-air balloon company, offers a lofty vantage of Letchworth canyon and its waterfalls. Balloons Over Letchworth is operated by Liberty Balloon Company, 6730 Barber Hill Rd., Groveland; (585) 243-3178. Book online at www.balloonsoverletchworth.com.

Accommodations

Letchworth State Park campgrounds have 270 electric sites and five areas with cabins. Reservations: (800) 456-2267; www.reserveamerica.com. The completely restored Glen Iris Inn also offers accommodations and serves meals; (585) 493-2622; www.glenirisinn.com.

20 Niagara Falls State Park

Start with the falls, and then head downriver to experience the power of the Niagara River as it cuts a spectacular dividing line between the United States and Canada.

Start: At the trailhead building in Niagara Falls State Park, across from the Discovery Center
Distance: The Great Gorge Railway Trail is 2.2 miles out-and-back, and the trail through Devil's Hole State Park is 2.5 miles out-and-back.
Approximate hiking time: 2 hours
Difficulty: Easy for the Great Gorge; Devil's Hole is a moderate hike because of 300 stone steps
Elevation change: About 200 feet
Trail surface: Chiseled stone, rock, gravel, and dirt
Seasons: Spring through fall; these trails may close in winter, so call before visiting
Other trail users: Hikers only
Canine compatibility: Leashed dogs permitted (clean up after animals)

Land status: Niagara Falls and Devil's Hole State Parks
Nearest town: Niagara Falls
Fees and permits: None
Schedule: Open daily dawn to dusk
Maps: https://parks.ny.gov/documents/parks/NiagaraFallsNiagaraGorgeTrailMap.pdf; also available from the Niagara Falls Gorge Discovery Center
Trail contact: Niagara Falls State Park, 332 Prospect St., Niagara Falls; (716) 278-1794; www.niagarafallsstatepark.com
Special considerations: Take special care when hiking in winter. While rocks line the path on the riverside, the trails are icy and may be slicker because of spray from the river and falls.

Finding the trailhead: Great Gorge Railway Trail: From Niagara Falls, take the Robert Moses Parkway north to the Niagara Gorge Discovery Center. The trailhead is behind the trailhead building, located across from the Discovery Center. GPS: 43.08211, -79.05081
Devil's Hole State Park: From Niagara Falls, take the Robert Moses Parkway north past the Niagara Gorge Discovery Center to the park. Watch for Devil's Hole State Park, and the trailhead is on the left side of the parkway. GPS: 43.13342, -79.04729

The Hike

When it comes to awe-inducing power and the thrill of swirling rapids, few rivers in the northeastern United States can match the Niagara—especially in the miles after Niagara Falls tumbles from its 176-foot height into the basin below. To appreciate the river's force and its influence on the sedimentary rock walls that contain it, descend into the gorge on the gentle Great Gorge Railway Trail.

One of eight trail choices you'll find along this stretch of the river, the Great Gorge Railway Trail offers a gentle, paved slope downward, with gorge walls rising slowly but imposingly over hikers as you descend. Beginning with four excellent overlook points along the gorge rim—each with interpretive displays supplied by the park—this trail provides stunning views of the American Falls through the arch of the Rainbow Bridge, while telling stories of the falls' industrial heritage, its hospitality to flora and fauna, and its place in the nation's history.

From the Devil's Hole Trail, you can see both the US (left) and Canada (right) on the Niagara River. PHOTO BY NIC MINETOR

After the fourth overlook, the trail slopes steadily but gradually downward, bringing you within touching distance of the gorge walls. Hanging gardens cling to these walls as water seeps through cracks in the dolostone, covering portions of the rock with verdant foliage in spring and summer. In winter and early spring, look for icicles suspended like stalactites from outcroppings and ledges above.

The Great Gorge trail ends under the Whirlpool Bridges—two routes into Canada for cars and trains—and at a chain-link fence. Beyond the fence the Whirlpool Rapids Trail begins, but this section is closed to the public. Steep slopes make this area dangerous and impassable to hikers. To return to the gorge rim, retrace your steps up the paved trail.

If you enjoyed the Great Gorge but you still feel energized enough for a second hike, make the short drive from the Discovery Center to Devil's Hole State Park, just a couple of miles down Robert Moses Parkway. Nearly obscured from view until you're standing at its rim, the Devil's Hole area can be startling at first glimpse: a deep gouge in the Niagara Gorge—actually a side gorge, eroded by an outlet of an ancient glacial lake (long since run dry) and now filled with thriving vegetation.

Legends abound about the mischief emitted by this yawning chasm. Long ago the Seneca people believed that the Great Spirit pushed back the Great Falls of Onguiaahra (what we now call the American Falls) for several miles to punish them for their wars with other tribes, until this gouge stood open and free of water—and the Evil Spirit trapped in this hole became free to wreak havoc. Seneca men determined to explore the cave and challenge the wayward spirit went down into the hole . . . and never returned. One did emerge eventually, but he blathered like a madman. Even the great explorer Robert La Salle succumbed to the lure of Devil's Hole, venturing in alone to hear the prophecy spoken by the Spirit—and then ignoring its warnings that further westward exploration would lead to his doom. Just as the Evil Spirit predicted, La Salle ventured deep into what would become the territory of the Louisiana Purchase, lost nearly everything he had, and died at the hands of a mutineer who wanted no more of the explorer's leadership.

The oracle, such as it is, has been silent for centuries since, so your descent into Devil's Hole will likely not lead to a forecast of your personal doom. Just follow the series of stone and concrete staircases around the perimeter of the side gorge until it comes to ground just a few feet above water level—an extraordinary place from which to view the river's pounding rapids, standing waves, and daunting rock formations.

The steep stairs—some 300 steps in all—are only the beginning of the adventure here. This is an active gorge where rock falls are commonplace, so it's likely that the trail will be overrun in some spots by fallen dolostone and other sedimentary rock. Wear sturdy footwear with closed toes, and be prepared to step over piles of shale and sandstone as you make your way along this 1-mile trail.

If you're up to the challenge, the payoff here is rich: Viewing the river's swirling waters, still agitated from their tumble over Niagara Falls, can be one of upstate New York's sublime wilderness experiences. Rapids in this part of the river are rated Class

III, but you'll see Class V whitewater if you continue past the Whirlpool staircase on the Whirlpool Rapids Trail.

A second set of steps awaits you at the end of the gorge portion of this hike, but these are not as steep, and they include gently inclined switchback trails between staircases. You're welcome to retrace your steps down the Devil's Hole Trail to return to your car, but I recommend climbing out of the gorge here at the end, and walking back to the trailhead along the Rim Trail at the top.

Miles and Directions

Great Gorge Railway Trail:

0.0 Begin the trail behind the trailhead building, outside the Niagara Gorge Discovery Center. Several trails begin here. You're following Trail 4.

0.1 Here is the first overlook. An interpretive sign gives details about the concrete structure here.

0.2 Turn left at this intersection and go down the steps (or around on the ramp).

0.3 This is the second scenic overlook. To your left, you can see Niagara Falls through the Rainbow Bridge.

0.4 From the third overlook, you can see the Whirlpool Bridges and the beginning of the Whirlpool Rapids. This is a particularly good spot to view gulls and other birds.

0.5 You've begun the descent into the gorge. At this fourth overlook, you have a great view of the Whirlpool Bridges, and the interpretive display tells the story of several bridges that have spanned this river. In about 350 feet the American Falls Gorge Trail goes off to your left and behind you. Continue straight on the Gorge Railway Trail as you descend into the gorge.

1.1 You've reached the end of the trail, under the Whirlpool Bridges and at the chain-link fence. On either side of the gorge near the bridges, you can see the foundations of a former railroad bridge that preceded these steel structures. This is the end of the Great Gorge Railway Trail. Turn around and retrace your steps to the trailhead near the Discovery Center.

2.2 You are back at the Discovery Center. If you wish, drive from here to Devil's Hole State Park.

Devil's Hole State Park:

0.0 If you've come up the Robert Moses Parkway from Niagara Falls, park in the area across the road from the park. Take the pedestrian walkway over the road to the gorge rim. The trailhead is to the right, near the Niagara Power Project scenic overlook. If you arrive on the parkway from the north, the park entrance is on your right.

0.3 Here are the stairs to the power plant overlook. The largest electricity producer in New York State, the recently modernized Robert Moses Niagara Power Plant diverts water from the river and into the plant, generating 2.4 million kilowatts of carbon-free electricity through the power of water. The stairs down into the gorge begin at the end of this platform.

0.5 You've come down 0.2 mile of stairs to the trail, just above water level. Turn left and begin to follow the trail along the river gorge. There are some narrow points in the trail with steep drop-offs, and some areas are obscured by fallen rock. Some huge boulders seem to block the trail, but the path usually winds between them.

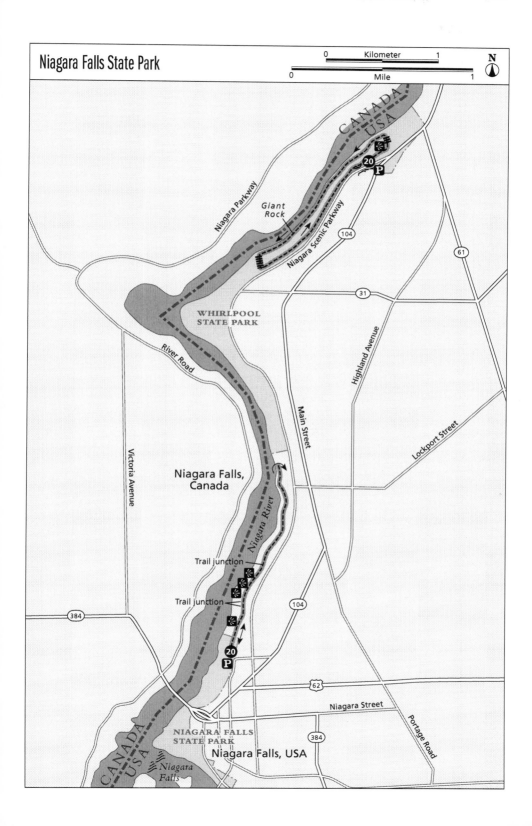

Niagara Falls State Park

0   Kilometer   1

0   Mile   1

N

CANADA
USA

20
P

Niagara Parkway

Giant
Rock

Niagara Scenic Parkway

104

61

31

WHIRLPOOL
STATE PARK

River Road

Highland Avenue

Main Street

Lockport Street

Victoria Avenue

Niagara Falls,
Canada

Niagara River

Trail junction

Trail junction

384

104

20
P

62

Niagara Street

Portage Road

CANADA
USA

NIAGARA FALLS
STATE PARK

384

Niagara Falls, USA

Niagara
Falls

1.3 Here is Giant Rock, an impressive chunk of dolostone fallen from the Lockport formation above you. (From the Canadian side of the river, you can see the hole in the wall that this rock once occupied.)

1.5 Whirlpool staircase. The Whirlpool Rapids Trail continues straight ahead—a challenging hike, with some boulder-hopping. You are welcome to proceed down this trail to see the famous whirlpool and rapids. If you prefer, head up the stairs to the rim.

1.7 You've reached the Rim Trail. Turn left and walk along the rim to the Devil's Hole trailhead and your vehicle.

2.5 Arrive at the parking area.

Hike Information

Local Information
Niagara Falls USA Visitor Center, 10 Rainbow Blvd., Niagara Falls; (877) FALLS-US. Note that if you plan to cross the border into Canada, a US passport or enhanced driver's license is required.

Local Events/Attractions
The **Maid of the Mist,** one of the most famous and popular attractions in the world, takes visitors on an electric-powered sightseeing boat to the base of the falls, where you can hear and feel the power of 600,000 gallons of water rushing downward every second. Souvenir ponchos are provided, but expect to get wet as the spray bathes your face and body. Daily tours take place from April 15 through the first Sunday in November. Niagara Falls State Park, (716) 284-8897; www.maidofthemist.com.

Accommodations
Niagara Falls Campground & Lodging, 2405 Niagara Falls Blvd., has sixty-five campsites. Reservations: (716) 731-3434; www.niagarafallsusa.com/directory/niagara-falls -campground-lodging/.

Organizations
Destination Niagara USA, Niagara Falls State Park, 10 Rainbow Blvd., Niagara Falls; (877) FALLS-US; www.niagarafallsusa.com/niagara-falls-state-park/

Honorable Mentions

K Alabama Swamps Trails

At the site of ancient Lake Tonawanda, the vast marshes north of the town of Alabama represent a critical wildlife habitat and an exciting natural area. Together, Iroquois National Wildlife Refuge (NWR) and the adjoining Oak Orchard and Tonawanda Wildlife Management Areas (WMA) open the public's access to 20,000 acres of prime wetland, maintained in a fairly wild and protected state. Nesting bald eagles find favor with the habitat. Spring migrations swell the bird counts, with tens of thousands of ducks, geese, and other waterfowl crowding the open water.

Five easy walks between 0.5 mile and 5 miles long introduce these wildlands. In Iroquois NWR the 1.2-mile Kanyoo Trail leads to an observation tower; the 5-mile out-and-back Feeder Road trail provides the best route for viewing waterfowl on many ponds; the 3-mile out-and-back Onondaga Nature Trail follows the edge of Onondaga Marsh and woodland; and the delightful Swallow Hollow Trail provides a 2-mile marsh boardwalk and dike loop where warblers and vireos congregate in spring and fall. The nature paths at Oak Orchard Environmental Education Center shape a fifth hike—they explore North Marsh and its open-water shore. Onondaga Nature Trail is closed to hiking during shotgun deer season, and you may choose to avoid Feeder Road during its two months of hunting season. Contact the NWR for dates. Side dikes off Feeder Road are closed during nesting season, March 1 to July 15; heed all notices. Access a map of Iroquois NWR at https://cnyhiking.com/IroquoisNWR.htm.

From the junction of NY 63 and NY 77 in Alabama, go north on NY 63 for 0.8 mile and turn left (west) onto Casey Road to reach the refuge headquarters in 0.6 mile. Continue west on Casey Road another 0.8 mile and turn northwest onto NY 77 (Lewiston Road) to reach the marked trailhead for Kanyoo Trail on the right in 0.9 mile. Gated Feeder Road lies east off NY 77, 300 feet farther north. GPS: 43.116774, -78.431364

For the other three trails, from the junction of Casey Road and NY 63 (east of the headquarters), go north on NY 63 for 0.1 mile and turn right (east) onto Roberts Road. In 1.1 miles turn north on dirt Sour Springs Road to reach Onondaga Nature Trail on the right in 0.8 mile. For Swallow Hollow Trail and the Oak Orchard nature trails, stay east on Roberts Road, go 1.5 miles past its intersection with Sour Springs Road, and turn north onto Knowlesville Road. Find Swallow Hollow Trail on the left in 1.8 miles and Oak Orchard on the right, 0.1 mile farther north. GPS: 43.125990, -78.325068

Contact: Iroquois NWR, 1101 Casey Rd., Basom; (585) 948-5445; www.fws.gov/refuge/iroquois; Oak Orchard Environmental Education Center, New York

State Department of Environmental Conservation, Region 8, 6274 East Avon–Lima Rd., Avon; (585) 226-2466; www.dec.ny.gov/outdoor/24442.html

L Tifft Nature Preserve

Near the Lake Erie shore, this 264-acre urban sanctuary marks a success story in land reclamation. Its low grassland hills (formerly a small landfill), wetland woods, thickets, ponds, and a 75-acre freshwater cattail marsh support a thriving bird population while offering a peaceful retreat from Buffalo's city pace. Five miles of trail and three boardwalks tour the preserve. The individual nature trails range from a fraction of a mile to 1.3 miles in length, visiting viewing blinds, mounds, wetlands, Berm Pond, Warbler Walk, and Heritage Boardwalk. Trails are open dawn to dusk. Access to Tifft's grounds, boardwalks, and trails is free and open to the public, but donations are gratefully accepted.

From NY 5 in south Buffalo, take the Tifft Street/Fuhrmann Boulevard exit. Westbound traffic will head 0.5 mile south from the exit, turn left under the freeway, and again turn left onto a one-way road, merging with the traffic exiting from NY 5 East. Go 0.5 mile north on the one-way road to reach the preserve parking lot on the right (east). Locate the trailheads near the visitor center cabin or 0.1 mile east of the cabin, where the service road crosses a bridge over the southeast arm of Lake Kirsty. GPS: 42.846233, -78.859361. Tifft Nature Preserve, 1200 Fuhrmann Blvd., Buffalo; (716) 825-6397; www.tifft.org.

Chautauqua-Allegheny Region

Historically, the Seneca Nation of the Iroquois Confederacy occupied this southwest corner of New York and fulfilled its role as western gatekeepers until French explorers arrived in 1679. Edged by Lake Erie, the region became a focal point when the French discovered the route connecting Lake Erie's Barcelona Harbor with Chautauqua Lake, making it key as a future trade route. Soon the English joined the pursuit of what became known as the Portage Trail, and when the Seneca also attempted to defend this route, the slim trail became one catalyst for the French and Indian War.

It took more than one hundred years to resolve ownership of this land, but in 1798 it finally came into the hands of the new Americans. Soon the Chautauqua region became a manufacturing hub, with pot ash, pearl ash, and black salts among its products. Over time, farming began to dominate the area's open lands, and Chautauqua County became the largest producer of concord grapes in the world—so much so that Welch's, the makers of the nation's most popular grape jam, jelly, and juice, built its main plant just over the Pennsylvania border from this region. Grape arbors, vineyards, and wineries figure prominently in the rural countryside. Beyond grapes, Amish communities, farmstands, Victorian villages, and historic sites contribute to the charm of this lightly populated region.

The local geography includes the long, flat summits and V-shaped valleys of the Allegheny Plateau, the Upper Genesee River, Chautauqua Lake, and the Chautauqua Creek Gorge. Four seasons give the land a changing face, inviting frequent returns.

The jewel in Chautauqua's crown is Allegany State Park, 65,000 acres of hills, mountains, lakes, and trails. The largest park in the state system, Allegany has two developed lake areas, Red House and Quaker, forming the two-chambered heart of this vast park playground. The park features a soothing landscape of mixed hardwood-conifer forests, boulder caves, wildflower meadows, and relaxing waters—the ideal escape for the frazzled and the harried. The understated beauty of this natural backdrop pairs neatly with the famed Chautauqua Institution, a world-renowned cultural center for music, art, lecture, and contemplation.

Here in the southwesternmost corner of New York State, a pair of long-distance trails, the Earl Cardot Eastside Overland Trail and the Fred J. Cusimano Westside Overland Trail, string through DEC forest parcels and along private land. Abandoned railbeds, nature trails, paths to summits, stony realms, hushed forests, and inviting shores engage hikers, snowshoers, and cross-country skiers for year-round fun.

21 Fred J. Cusimano Westside Overland Trail

Between Sherman and Panama, this long-distance linear trail strings 24 miles through a series of state forests in Chautauqua County, traversing agricultural easements in between. Changing forest, meadow and pond habitats, and rural and forest views vary the way. Multiple trailheads allow you to decide how long your hike should be. Established shelters allow for overnight stays and stargazing, urging you to lengthen your Westside sojourn.

Start: At the northern trailhead
Distance: 19.2 miles point-to-point
Approximate hiking time: 1 to 2 days
Difficulty: Strenuous when hiking the full 19 miles of the selected hike
Elevation change: This rolling trail travels between 1,500 and 1,850 feet in elevation.
Trail surface: Earthen path, mowed track, woods road, rural and forest roads
Seasons: Open year-round, hiking is best spring through fall
Other trail users: Mountain bikers, snowshoers, cross-country skiers, hunters (on public lands in fall)
Canine compatibility: Dogs permitted (as a courtesy, leash animals when crossing private lands)
Land status: New York State Forest, as well as county and private land
Nearest town: Panama for minimal services; otherwise, Chautauqua
Fees and permits: None
Schedule: No time restrictions, but occasional temporary closures because of logging

Map: https://hikechautauqua.com/wp-content/uploads/2019/04/PR_WESTSIDE_BACK.pdf. The map is necessary to locate trailheads.
Trail contact: Chautauqua County Parks Department, 3 N. Erie St., Mayville; (716) 661-8417; https://chqgov.com/parks-and-trails/parks-trails
Special considerations: Be alert for arrows and blazes showing the changes in direction. Some sections are overgrown or subject to mud. Respect easements through and along private lands, which are open to hikers only. There is no camping within 150 feet of road, trail, or water and none on private land. Any overnight forest stay longer than three nights at one site requires a New York State Department of Environmental Conservation (DEC) permit. Contact the DEC Region 9 suboffice in Falconer. The designated camp shelters offer basic amenities, including latrines and working wells. All DEC rules apply for fire building and wood collecting. Trailheads are well signed and the trail is generally well blazed. Wearing blaze orange during the fall hunting season is a wise precaution. The trail is closed to all-terrain vehicles (ATVs) and horses.

Finding the trailhead: For the northern terminus, from I-86, take exit 6 at Sherman and go north 0.4 mile on NY 76, turning right (east) onto NY 430. Proceed 7.3 miles and turn left onto Hannum Road. Follow Hannum Road for 3.1 miles to find the trailhead at road's end (last 0.8 mile on dirt). GPS: 42.240076, -79.586862

For the hike's southern terminus, from the junction of NY 474 and County Road 33 in the village of Panama (5.6 miles south of I-86), go 1.8 miles west on NY 474. Trailhead parking is north off NY 474. GPS: 42.075085, -79.518249

Trail shelters offer a dry overnight wayside on the Westside Overland Trail.

The Hike

From the trailhead, begin heading south. Pass through rolling, second-growth woods of maple, black locust, ash, and hop hornbeam. After a closed road and drainage crossings, walk south on Summerdale Road until the foot trail resumes to your left; follow it through a stretch of private land.

Cross NY 430 and enter Mount Pleasant State Forest. Beyond a meadow break, oaks appear in the upper canopy, and ferns, wild raspberry, horsetail reed, and poison ivy contribute to the tangle. Where the trail traverses a bog, spiny-armed spruce and hardwoods face off.

Cross Brodt Road, where a dense spruce grove swallows or abuts the trail. Mud often exceeds the logs' reach at a bog crossing. The trail bears right where a grassy track merges on the left. Big maple or beech attract note. The trail then drops down to a footbridge crossing, crosses a gravel road and a couple more creek bridges, and jogs right on East Brumagin Road before resuming its southward trajectory on a woods road.

Mixed forest leads to a pair of three-sided log shelters, available on a first-come, first-served basis. Follow the dirt road away from the shelters. The trail rolls from red pine plantation to field, with an artificial pond to the left often visited by geese and ringed by grass and shrubs. Cross a gas well track and pass abandoned apple trees to leave the state forest, and briefly follow the unpaved Titus Road. Southbound travel resumes shortly through private land.

Follow the trail along a section of fence and plank boardwalk and skirt a wet meadow and shrub corridor, returning to the woods and tracing straight lines along fences. Be alert for the blazes indicating turns, especially where the trail is overgrown. I-86 briefly becomes a part of the terrain, but you won't be on the highway for long. Pass a field and stay on the trail as it crosses under the interstate on Wait Corners Road. On the east side of this road, continue again on private land. Field segments hold the hike's vistas and offer different wildlife viewing. Wild turkey, barred owl, and northern harrier may capture attention.

The trail follows Bates Road (used by area Amish) east to resume its way south at the top of the hill. The hilltop trail then draws a seam between rolling fields. All the rural icons are here: hay bales, fields, silos, barns, and huddles of black-and-white Holstein dairy cows. Blue-capped fence posts act as guides; step stiles keep animals away from fence crossings.

From Stebbins Road, enter Edward J. Whalen Memorial State Forest and red pine plantation on mowed path with a mild incline. Cross a cable corridor, beginning a gentle descent between spruce plantation and maple hardwood forest. Footbridges span the deeper hollows. Cross a ramped footbridge over a tinsel flow shadowed by hemlocks. Mature American beech trees, threatened by beech leaf and beech bark diseases, continue to hold their own here.

The trail climbs to sun-drenched, unpaved Eggleston Hill Road; follow it to the left, and keep left at the junction. The hike then resumes south, entering the towering North Harmony State Forest. Some routes veer left along this stretch of trail; continue straight.

At a cattail-edged bass pond, follow the trail along the east shore to the Adirondack-style shelters of Panama Campsite, overlooking the pond, meadow, and reflected forest. Tamaracks rise above camp. Pass east of the shelters and begin a sharp climb that leads to the crossing of a two-track. From here, the trail parallels Warner Road to the right before crossing over it to continue south. Travel the southern half of North Harmony Forest to Snake Forest Road (a truck trail). Trace it briefly left before resuming right on a foot trail.

The crossing of Wiltsie Road marks the last interruption until NY 474, where our suggested trek ends. Travel a meadow swath, pass spiny hemlock, and view big birches near the footbridge over the headwaters of Little Brokenstraw Creek. Watch out for mountain bikers on the NY 474 access.

Miles and Directions

0.0 Start from the northern trailhead (Trailhead A, the Hannum Road trail parking). Round the boulder barricade and ascend south on blue-blazed trail into Chautauqua State Forest. *Note:* Hiking north leads to Chautauqua Gorge.

1.0 Reach Summerdale Road and follow it right (south).

1.5 Resume on trail, heading left (east).

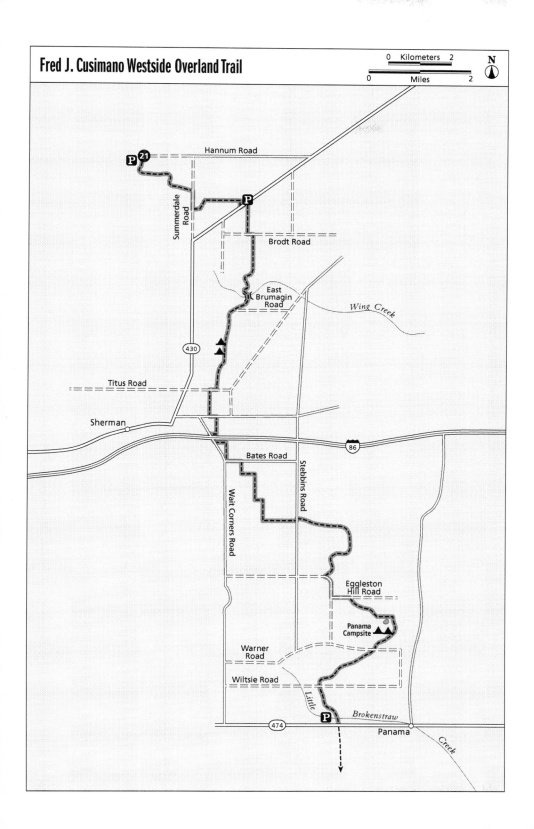

Fred J. Cusimano Westside Overland Trail

0   Kilometers   2

0   Miles   2

N

Hannum Road

P 21

Summerdale Road

P

Brodt Road

East Brumagin Road

Wing Creek

430

Titus Road

Sherman

Bates Road

86

Wait Corners Road

Stebbins Road

Eggleston Hill Road

Panama Campsite

Warner Road

Wiltsie Road

Little

Brokenstraw

474

Panama

Creek

3.0	Cross NY 430 to enter Mount Pleasant State Forest at a large trailhead parking lot. **Option or bailout:** This site offers an alternative start or a place to shorten the hike.
3.8	Cross Brodt Road, a single-lane dirt country road.
5.8	Follow East Brumagin Road right for 0.3 mile and then resume south on an old woods road.
6.5	Reach shelters. Follow the dirt road beyond the shelters to the right for 0.1 mile to resume south.
7.4	Head right 0.2 mile on dirt Titus Road to resume hiking south along private property.
8.4	Follow a county road left to pick up the southbound trail next to a fence line.
9.3	At the foot of a field, turn right (west), crossing over a fence step-stile to follow Wait Corners Road south under I-86. Resume the trail as it continues on the east side of Wait Corners Road.
10.0	Follow Bates Road east 0.5 mile to continue south on the trail at the top of the hill.
12.6	Angle left across Stebbins Road to enter Edward J. Whalen Memorial State Forest.
13.6	Follow a truck road right 0.8 mile to pick up the southbound trail. Be alert for blazes.
14.8	Follow Eggleston Hill Road left 0.3 mile to a road junction and again turn left per arrows.
15.5	Enter North Harmony State Forest.
16.4	Reach the Panama Campsite shelters; on leaving, pass east of the shelters.
17.0	Cross Warner Road.
18.4	Cross Wiltsie Road.
19.2	End at the NY 474 trailhead (west of Panama). **Option:** You may continue south on the Westside Overland Trail, crossing the highway and edging private land. Carry the brochure and watch for blazings. You'll end at Town Line Road (24 miles).

Hike Information

Local Information

Chautauqua County Visitors Bureau, Main Gate, NY 394, Chautauqua; (716) 357-4569; www.tourchautauqua.com

Local Events/Attractions

The internationally known **Chautauqua Institution** is celebrated for its lecture and concert series, its restful grounds, its National Historic Landmark architecture, and its atmosphere for betterment of learning and spiritual renewal. Chautauqua Institution, 1 Ames Ave., Chautauqua; (716) 357-6250; chq.org.

22 Allegany State Park, Red House Headquarters–Eastwood Meadows Loop

The biggest park in the state system, this "wilderness playground" in southwestern New York brings together even-height ridges, V-shaped valleys, man-made lakes, second-growth forests, and block-fractured boulder realms. Two recreation areas, Red House and Quaker, make up the park. No single trail can showcase the full offering, but the Red House Headquarters–Eastwood Meadows Loop offers a good peek at what's here and travels a stretch of trail common to three long-distance trails: North Country, Conservation, and Finger Lakes. You'll want to add one or more of the optional trails because this great park is worthy of the extra time.

Start: At the Red House Administration Building

Distance: 10.9 miles out-and-back on lasso-shaped trail

Approximate hiking time: 6 to 7.5 hours

Difficulty: Moderate due to terrain

Elevation change: This hike has about an 800-foot elevation change.

Trail surface: Earthen path

Seasons: Open year-round, best for hiking spring through fall

Other trail users: Snowshoers

Canine compatibility: Leashed dogs permitted (proof of shots required), but no pets in buildings, bathhouses, or along cross-country ski trails

Land status: New York State Park

Nearest town: Salamanca

Fees and permits: Park admission fee

Schedule: Park open 24 hours, daylight hours for trails (Exception: Trail camping is allowed at the designated lean-tos along the North Country Trail, but only after you have first contacted park police about your plans and your hiking group and have police approval; (716) 354-9111. There is no other trail camping in the park.)

Maps: https://parks.ny.gov/documents/parks/AlleganyRedHouseAreaTrailMap.pdf; Finger Lakes Trail Conference map, Sheet M1/CT1 (purchase at https://fingerlakestrail.org/product-category/maps/map-sets/)

Trail contact: Allegany State Park, 2373 ASP, US 1, Suite 3, Salamanca; (716) 354-9101; https://parks.ny.gov/parks/alleganyredhouse/details.aspx; https://parks.ny.gov/parks/alleganyquaker/details.aspx

Special considerations: When exploring 65,000-acre Allegany State Park, keep to trails and carry maps so as not to get lost. Never push beyond your wilderness aptitude. Hunting occurs anywhere in the park except at the lakes areas, so rangers advise you to wear blaze orange during deer-hunting season (Oct into Dec). On Sunday the park closes to hunting, again allowing worry-free hiking.

Finding the trailhead: For the Red House Recreation Area: From the Southern Tier Expressway (I-86) west of Salamanca, take exit 19, reaching the entrance station in 0.7 mile. The trails radiate from the lake area, off ASP Routes 1, 2, and 2A. The featured hike starts at the Red House Administration Building on ASP 1. GPS: 42.100286, -78.749691

For the Quaker Recreation Area: From I-86 west of Salamanca, take exit 18 and go 4 miles south on NY 280 to the entrance station. Find trails off ASP Routes 3 and 1. GPS: 42.011192, -78.827351

The Hike

The described lasso-shaped hike starts south from the Red House Administration Building to Eastwood Meadows Loop. It begins on a blue park trail and continues south along the shared long-distance route of the park's big three: the North Country Trail (NCT), the Finger Lakes Trail (FLT), and the Conservation Trail (CT), before adding the loop.

As an alternative, this hike can be fashioned into a 4.6-mile shuttle hike (without the meadow loop) or 7.3-mile shuttle hike (with the meadow loop) by spotting a vehicle at the North Country or close-by Eastwood Meadows Trailhead. Both parking areas are on ASP 1, about 4 miles south of the park campground.

From the back of the administration building, ascend left past an old foundation toward a trail sign in the power line corridor. The sign indicates "Conservation Hiking Trails, 2.3 miles." Continue your ascent in uneven spurts following the blue state park trail among hardwoods and meadow clearings. Noise from the campground rides upslope but quickly vanishes. Mossy rock slabs contribute to the forest character.

A side trail that connects to the long-distance trails in the Beck Hollow Area arrives on the right; keep south on the blue trail. It ascends through an area of large upturned roots, then levels, passing among successional hardwoods, groves of hemlock, and pockets of young beech and shrubs, eventually coming to a drainage crossing.

Where you come upon a North Country Trail bivouac area and meet up with the shared white-blazed route of the NCT, FLT, and CT, follow the white blazes left (south), continuing toward Eastwood Meadows Loop. An idyllic stroll unrolls before you. The modest gradient and trouble-free path allows you to enjoy views of the surroundings. A midstory of mountain elder, red-berried in fall, alternates with the spatially open forest. Later, where a hemlock-hardwood forest enfolds the route, ferns embroider the trail's sides and some bare branches open up the cathedral.

After a lengthy walk you reach a trail junction. Take the trail on the right to add Eastwood Meadows Loop. When you meet a grassy woods road, turn right to reach the actual loop; then head left for a clockwise tour.

An eastern newt brings woodland hikers to their knees.

The consistent views of the forest soothe the eyes and soul. Bigtooth aspens whisper in the canopy. In about 100 feet the loop swings right to begin its return. Here you'll find a limited opening with a view that expands west across a meadow clearing and the Bay State Brook drainage to spotlight an Allegany ridge.

The loop's return then descends through a similar forest with a shrubby understory of nettles and brambles. Although not exactly a gauntlet, at times you will need to evade the prickly overhang. Black-cherry trees stand as giants in the woods. Close the loop and return to the white-blazed trail.

Backtrack on the NCT, FLT, and CT to the bivouac area, and return via the blue state park trail to the Red House Administration Building. Or if you arranged a shuttle vehicle, continue south (right) on the white-blazed trail to the ASP 1 trail parking areas, alternately passing through stands of beech, maple, and hemlock and the shrubby meadow and fern clearings from the site's former ski runs.

Miles and Directions

0.0 Start behind the Red House Administration Building and ascend left toward the trail sign in the power line corridor.

0.1 Reach the trail sign for Conservation Hiking Trails. Continue ascent on blue state park trail.

1.5 An orange connector to the long-distance trails heads right. Continue forward on blue trail.

2.3 Meet the shared white-blazed long-distance route at a bivouac area. Follow the white blazes left (south) toward Eastwood Meadows Loop. *Note:* Turning right (north) on the white-blazed route leads toward Beck Hollow and the Beck Hollow trail shelter.

4.1 Reach a junction. Turn right and keep right at a grassy woods road for Eastwood Meadows Loop. *Note:* If you continue south on the white-blazed trio, you'll reach trail parking on ASP 1 in 0.5 mile (a shuttle hike option).

4.4 Reach the loop junction and turn left (clockwise).

5.5 Locate a vista, where the loop swings right for the return leg.

6.5 Close the loop. Return to the 4.1-mile junction.

6.8 Back at the junction, backtrack north to the administration building. *Note:* If you arranged for a shuttle vehicle, bear right, coming out at the ASP 1 trail parking lots in 0.5 mile.

8.6 Return to the bivouac area junction. Follow the blue state park trail right.

10.9 End back at the Red House Administration Building.

Options

Red House Hiking Options

The 0.7-mile loop of the **Red Jacket Trail** begins on the west side of the Red House Administration Building. The trail's rustic stone stairs, bridge, and path lead uphill to a marked trail junction beneath a power line; go right, coming to the loop junction. The hike's split-level loop contours a maple, black cherry, and hemlock treed slope above Red House Lake. The understory displays half a dozen fern varieties; pines claim the lower slope. Deer browse near the trail at first and last light. Rustic

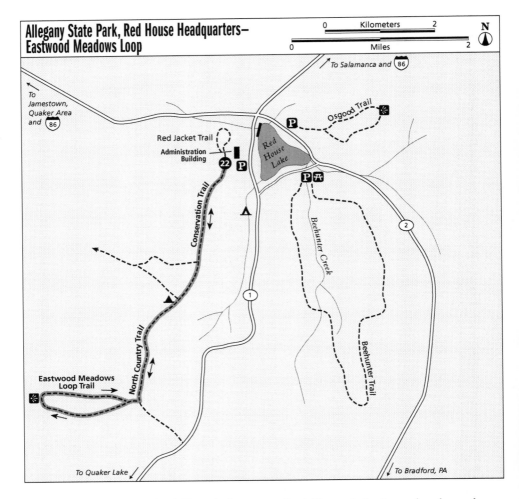

0   Kilometers   2

0   Miles   2

N

To Salamanca and (86)

To
Jamestown,
Quaker Area
and (86)

Osgood Trail

Red Jacket Trail

Administration
Building

22

Red
House
Lake

Conservation Trail

Beehunter Creek

2

North Country Trail

Eastwood Meadows
Loop Trail

Beehunter Trail

1

To Quaker Lake

To Bradford, PA

benches offer open and leaf-filtered glimpses at Red House Lake, its outlet, the park bikeway, and a round-topped hill. Midway, a recessed stone wall and a tree-masked rusted steel tower hint at the ski jump that once stood here.

The 2.7-mile **Osgood Trail** travels the round-topped hill at the northeast end of Red House Lake. It starts off McIntosh Trail, east of the ASP 1–ASP 2 junction. Chipmunks, songbirds, woodpeckers, and deer make surprise appearances here. Pass through the fruit tree corridor into the hemlock-pine woods, ascending to the loop junction. Continue uphill; the unmarked trail to the right closes the loop. Where the trail contours above the McIntosh drainage, flat rock slabs punctuate the forest. At the hill's meadow crown, a break in the tree rim funnels views west; the ensuing descent passes through an attractive meadow plateau drained by springs. Be watchful where the trail traverses mossy slabs. A well-worn false trail heads straight downhill as the primary trail curves right, bringing the loop and hike to a close.

South of Red House Lake, the 6.5-mile **Beehunter Trail** travels the ridges drained by Beehunter Creek to form a loop. The trail ascends steadily and steeply, attaining the ridge spine for a more comfortable tour. Thick grasses spread beneath an open forest of oak, maple, ash, and hemlock. To the east, filtered views span the Beehunter Creek drainage. In places, mossy, slick rocks compose footing. Cross 15-foot-wide Beehunter Creek; wading may be necessary if the water is high. Parklike forest, red-berried elder in August, and a fern-draped split rock characterize the ridge ascent and descent. Beyond a hemlock grove, follow a woods road across a service road and field to a trailhead sign. There a dirt road leads you back to the bike trail and the last Beehunter Creek crossing. End at the picnic area.

Quaker Hiking Options

This area's sampling travels ridges, tops peaks, explores a boulder realm, and visits a natural spring.

The 5-mile out-and-back **Mount Tuscarora Trail** starts south of the Quaker entrance station; there is road-shoulder parking only. Its foot trail ascends through dark hemlock-hardwood forest, passing parallel to a drainage. With a burst of climb, top and trace the ridge. Indian pipe, baneberry, huckleberry, witch hazel, striped maple, beech, and small oaks frame travel. Claim the first summit (elevation 2,064 feet) at 2.25 miles and the upper plateau (elevation 2,144 feet) at 2.5 miles. Here stands an abandoned fire tower, missing its lower flight of stairs and several of its landings. The tower now serves only as a landmark, and trees enfold the site. While the ridge trail continues to Coon Run Road, backtrack as you came. (Note: The park's Summit Fire Tower on South Mountain above Red House Lake has been restored.)

The 2.5-mile **Three Sisters Trail** travels a loop visiting only one sister, West Sister, and begins west of the rental office (west of the ASP 1–ASP 3 junction). Pass into a pine-hardwood forest with a shrubby understory, skirt a pine-hemlock stand, and cross under a power line to cross a footbridge. The trail traverses both grassy meadow and open forest—a virtual sauna on sunny, humid days. Pockets of bee balm, a red member of the mint family, adorn the drainage in early summer. The steady ascent can be rocky, with rustic corduroys aiding passage at soggy reaches. The forest fills out and the trail tops and follows the ridge left to summit West Sister (1.4 miles) but finds no views. On your descent, beware: The grassy footpath can be slippery when wet. Cross a natural spring on a rock slab and pass under the power line to meet and descend Ranger Trail (a road) near cabins 1, 2, and 4. Just before you reach ASP 3, a footpath heads left, bringing the hike to its end.

For the 3-mile out-and-back **Bear Caves–Mount Seneca Trail,** the preferred access is the eastern one (1.4 miles east of the ASP 1–ASP 3 junction). The trail heads north off ASP 3. Bring flashlights to look into the boulder caves, and come prepared for some stooping and squeezing in the small rooms and passages less than 200 feet long. Naturalist-led tours will help you locate the openings. This trail ascends the steep, boulder-strewn slope on a wide, worn path, reaching an entire community of the massive boxy boulders and outcrops. Cross-bedding, balanced rocks, eroded nooks, fissures, and overhangs, plus the adorning mosses, lichens, and ferns, make this a fascinating route. At the base of the rocky realm, follow the primary trail to the right; a secondary trail rounds to the left. Cross the woodsy top of the rocks; then where the trail is again at the rocks' base, tour the familiar Allegany forest. The crossing of Slide Hollow may require wading during high water. The trail contours, then turns sharply right for a steep assault on Mount Seneca. Clintonia, trillium, and mayflower decorate the floor in early spring, while dame's rocket, daisies, and other wildflowers take over in summer. Emerge at the summit (1.5 miles), viewing the wooded ridge of Mount Onondaga to the northeast and the immediate peak to the east. Although the trail continues, return as you came.

The 0.5-mile out-and-back **Bear Springs Trail** begins on the west side of ASP 1, 2.2 miles north of the ASP 1–ASP 3 junction. Enter a woods of maple, black cherry, and hemlock to the left of the sign. The trail slowly descends to the lush ferns of the open forest floor, with a profusion of woods flora not seen elsewhere in the park. Oxalis, mayflower, trillium, and whorled pogonia and other orchids contribute to the array. Soon after crossing a drainage, the trail reaches the 6-foot-high stonework grotto protecting the springs. Although the trail continues to travel through field and hardwood forest, return as you came.

Hike Information

Local Information
Cattaraugus County Tourism, 303 Court St., Little Valley; (800) 331-0543; www .enchantedmountains.com

Local Events/Attractions
Just north of Randolph, you can explore the backroads and hillsides that are home to an **Old Order Amish community.** While touring this lovely countryside, you can glimpse the simple life of the Amish and purchase their quilts, furniture, and baked goods at their shops and roadside stands, but never on Sunday. Contact Cattaraugus County Tourism, or visit https://amishtrail.com/what-see.

Accommodations
Allegany State Park campgrounds are open year-round and have a total of 303 campsites, 336 cabins, and 8 cottages and 2 group camps. Reservations: (800) 456-2267; www.reserveamerica.com.

Honorable Mention

M Deer Lick Nature Sanctuary

Southeast of Gowanda, this 400-acre National Natural Landmark wins you over with familiarity versus drama. Quiet hardwood forests, dark hemlock stands, lush meadows, and gentle creeks are the hallmarks of this sanctuary owned by the Nature Conservancy (TNC). Bordered to the north by the South Branch Cattaraugus Creek and New York State's Zoar Valley Multiple-Use Area, the sanctuary completes the puzzle of unbroken open space that forms a vital natural wildlife corridor. A relaxed 5-mile day hike strings together the four color-coded trails of this sanctuary, but any of the trails will do on its own. Pets, smoking, and picnicking are prohibited at the preserve, which is open daylight hours only.

From central Gowanda, go south on US 62 for 0.5 mile and turn left (east) onto Hill Street. In 0.4 mile turn right onto Broadway Road, and in another 0.6 mile turn left onto Point Peter Road. Stay on Point Peter Road for 2.3 miles and turn left to enter the sanctuary (0.5 mile past the Point Peter Road–Forty Road fork). Find a small parking area, trail register, and pit toilets near the trail's start. GPS: 42.420010, -78.905277. Contact the Nature Conservancy, Central and Western New York Office, 274 North Goodman St., Suite B261, Rochester; (585) 546-8030; www.nature.org.

Finger Lakes Region

T he eleven long, thin, glacier-gouged Finger Lakes look as if Mother Nature raked her fingers down the state's middle, and in a way, that's exactly what happened here at the end of the last ice age. Extending from just south of Rochester through the state's Southern Tier, these lakes formed a landscape reminiscent of the German wine country—and, coincidentally, the fertile soil and distinct change of seasons created exactly the cold-weather climate for many of the same wine grapes grown in that European region. The Finger Lakes are known best for their Riesling and Gewürztraminer varieties, as well as its Cabernet Franc and a wide range of grapes bred specifically for northeastern United States climates. Meanwhile, in among the thousands of acres of vineyards are gorges that conceal some of the most iconic hiking in the state, aided by tumbling waters that continue to carve these rock walls into fantastic structures. A gently rolling, bumpy terrain of drumlins sits to their north, while an impenetrable rock deposit—the Valley Heads Moraine—rises to the south.

The city of Rochester and its Lake Ontario shoreline form the northwestern corner of this region, with its own network of trails radiating like spokes from Genesee Valley Park. It's one of three parks in Rochester designed by world-famous landscape architect Frederick Law Olmsted. Genesee Valley Greenway extends south from the park, and the urban Genesee Riverway Trail leads north to Lake Ontario; both of these are featured in this book. The Rochester segment of the Erie Canalway Trail also crosses the park and continues east to Albany and west to Lockport. This supremely walkable area benefits from gently rolling hills and fairly level terrain.

At the Seneca-Cayuga County border northeast of Seneca Falls, Montezuma National Wildlife Refuge occupies a remnant ancient lake formed when the glaciers melted. Today these wetlands are carefully managed by the US Fish and Wildlife Service to provide native plant life and food to migrating waterfowl. The results of this effort have made Montezuma a migratory hub: Hundreds of thousands of ducks, geese, terns, swans, and shorebirds stop here during spring and fall migration, drawing birders from throughout the Northeast.

This region holds claim to New York's tallest single-drop waterfall (Taughannock Falls), the lone national forest in the state (Finger Lakes National Forest), the birth of the women's rights movement in Seneca Falls, and the founding of the Church of Jesus Christ of Latter-Day Saints at Hill Cumorah in Palmyra, outside of Rochester. The long-distance Finger Lakes Trail traverses the forest of the same name and serves as part of the new Empire State Trail. Transportation history, early settlement, Native American lands, and Revolutionary War sites all contribute to the stories the Finger Lakes can tell about New York.

Boardwalks shape pleasing family walks along Beaver Lake.

On the region's eastern side, the lands around the city of Syracuse were originally the territory of the Onondaga Nation, "the keepers of the council fire" and one of the Six Nations of the Haudenosaunee (Iroquois). Between 1788 and 1822, the Onondaga Nation lost nearly all of its land through its dealings with the newly formed American government. Today, this Nation's territory covers 7,300 acres south of Syracuse near Nedrow. Salt deposited here some 400 million years ago by an evaporating sea attracted the Onondaga people—and later the white settlers—to the Syracuse area. The construction of the Erie Canal allowed the region to fully exploit the resource, bringing with it ready-made markets. For more of this salty tale, visit the Salt Museum on the grounds of Onondaga Lake Park in northwest Syracuse.

23 Genesee Riverway Trail

One of the newest developed trails in the greater Rochester area, this splendid urban hike connects Lake Ontario, several parks designed by Frederick Law Olmsted, three major downtown waterfalls, and some of the city's most attractive old neighborhoods.

Start: At the marina at the Port of Rochester, where the Genesee River meets Lake Ontario
Distance: 13.0 miles one-way (best as a shuttle hike)
Approximate hiking time: 5 hours
Difficulty: Easy
Elevation change: The trail is virtually flat.
Trail surface: Mostly pavement
Seasons: Spring through fall are the prettiest months, though most sections of the trail are plowed in winter.
Other trail users: City residents, bicycles, roller skaters
Canine compatibility: Dogs permitted on leash

Land status: City of Rochester
Nearest town: Rochester
Fees and permits: None
Schedule: Year-round
Map: www.cityofrochester.gov/grt/
Trail contact: City of Rochester Recreation Bureau, 400 Dewey Ave., Rochester; (585) 428-6755; cityofrochester.gov/parks
Special considerations: This is an urban trail that uses city streets for parts of its length. Take the same precautions you would in any major city when walking this trail: Hike in daylight hours, pay attention to people around you, and leave your valuables at home.

Finding the trailhead: From I-590 North in Rochester, take exit 10A to merge onto NY 104 West. In 4.5 miles turn right onto Lake Avenue. Drive 4.5 miles to Ontario Beach Park, and turn right on Corrigan Street and into the marina parking area. Park near the Port of Rochester. GPS: 43.25632, -77.60755

To reach the other end of the trail on the Erie Canal at Genesee Valley Park, take I-590 South to I-390 North, and take exit 17 toward NY-383 (Scottsville Road). Turn left at the fork, and take Scottsville Road to its end at Genesee Street. Turn right on Genesee and into Genesee Valley Park. Continue to the parking lot near the tennis courts. GPS: 43.12356, -77.64003

The Hike

Facing the Port of Rochester, you have the option of beginning the hike immediately by turning right onto the paved walkway or turning left and walking out along the pier to the modern lighthouse. If you start with the pier, you can enjoy wonderful views of Lake Ontario, the smallest of the Great Lakes but not in any way diminutive, before starting the hike south toward the city.

Heading south, note the green Genesee Riverway Trail signs—these clearly mark the route. Pass the 1822 Charlotte-Genesee Lighthouse (formerly known as Rochester Harbor Light), which is open to visitors from early May through the end of October. Much closer to Lake Ontario when it was built, the lighthouse stands in its original spot—but when the city built piers to prevent sand bars from forming across the mouth of the river, the natural deposits of sand created a beach that extended

Ninety feet tall, High Falls cascades mightily in the middle of downtown Rochester.
PHOTO BY NIC MINETOR

farther out into the lake each year. The lighthouse was deactivated in the early 1880s. It's just forty-two steps to the top, if you're thinking of making a side trip to climb the lighthouse.

Continue along the river to the Genesee River Turning Basin, with its 3,572-foot-long elevated walkway. In the late nineteenth century, large ships came to Rochester by way of Lake Ontario to load coal brought into this basin by the B&O Railroad, taking it across the lake to Canada. Today this walkway provides close-up views of the basin from just above the water level, giving new perspective and dimension to the river gorge that surrounds it. If you're looking for a short walk, many hikers turn around here and head back to the Port of Rochester, completing a 4.4-mile out-and-back route.

To continue on a daylong hike, enter Turning Point Park on the steepest uphill portion of the hike—a pretty mild incline—and keep heading south on the paved path. Soon the route joins city sidewalks to follow Lake Avenue through Riverside and Holy Sepulchre Cemeteries, two of the oldest cemeteries in Rochester. This is the final resting place of Francis J. Tumblety, the most likely suspect in the Jack the Ripper murders in London, England, in the late nineteenth century. He was never tried for the crimes, but the creepy legend brings many visitors to his gravesite every year.

Next the route passes Seneca Park, one of three parks in Rochester designed by renowned landscape architect Frederick Law Olmsted. As the path breaks away from Lake Avenue and turns slightly east, it passes along Maplewood Park, where Rochester's most prolific rose gardens bloom with great abandon in June.

Cross Driving Point Park and enter Lower Falls Park to see the first of three waterfalls in the heart of the city. Lower Falls is the smallest of the three and is closely followed by Middle Falls, busily generating power for Rochester Gas & Electric. Follow the walkway through the RG&E area for some excellent views of the roaring falls from an elevated bridge.

From here, continue south and east to St. Paul Street, through a city neighborhood and on to the middle of downtown Rochester. A new state park is in the planning stages here at High Falls, a thundering 90-foot waterfall with a number of scenic overlooks for your viewing pleasure. Soon trails may lead down to the bottom of this falls, with places where you will be able to picnic or just relax and enjoy the view. Across the footbridge between the High Falls commercial district and St. Paul Street, the Genesee Brewery's own pub and restaurant is an excellent place to stop for lunch or libations.

The route through the city now follows the river closely, and you have the option of walking on either side of the river as you choose. The western route takes you to Corn Hill Landing with its restaurants and shops, and then continues peacefully to Genesee Valley Park. The eastern side features Bausch & Lomb Riverside Park and Mt. Hope Cemetery—where women's rights activist Susan B. Anthony and orator and abolitionist Frederick Douglass are buried, along with a wide range of more local

Genesee Riverway Trail

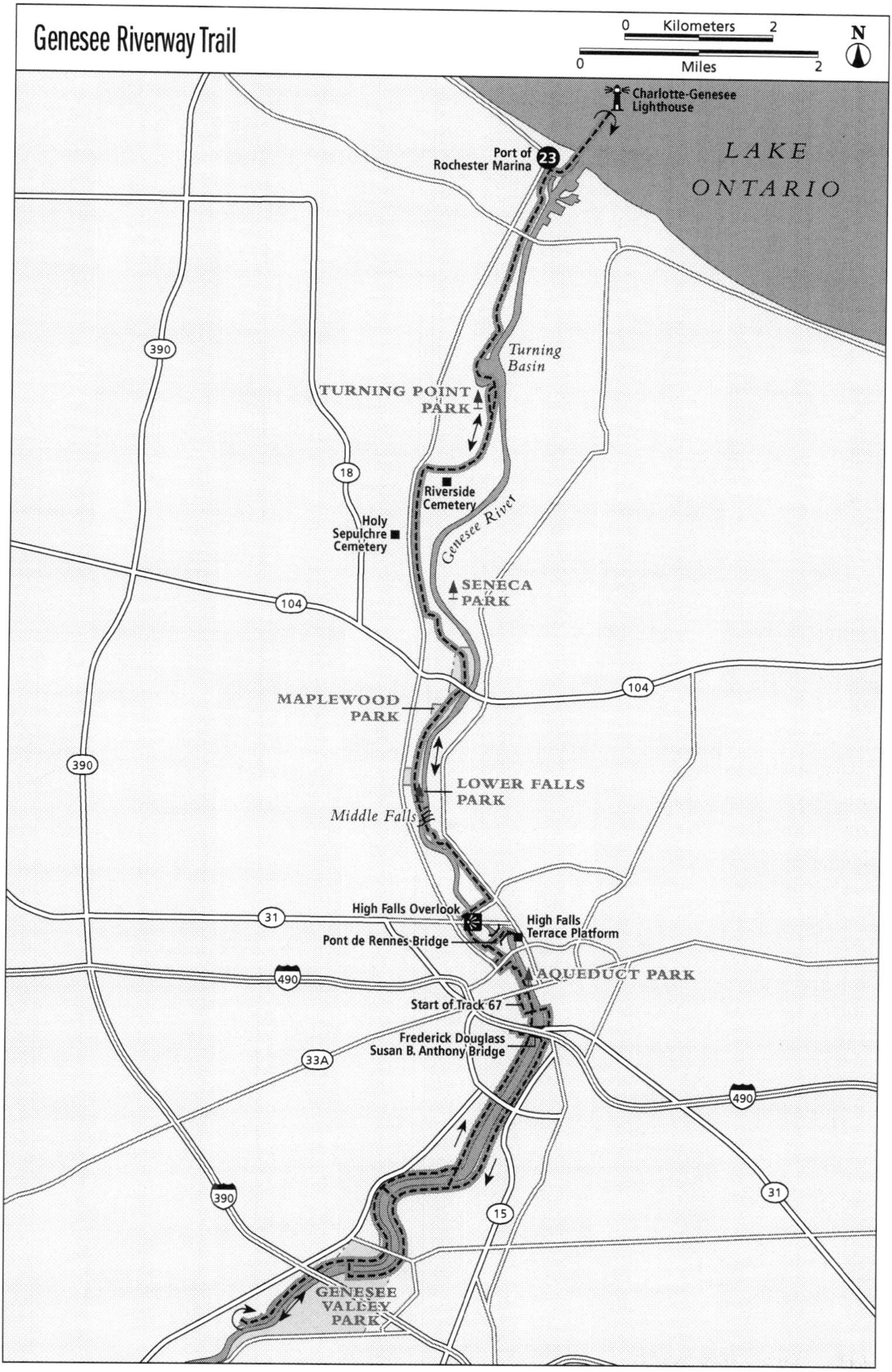

0 Kilometers 2
0 Miles 2

N

Charlotte-Genesee Lighthouse

LAKE ONTARIO

Port of Rochester Marina **23**

Turning Basin

TURNING POINT PARK

Genesee River

Riverside Cemetery

Holy Sepulchre Cemetery

SENECA PARK

390

18

104

MAPLEWOOD PARK

104

LOWER FALLS PARK

390

Middle Falls

High Falls Overlook

31

Pont de Rennes Bridge

High Falls Terrace Platform

AQUEDUCT PARK

490

Start of Track 67

Frederick Douglass Susan B. Anthony Bridge

33A

490

31

390

15

GENESEE VALLEY PARK

luminaries (notably John Bausch and Henry Lomb, who founded the corporation that bears their names). The parklike setting draws many visitors to stroll between the tombstones and enjoy the stately trees and songbirds.

The trail ends at Genesee Valley Park, another Olmsted project. Here you will find a confluence of major trails that cross Rochester: The Genesee Greenway Trail begins here, and the Erie Canalway Heritage Trail crosses the park on its way east and west.

Miles and Directions

0.0 Begin at the Port of Rochester.

2.0 Reach Turning Point Park. From here, the route parallels Lake Avenue.

3.0 Riverside Cemetery comes into view on the right.

4.5 At Maplewood Park cross Ridgeway Avenue and continue through the park along the river gorge.

6.5 Cross Driving Park Boulevard and enter Lower Falls Park, which contains both Lower and Middle Falls.

7.5 Reach High Falls Terrace Park, where you can view High Falls from a number of vantage points.

8.0 Choose either the east or west bank of the river on which to continue to follow the Genesee Riverway Trail signs. Both end at the same place in Genesee Valley Park.

13.0 The trail ends at Genesee Valley Park.

Hike Information

Local Information
Visit Rochester, 45 East Ave., Rochester; (585) 279-8300; www.visitrochester.com

Local Events/Attractions
The 150-acre **Highland Park,** the third of the Olmsted-designed parks in Rochester, holds the largest collection of lilacs of any city in America. More than 1,200 lilac shrubs feature hundreds of varieties, and other collections include 700 varieties of rhododendron, azaleas, mountain laurel, and andromeda, 35 varieties of magnolias, and its famous pansy bed with more than 10,000 plants placed in a new pattern every year. Highland and Goodman Streets in Rochester; www.monroecounty.gov/parks-highland.

Accommodations
Webster Park Campground is open May 1 to October 31 and features forty-five campsites. 255 Holt Rd., Webster. Reservations: (585) 872-5326; https://webapps.monroecounty.gov/mcparks/reserve/camp.

24 Genesee Valley Greenway State Park Trail

A repurposed abandoned canal and railway corridor, the Greenway has become one of western New York's prettiest and most frequented trails. This tree-lined section provides a lovely hike along farmers' fields and a nature preserve.

Start: At the trailhead on Morgan Road in Scottsville
Distance: 8.2 miles out-and-back
Approximate hiking time: 3 hours
Difficulty: Easy
Elevation change: The trail is virtually flat.
Trail surface: Mowed path
Seasons: Year-round, spring through fall are best for hiking
Other trail users: Bicyclists, cross-country skiers, snowshoers, birders
Canine compatibility: Dogs permitted on leash
Land status: New York State Park
Nearest town: Scottsville or Chili

Fees and permits: None
Schedule: Year-round
Map: https://parks.ny.gov/documents/parks/GeneseeValleyGreenwayGeneseeValleyGreenwayTrailMap.pdf
Trail contact: Genesee Valley Greenway, 1 Letchworth State Park, Castile; (585) 493-3614; https://parks.ny.gov/parks/geneseevalleygreenway/
Special considerations: Trail can be very muddy in transitional seasons. The trail is very popular with bicyclists, including mountain bikers; watch for fast cycles.

Finding the trailhead: From I-390 North or South, take the Scottsville Road (NY 383) exit. Turn south on NY 383 and continue south for about 9 miles to Morgan Road. Turn right onto Morgan Road. The trailhead will come into view on your right (look for the yellow gates). Park on the side of the road near the trailhead. GPS: 43.05053, -77.72827

The Hike

New York residents have a passion for saving abandoned railroad beds, and nowhere is their fine work more in evidence than here in the Greenway. Now a 90-mile trail that begins north of Genesee Valley Park and extends all the way to Hinsdale, New York, on the Pennsylvania border, the Greenway follows the path of the Genesee Valley Canal and the Rochester branch of the Pennsylvania Railroad, turning land that had fallen into disuse into an open recreational corridor.

You may wish to hike the entire length of this bucolic trail, but through-hiking it is tricky, as there are few adjacent campsites. And despite its recent elevation to state park status, it crosses a great deal of private land. Showcased here is a sampling of what you will find along this route. If this whets your appetite for more, you may want to plan a much longer trek that makes use of the Greenway's connection to the Finger Lakes Trail, the Erie Canal Recreation Way, the Erie Attica Trail, and the Lehigh Valley Trail. These may afford you side trips to campgrounds and other support for a through-hike.

The Genesee Valley Greenway replaced the Rochester branch of the Pennsylvania Railroad.
PHOTO BY NIC MINETOR

The hike described here begins at Morgan Road, at the south end of a particularly pleasing trail segment that passes through privately owned farmland and the Brookdale Preserve, a protected property of the Genesee Land Trust.

About 1.3 miles up the trail between Morgan and Brook Roads, you'll see a fine example of a stone lock, an exceptionally well-preserved artifact from the Genesee Valley Canal. Built in the late 1830s, this canal formed a connecting route from the Erie Canal down into New York State's Southern Tier, expanding the transportation of goods and materials into rural areas. The land surrounding this trail section produces a remarkable display of wildflowers in spring, and blue-winged warblers, eastern bluebirds, and field sparrows have been recorded as area breeders.

Cross Brook Road and continue into the "tunnel of green," the thick forest canopy that shelters this trail section. To your left, the Brookdale Preserve's wooded wetland can be filled with birds in spring and summer, and spring peepers begin to sing here with the first warm evenings in March. Amphibian lovers will find at least six species of frogs here: Spring peepers, western chorus, wood, northern leopard, tree, and green frogs have all been recorded on warm spring and summer evenings. The wooded areas on the right side of the trail are privately owned but no less loaded with resident birds and other creatures.

When you reach Ballantyne Road, cross here and continue north on the trail for another 0.4 mile to see one of the largest canal culverts in New York State. This double-arched culvert (under the trail) was constructed to redirect Black Creek

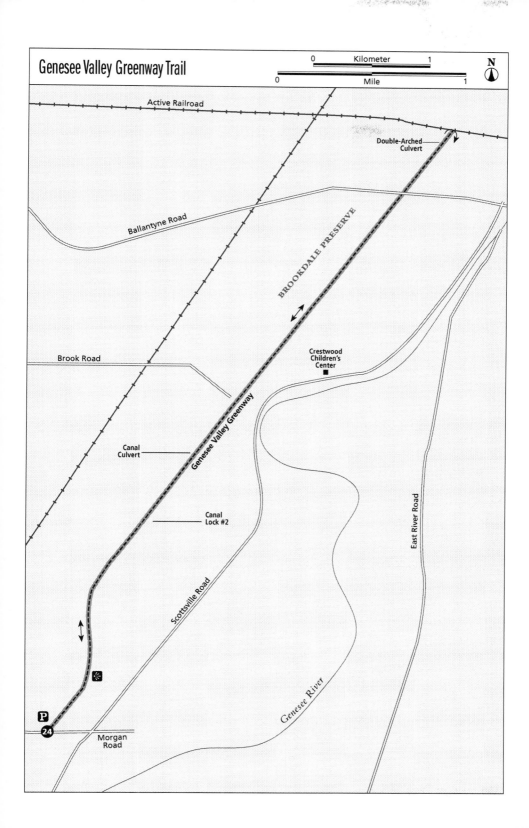

Genesee Valley Greenway Trail

Kilometer

Mile

N

Active Railroad

Double-Arched Culvert

Ballantyne Road

BROOKDALE PRESERVE

Brook Road

Crestwood Children's Center

Genesee Valley Greenway

Canal Culvert

Canal Lock #2

Scottsville Road

East River Road

Genesee River

P

24

Morgan Road

under the Genesee Valley Canal. From here, your route north ends at the active CSX Railroad tracks. The Friends of the Genesee Valley Greenway continue to explore options for creating some kind of trail passage over or around these tracks, but for now, we will use this as a turnaround point and begin walking south to return to Morgan Road.

Miles and Directions

0.0 Park at the trailhead and begin your walk north at the Morgan Road entrance to the trail. Continue straight.

2.0 Cross Brook Road.

2.3 The trail crossing here to the left goes into Brookdale Preserve.

2.6 Cross the gas pipeline right-of-way.

3.5 Cross Ballantyne Road.

4.1 Railroad tracks and turnaround point. Turn south.

8.2 Arrive back at Morgan Road.

Hike Information

Local Information

Visit Rochester, 45 East Ave., Rochester; (585) 279-8300; www.visitrochester.com

Local Events/Attractions

Oatka Creek Park in Scottsville offers some of the most pleasant hiking in the area throughout its 461 acres, as well as a haven for breeding birds including yellow-billed cuckoo, scarlet tanager, eastern towhee, and many warblers, vireos, and other songbirds. Fishing in the creek is encouraged. Open daily sunrise to sunset. 9797 Union St., Scottsville; (585) 753-7275; www.monroecounty.gov/parks-oatka.

Accommodations

Genesee Country Campground is open May 1 to October 31 and features 109 campsites. 40 Flint Hill Rd., Caledonia. Reservations: (585) 538-4200; https://genesee countrycampground.com.

25 Beaver Lake Nature Center

At this 650-acre Onondaga County Park northwest of Syracuse, 9 miles of superbly groomed nature trails and boardwalks explore lake, marsh, meadow, and woods habitats. Thirty thousand spring-migrating Canada geese and thousands of other migrating waterfowl swell the resident bird populations. The trails serve all levels of ability, and repeat tours bring new appreciation—just ask the park's "100 milers" who regularly walk the eight trails. The Lake Loop, featured here, is the shining core. The site's interpretive panels, benches, observation platforms, blind, and high-powered binoculars enhance discovery.

Start: At the visitor center, Lake Loop trailhead
Distance: 3.0-mile loop
Approximate hiking time: 1.5 to 2 hours
Difficulty: Easy
Elevation change: The trail is virtually flat.
Trail surface: Boardwalk and woodchip path
Seasons: Best for hiking spring through fall
Other trail users: Cross-country skiers (The Lake Loop is exclusive to cross-country skiers in winter; adjacent trails serve snowshoers. In winter, snowshoes are available for rent.)
Canine compatibility: Dogs not permitted
Land status: Onondaga County Park
Nearest town: Baldwinsville

Fees and permits: Vehicle entrance fee
Schedule: Year-round, grounds: 7:30 a.m. to posted closing time (varies with season); building opens 8 a.m.
Map: https://onondagacountyparks.com/parks/beaver-lake-nature-center/trails/
Trail contact: Beaver Lake Nature Center, 8477 East Mud Lake Rd., Baldwinsville; (315) 638-2519; https://onondagacountyparks.com/parks/beaver-lake-nature-center/
Special considerations: Seasonally, this site can be buggy, so carry insect repellent. The Lake Loop may flood seasonally; in wet seasons, call before visiting.

Finding the trailhead: From New York State Thruway I-90, take exit 39, go north on I-690/NY 690 for 5.8 miles, and take the second Baldwinsville exit onto NY 370 as indicated for the nature center. Go west on NY 370 for 2 miles, then turn right on East Mud Lake Road, following the signs. The nature center is on the left in 0.7 mile. The Lake Loop starts to the right of the visitor center; the other named trails start to the center's left. Attractive signs identify each trail. GPS: 43.180809, -76.401503

The Hike

A woods walk characterizes the early distance of the Lake Loop, which seldom hints at the centrally located 206-acre glacial lake—the site's namesake, Beaver Lake. The wide wood-chip path travels among spruce-pine woodland, towering tulip and beech trees, and a congestion of young, spindly maples. Virginia creeper, mayapple, and various ferns contribute to the understory.

Where a boardwalk carries you across the lake outlet, white water lilies decorate the flow in summer, and turtles sometimes sun on logs. Highbush blueberry, alder,

Canoeing and kayaking are popular at Beaver Lake.

nettles, ferns, and cattails rise among the wetland tangle. Ahead, an elevated bench overlooks Beaver Lake, and later, duckweed coats a small inlet where interesting fungi may decorate a log.

Wide foot trail replaces the boardwalk, and soon after, side trails branch right to three lean-tos and left to a canoe landing site. Canoes and kayaks are popular ways to explore the lake; rentals are available. (See park page for season and details.) In the wet ash-maple woodland, poison ivy abounds. Back on the boardwalk, pass a small pond with rimming cattail and pickerelweed.

The trail then passes through pine plantation and meadow, skirting below the Vann Road lake overlook. As the Lake Loop continues, a spur accesses the parallel loop of the Three Meadows Trail. Hemlock hollows and transition woods now alternately claim attention on the loop. Travel is again removed from the Beaver Lake shore. A small wetland pond sits trailside. On the way back to the visitor center, pass the Hemlock Hollow, Bog, and Lakeview trailheads, which suggest side trips.

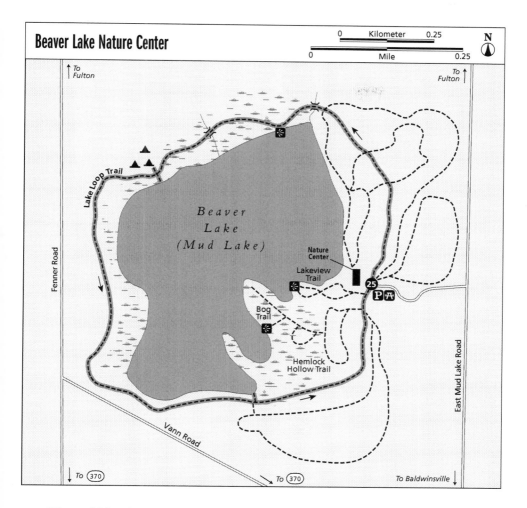

Beaver Lake Nature Center

To Fulton

To Fulton

Lake Loop Trail

Fenner Road

Beaver Lake (Mud Lake)

Nature Center

Lakeview Trail

Bog Trail

Hemlock Hollow Trail

East Mud Lake Road

25

P

Vann Road

To 370

To 370

To Baldwinsville

Miles and Directions

0.0   Start from the visitor center trailhead and head right, following the Lake Loop counterclockwise.

0.5   Cross the boardwalk over the lake outlet.

1.2   Reach the shelters and canoe landing.

2.5   Pass the spur to Three Meadows Trail.

3.0   Arrive back at the visitor center.

Options

The final leg of the Lake Loop provides access to both the Hemlock Hollow Trail and the Lakeview Loop, which suggest options to extend the hike. Because the Hemlock

Hollow Trail is the lone access to the Bog Trail, likely you'll choose to combine these two walks.

The **Hemlock Hollow Trail** swings a 0.4-mile loop through a dark hemlock woods with oak, birch, beech, and interspersing witch hazel. Midway, the 0.6-mile ladle-shaped **Bog Trail** branches west, traveling boardwalk and trail along a former island, now a marshy Beaver Lake peninsula. By keeping right at the two initial Bog Trail junctions (the ladle loop), you can first explore the length of the peninsula (the handle). Spurs off the "handle" lead to a bog-pond overlook, a one-story lake observation platform, and a couple of lakeshore accesses. At the lake platform, a good pair of binoculars will pull cross-lake great blue herons and green herons into close scrutiny. On your return take the boardwalk (ladle) loop, capping your bog visit with marsh study. Sweet gale, pickerelweed, cranberry, boneset, and carnivorous pitcher plant are among the finds here.

The wheelchair-accessible 0.3-mile **Lakeview Loop** draws a figure eight through similar deep woods, with plaques explaining the intricate habitat interactions. A beautiful big oak marks the second loop junction. Off the second loop, spurs lead to two lake vistas. At the larger viewing stop, benches and telescopes are provided, including one telescope low enough for comfortable use from a wheelchair. An osprey snatching a fish from the lake, the growing wake of a beaver, or some 30,000 migrant geese waiting for the spring thaw in Canada can dazzle onlookers. Late March to early May and late October through November mark the peak times for viewing Canada geese. In fall, ducks, including ring-necked duck, gadwall, American wigeon, ruddy duck, and hooded and common mergansers, stop over on the lake on their way south.

Hike Information

Local Information

Visit Syracuse, 109 S. Warren St., Suite 10, Syracuse; (315) 470-1910; www.visit syracuse.com

Local Events/Attractions

The **Onondaga Lake Park** complex in northwest Syracuse includes a carousel, skate park, dog park, walking trails, and boating, as well as the Salt Museum (salt was an early Syracuse industry) and the re-created Skä•noñh—Great Law of Peace Center (formerly known as "Sainte Marie among the Iroquois" French Mission) that stood on this lakeshore (1656–1658). At the latter, volunteers in period dress introduce life skills of the seventeenth century. The museum here explains the cultures of the Haudenosaunee (Iroquois), the French, and the meeting of the two. Onondaga Lake Park, 106 Lake Dr., Liverpool; (315) 453-6712; https://onondagacountyparks.com/parks/onondaga-lake-park/.

26 Interloken National Recreation Trail

Northeast of Watkins Glen, the gentle ridges and open flats of New York State's one and only national forest were once inhabited by Iroquois Indians, and later partitioned into military parcels issued in payment to veterans of the Revolutionary War. Through a farmer's relief act in the Great Depression, the lands returned to government hands, and today they serve recreational users. This linear multiuse National Recreation Trail (NRT) strings north to south through the national forest, exploring natural and planted forest stands, open meadows, shrubby transitional lands, and pond habitats. The diversity supports fish, birds, and mammals.

Start: At the northern trailhead
Distance: 12.0-mile shuttle
Approximate hiking time: 6.5 to 8 hours
Difficulty: Moderate
Elevation change: The trail has a 550-foot elevation change, with its low elevation of 1,300 feet in the south, its high elevation of 1,850 feet on Hector Backbone.
Trail surface: Earthen path, grassy tracks, and boardwalk crossings
Seasons: Open year-round, best for hiking spring through fall
Other trail users: Hunters, cross-country skiers (This is primarily a foot/cross-country ski trail, but limited marked stretches may be shared with horse riders or mountain bikers.)
Canine compatibility: Leashed dogs permitted (cleanup required)
Land status: US Department of Agriculture
Nearest town: Watkins Glen
Fees and permits: None

Schedule: No time restrictions, but there is a 14-day limit in the forest for camping
Map: www.cnyhiking.com/InterlokenTrail.htm
Trail contact: Finger Lakes National Forest, Hector Ranger District, 5218 NY Route 414, Hector; (607) 546-4470; www.fs.usda.gov/main/gmfl/home
Special considerations: Where the trail is shared-use, be alert for horse riders and yield the right-of-way to them. There is no camping within 50 feet of the trail, and you should wear fluorescent orange during hunting season (late Sept into Dec). You may encounter occasional blowdowns on the trail, and despite such improvements as boardwalks and gravel, muddy patches still exist. The forest service is always on the lookout for volunteers to help maintain this trail. Metal stakes, wooden signs, and orange markings variously indicate the trail.

Finding the trailhead: From the NY 227–NY 96 junction in Trumansburg, go north on NY 96 for 1.5 miles and turn left onto NY 143, proceeding 4.8 miles. Turn right onto NY 146 for 1 mile and then go left onto Parmenter/Butcher Hill Road for 0.6 mile. The northern trailhead is on the left. GPS: 42.572113, -76.794218

For the southern trailhead, at the NY 5–NY 79 intersection in Burdett, go 0.9 mile east on NY 79 and turn left onto Logan Road (County Road 4) for 1.1 miles. Turn right onto Wyckoff Road. In 0.5 mile head right on Burnt Hill Road for 0.4 mile. The trailhead is on the left. GPS: 42.442760, -76.813816

New York's lone National Forest houses the Interloken Trail.

The Hike

Beginning at the northern trailhead, the National Recreation Trail (NRT) enters a mature mixed woods with a lush understory. Cross an aspen-shrub complex, a woodlot of young maples and pines, and an open meadow. Shortly after you cross Townsend Road, a 10-foot-wide drainage may require wading in high water. Veer left for a mild ascent to pass through a gate.

You next wade through knee-high grasses, descending to and crossing Seneca Road. Bypass the No-Tan-Takto Horse Trail and traverse an aspen-shrub complex, reaching Teeter Pond. This expansive marsh and open water attract wildlife and anglers after warm-water fish species. Snags, shrub islands, and reflections of the cloud-filled sky can add to its welcome. Pass to the right of the pond.

A full mixed forest lines the trail to the next gate at the corner of a large pasture. Follow the diagonal-staked course of the NRT across Teeter Grassland. The trail again parts deep grasses sprinkled with clover, daisy, and buttercup. A row of maples guides you out the gate to Searsburg Road. Close any gates that you open, because cattle grazing is used as part of forest management.

Upon crossing Searsburg Road, a mowed swath enters the woods for a gentle climb, but muddy passages can weigh down boots. A leafy abundance stretches from the lower story to the canopy. An occasional bright azalea patch seasonally steals the stage. Warblers can enliven the woods.

At a signed junction with the Backbone Trail, continue straight for the NRT, traversing a pine plantation with accents of fairy slipper. Back in oak-maple woodland,

The Interloken Trail travels open fields and lush woods.

you'll skirt a private property on the right; keep to the trail. A thinned forest of big trees and boardwalks precedes the shrubby outskirts of Foster Pond.

While touring the pond outskirts, keep to the tracked path straight ahead. The Backbone Trail (northbound) heads left, and in 200 feet its southbound counterpart journeys right. Afterward, the Interloken NRT rounds the south shore of Foster Pond. Keep alert for an upcoming turn to the right. This is the first of three junctions where side trails branch east to Potomac Road. Thick vegetation encloses the trail before you return to woods.

Next, follow Picnic Area Road right (west) to pick up the southbound NRT past Blueberry Patch Recreation Area. You enter an oak-conifer transition habitat with tall shrubs. At back-to-back junctions, proceed straight. Pass from a younger woods of maple and bigtooth aspen to a more mature, mixed complex, coming to a gate and another stretch through pasture. As the footpath angles uphill to the left, a microwave tower may be visible to the east. Ridges and farmland sweep west. Despite the tall grasses that overhang it, the path is more passable than it first appears.

From Mathews Road, return to woods, soon passing among snags and 8-foot-tall shrubs. After you cross the overgrown corridor of Burnt Hill Trail, the NRT enters a rolling meander through planted and natural woods. The NRT briefly merges with the Gorge Trail. An area of mature oaks and more conifer plantations brings you to a levee of a wildlife pond at a corner on Burnt Hill Road. The duckweed-covered crescent can percolate with frogs, but watch out for poison ivy.

Continue straight past South Slope Trail and, upon meeting the Finger Lakes Trail (FLT), bear left. A lean-to sits in the nearby grassy clearing. Proceed forward,

NATIONAL RECREATION TRAILS

The National Trail System Act of 1968 authorized the creation of a network of recreational, scenic, and historical trails of outstanding caliber. Although the creation of each National Scenic Trail and National Historic Trail requires an act of Congress, National Recreation Trails (NRTs) may be designated by the secretaries of interior and agriculture. These public trails travel federal, state, county, and municipal lands through rural, urban, and natural wilds. More than 1,300 National Recreation Trails now exist, and they can be found in all fifty states, with new trails added annually. The trails range from a fraction of a mile to a whopping 485 miles in length.

following the FLT/Interloken Trail. With a rolling descent, the trail crosses a shrubby bog, skirting a frog pond, passing through a gap in a stone wall, and traveling along a boardwalk to end at the southern terminus.

Miles and Directions

0.0 Start from the northern trailhead and hike the NRT south.

1.2 Cross Townsend Road.

2.1 Cross Seneca Road.

2.2 Proceed forward past the No-Tan-Takto Trail.

2.5 Reach Teeter Pond; pass along the west shore.

3.3 Cross Searsburg Road.

4.4 Meet the Backbone Trail. Continue straight on the NRT.

5.7 Again meet the Backbone Trail and continue straight on the NRT.

5.8 Reach Foster Pond. Travel east along its south shore.

6.1 Reach a junction. Follow the NRT to the right. *Note:* The path straight ahead comes out at Potomac Road. (This is the first of three junctions where side trails branch east to Potomac Road.)

6.9 Reach Picnic Area Road. Follow the road right (west) 0.2 mile to resume southbound on the NRT (here a foot trail on the left).

7.4 Reach the first of back-to-back junctions. Proceed straight at each. *Note:* At the second junction the Ravine Trail heads right.

8.4 Cross Mathews Road.

9.1 Cross the overgrown Burnt Hill Trail.

9.6 Follow the Gorge Trail right for 0.1 mile and then proceed straight, where the Gorge Trail turns right.

10.2 Travel the levee of a wildlife pond.

10.5 Continue straight past South Slope Trail.

11.0 Meet the main Finger Lakes Trail (FLT) and bear left.

12.0 End at the southern trailhead.

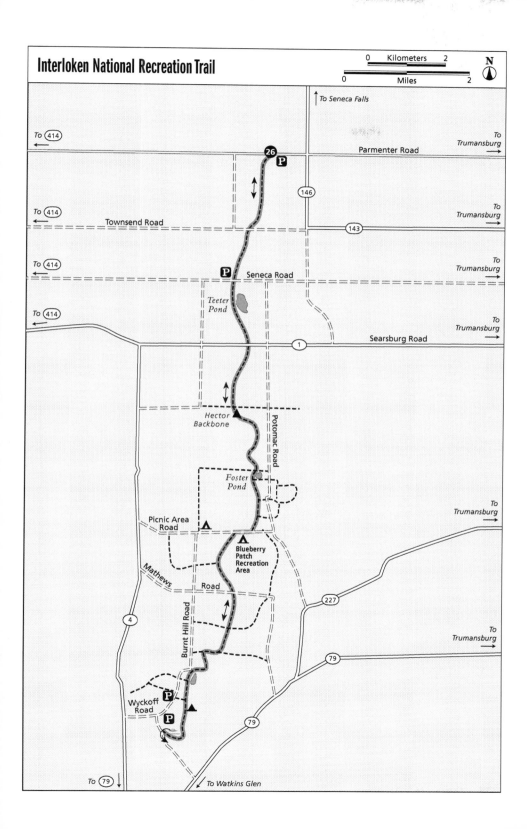

Interloken National Recreation Trail

Hike Information

Local Information

Seneca County Chamber of Commerce, 1 West Main St., Waterloo; (315) 568-2906; www.discoverseneca.com

Watkins Glen Area Chamber of Commerce, 214 North Franklin St., Highway 14, Watkins Glen; (607) 535-4300 or (800) 607-4552; www.watkinsglenchamber.com

Local Events/Attractions

Women's Rights National Historical Park (NHP) in Seneca Falls follows the history of the women's rights movement through museum exhibits, video, and guided tours. In 1848 Elizabeth Cady Stanton, Lucretia Mott, Harriet Cady Eaton, Margaret Pryor, and Mary Ann M'Clintock invited the public to the first Women's Rights Convention here in Seneca Falls. Stanton's home is among those toured. Women's Rights NHP, 136 Fall St., Seneca Falls; (315) 568-0024; www.nps.gov/wori.

Accommodations

Blueberry Patch Campground, open year-round but operated as walk-in only in winter, has nine fee sites available on a first-come, first-served basis. On Schuyler County Road 2, 4 miles east of NY 414.

Organizations

Finger Lakes Trail Conference helps maintain and map the trail. FLTC, 6111 Visitor Center Rd., Mount Morris; (585) 658-9320; www.fingerlakestrail.org.

27 Taughannock Falls State Park

The Finger Lakes Region boasts several prized east–west gorges with companion gorge and waterfall trails, but each pens a unique signature. Taughannock Falls autographs this park with a flourish. Cradled in an amphitheater of 400-foot cliffs and spilling 215 feet from a hanging canyon, the waterfall conjures images of Yosemite National Park in California and ranks as one of the tallest waterfalls east of the Mississippi River. The park's hiking trail duo neatly combines, so you can admire the falls canyon from belly and rim.

Start: At the Taughannock Falls trailhead
Distance: 5.0 miles combining the out-and-back interior trail with the rim loop
Approximate hiking time: 2.5 to 3.5 hours
Difficulty: Easy
Elevation change: The Gorge Trail segment has a 100-foot elevation change, the rim loop about a 550-foot elevation change.
Trail surface: Paved or surfaced walk and earthen path
Seasons: Best for hiking spring through fall
Other trail users: None
Canine compatibility: Leashed dogs permitted, cleanup required. (Because the interior trail can buzz with people, you'll have a better walk with your dog along the rim loop.)
Land status: New York State Park
Nearest town: Ithaca

Fees and permits: Park entrance fee
Schedule: Year-round, dawn to dusk; North and South Rim Trails closed in winter
Map: https://parks.ny.gov/documents/parks/TaughannockFallsTrailMap.pdf
Trail contact: Taughannock Falls State Park, 1740 Taughannock Blvd., Trumansburg; (607) 387-6739; https://parks.ny.gov/parks/taughannockfalls
Special considerations: There is no swimming in Taughannock Creek, and mountain bikes are prohibited. Stay on trails because of the danger of falling rocks. Icy conditions in winter or spring can result in temporary closures of the normally year-round Gorge Trail. The park allows bowhunting for deer in season (Oct to early Dec), but it's generally conducted away from trails. Pack in, pack out.

Finding the trailhead: From the junction of NY 13/34 and NY 89/96/79 (the corner of State and Meadow Streets) in Ithaca, head north on NY 89 for 9.1 miles. Turn left (west) to enter the trailhead parking lot. Trails leave from the southwest corner of the parking area. GPS: 42.545459, -76.599232

The Hike

The park trails start from a site once occupied by native Taughannock camps and a cabin that sheltered a soldier during the Revolutionary War. The interior trail and Falls Overlook on the north rim tender the best views of Taughannock Falls, but the rim loop grants perspectives on the canyon and its exciting creek.

First exploring the canyon interior, hike the 1-mile Gorge Trail (an interpretive trail with a paved walk) west upstream to the waterfall viewpoint.

Taughannock Falls is one of the highest waterfalls east of the Rocky Mountains.

Before reaching the falls, an impressive 15-foot-high ledge spans the 75- to 100-foot width of Taughannock Creek. At the ledge's northern corner, the water spills at an angle, its chutes carving deep channels into the sedimentary ledge. Torrents of melting ice and rock shaped the uniformly flat bedrock long ago. Hemlock, basswood, maple, and oak overhang the path.

Upstream a lower ledge spans the creek, and the steep wooded slopes yield to skyward-stretching cliffs. Barn, bank, northern rough-winged, and tree swallows; peregrine falcons; and common ravens dwell in the canyon alongside red-tailed hawks and plenty of American crows.

The sandstone-shale cliffs become more prominent, steep, eroding, and jointed, with boxy overhangs and tenuously held trees. Sycamores join the ranks. Across the bridge the waterfall amphitheater humbles onlookers. With multiple streamers and wisping spray, the 215-foot vertical falls plunges to an awaiting pool, 30 feet deep. Spray-nurtured greenery adorns the canted base of the 400-foot cliffs. You couldn't ask for a more lovely or authoritative stop sign.

Backtrack downstream to add the rim loop. Back at the trailhead, next to the trail information hut, you'll see where the South Rim Trail veers left; take it for clockwise travel.

Ascend the stairs of the South Rim Trail, top the rim, and turn right. A mixed deciduous-hemlock forest provides shade. Deer encounters are possible. After a half mile an open up-canyon view replaces the teasing canyon glimpses so far granted by the rim trail. This view spotlights the upper reaches of Taughannock Falls.

After the rim terrain pushes you out onto Gorge Road to round a steep side drainage, the trail and lightly used road remain closely paired. At a U-shaped scouring of the rim, a dizzying look down reveals the canyon bottom. Next, travel a broad, wooded plateau and round a deep rim gash. Cedar, birch, willow, berried shrub, tiger lily, daisy, and harebell adorn the trail corridor.

Cross the hiker bridge over Taughannock Creek before reaching a road bridge and the park boundary. Upstream a 100-foot falls spills at a hairpin turn of the now-pinched gorge. Downstream the prominent tree-capped rim, jutting points, vertical cliffs, and an ancient plunge pool washed by the slow-moving stream complete the scene. Following the North Rim Trail, pass through a small field, bearing right to follow the mowed shoulder of the park road, before returning to foot trail, now in a narrow hemlock-hardwood corridor near a wire-mesh fence.

At Falls Overlook you gain a bird's-eye view of the rock amphitheater and its star waterfall. This vantage reveals the upstream water flowing up to and over the abrupt ledge of the hanging valley, as well as the full length of the 215-foot drop. Taughannock House, a luxury hotel that operated here from the 1860s until the turn of the twentieth century, formerly claimed this view.

Descend past a picnic area and the campground. Views span downstream, taking in the broad creek bottom, wooded canyon, Cayuga Lake, and its east ridge. Stone

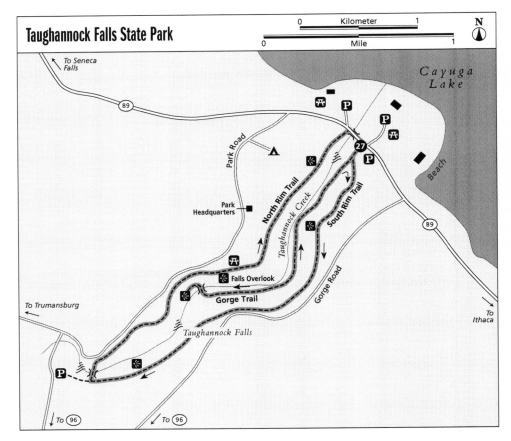

Taughannock Falls State Park

stairs lead to NY 89, at the north side of the Taughannock Creek bridge. Turn right, cross the bridge, and return to the parking area.

Miles and Directions

0.0 Start from the Taughannock Falls trailhead at the southwest corner of trail parking. Hike the Gorge Trail west upstream, staying inside the gorge.

0.7 Cross the footbridge of Taughannock Creek, reaching the Taughannock Falls viewpoint. Backtrack downstream to the South Rim Trail's start.

1.5 Follow South Rim Trail uphill and turn right on the rim.

3.3 Cross the Taughannock Creek bridge to the North Rim Trail. Follow the North Rim Trail downstream.

4.0 Reach Falls Overlook and continue downstream.

4.7 Meet NY 89, turn right, and cross the road bridge over Taughannock Creek.

5.0 End at trailhead parking.

Hike Information

Local Information

Taughannock Falls Overlook Visitor Center, 2381 Taughannock Park Rd., Trumansburg; (607) 209-0008 (May–Nov). **Ithaca/Tompkins County Convention & Visitors Bureau,** 110 North Tioga St., Ithaca; (607) 272-1313 or (315) 273-7482; www.visitithaca.com.

Local Events/Attractions

This area is noted for its **farmstands, U-picks, cideries, wineries, cheesemakers, and distilleries.** The Cayuga Lake Wine Trail links a dozen wineries on the west side of Cayuga Lake, as well as restaurants, distillers, goat dairies, a coffee roaster, museums, and more. Cayuga Lake Wine Trail, PO Box 123, Fayette, NY 13065; (315) 549-3034; www.cayugawinetrail.com.

Accommodations

Taughannock Falls State Park campground, open late March to mid-October, has eighty-seven sites, some with cabins, as well as three pavilions. Reservations: (800) 456-2267; www.reserveamerica.com.

28 Onondaga Trail

Southeast of Syracuse, this blue-blazed trail, an extension of the Finger Lakes Trail (FLT) and part of the North Country National Scenic Trail (NCT), rolls from rim to drainage, touring hemlock glen and hardwood forest between Spruce Pond and Chickadee Hollow Road. It then surrenders to roadway travel all the way to Cuyler before resuming as a foot trail passing through state forests to meet the main FLT. This hike features the northern Onondaga stretch to Chickadee Hollow truck road. On the way, you pass a hang-gliding site and many vistas, but mostly you enjoy a pleasant forest sojourn.

Start: At the northern (Spruce Pond) trailhead
Distance: 15.6 miles out-and-back
Approximate hiking time: 9 to 11 hours
Difficulty: Strenuous
Elevation change: The trail has a 750-foot elevation change, with the high point on Morgan Hill.
Trail surface: Earthen path, doubletrack, and woods road
Seasons: Open year-round, best for hiking spring through fall
Other trail users: Hang gliders, hunters, snowshoers, cross-country skiers
Canine compatibility: Dogs permitted but must be controlled at owner's side by leash or voice command
Land status: New York State Department of Environmental Conservation (DEC) and private land

Nearest town: Truxton
Fees and permits: None
Schedule: No time restrictions
Map: https://cnyhiking.com/OnondagaTrail.htm
Trail contact: New York State DEC, Region 7, 1285 Fisher Ave., Cortland; (607) 753-3095; www.dec.ny.gov
Special considerations: This trail travels both public and private lands, so keep to the trail, obeying posted notices. In Labrador Hollow Unique Area, there is no camping and no fires, and that goes for private land too. When following the woods roads, you need to keep a sharp eye out for the continuations of the foot trail. A long lapse between markers may indicate the need to backtrack and find the trail. Hang gliders must secure a special permit from the NYSDEC.

Finding the trailhead: From I-81, take exit 14 for Tully and go east on NY 80 for 4.5 miles, passing through Tully and merging with NY 91 North. At 4.5 miles turn south on gravel Herlihy Road, go 1.9 miles, and continue straight at the junction to reach the Spruce Pond Fishing Access in another 0.1 mile. There is parking for ten vehicles. GPS: 42.799212, -76.025723

The Hike

Going south from the trailhead, cross the earthen levee of square-shaped Spruce Pond to strike up a slope of beeches and maples, following blue blazes. A dark spruce plantation, aspen-ash woods, and an aisle of seasonally fragrant azalea in turn claim the way. Atop Jones Hill, cross private land that has been logged before entering Labrador Hollow Unique Area. As the trail passes above the steep western slope, faint side paths

Comforting woods advance the Onondaga Trail.

spur to the rim for seasonal views. Keeping to the trail, traverse the meadow gap of Hang Glider Leap, the official hang-glider takeoff. Here the view opens to the steep-sided north–south valley of oval Labrador Pond. This area is particularly spectacular in fall, when the forest-covered hillsides turn amber and crimson.

Next, follow the doubletrack south, descending the rim. Here, keep an eye out for the return to foot trail, which heads left into leafy forest. The tour again flip-flops between road and trail; keep left, still descending. A sharp descent leads to the gulf rim of Tinker Falls Creek. The severity of the slope restricts views of the 50-foot falls, which weeps from an overhang. Although tracked paths descend suicidally toward the falls, they are both unofficial and irresponsible, damaging terrain and risking injury. Do not approach the dangerous, sloughing edge or in any way attempt cross-country travel to improve your view. But taking a few steps to your right affords a relatively safe look into the cliff bowl and gorge. If you want to see the falls, a 0.3-mile DEC spur ascends along the creek from NY 91 to a base-of-the-falls view.

Proceed ahead, crossing Tinker Falls Creek just upstream from the overhang, and make a steep, angular ascent to a woods road. Be careful at the creek crossing, though; the rocks are mossy and the drop is precipitous. Follow the road grade a few steps to the left to pick up the foot trail on the right. The hike again alternates between a foot trail and woods road as it ascends away from the drainage. Cross the nose of a ridge and descend through plantations of spruce and tamarack to cross Shackham Road.

Cross the bridge over Shackham Brook. Soon after, cross Enchanted Hollow, where a side excursion up either side finds pretty cascades. The trail continues forward to contour a hemlock-spruce slope, pursuing Shackham Brook upstream, and then hooks left to travel parallel to and upstream along the aptly named Hemlock Brook. Beyond an 8-foot mossy waterfall and camp flat, you reach a lean-to overlooking the steep-sided drainage. Hemlock Brook is the prettiest spot on the trail,

POISON IVY

This skin irritant can be found just about anywhere in North America in the form of a low shrub or a climbing vine, having leaflets in groups of three. The urushiol oil it secretes can cause an allergic reaction in the form of blisters, usually about 12 hours after exposure. The itchy rash can last from ten days to several weeks. The best defense is to wear clothing that covers the arms, legs, and torso, and to be careful to remove and wash all clothing and shoes that may have come into contact with the plant. Urushiol is tenacious and will stay on shoes or clothing, surprising you later with an unexpected rash.

If you think you were in contact with the plants, wash with soap and water to remove any lingering oil from your skin. Should you contract a rash, use an antihistamine (e.g., Benadryl) to reduce the itching, and apply a topical lotion to dry up the area. If the rash spreads, consult your doctor.

so you might choose to snack or picnic here before moving on. After the crossing of Hemlock Brook, the trail climbs sharply away.

Back on a woods road, watch for the foot trail to descend left. After the trail dips through a steep side drainage, cross Morgan Hill Road. Side trails branch left to the Morgan Hill bivouac area. Continue to seek out the blue Onondaga Trail markers, as truck trails and snowmobile routes interweave the area. Woodpecker, grouse, and deer may make surprise appearances.

The hike passes through tree plantation and mixed woods, with a few big-diameter trees, to meet Chickadee Hollow Road, a lightly used truck trail. Although the Onondaga Trail continues to the right on this road, for this hike, turn back, returning the way you came.

Miles and Directions

0.0 Start from the northern (Spruce Pond) trailhead, cross the earthen levee, and strike uphill.

1.3 Enter Jones Hill–Labrador Hollow Unique Area.

1.5 Reach the hang-glider site. Follow the doubletrack descending south.

1.7 Look for and follow the foot trail heading left off the doubletrack.

2.5 Reach the gulf rim of Tinker Falls Creek. Keep to the trail, crossing Tinker Falls Creek upstream from the overhang.

4.0 Cross Shackham Road.

4.3 Reach Enchanted Hollow. **Side trip:** Upon crossing the hollow, you can detour upstream along the marked woods road, finding hollow views and a stepped cascade in 0.1 mile.

5.0 Reach the lean-to at Hemlock Brook. Descend to and cross Hemlock Brook on flat stones and then take the foot trail as it angles sharply uphill. **Bailout:** The lean-to makes a satisfying ending for a 10-mile out-and-back hike.

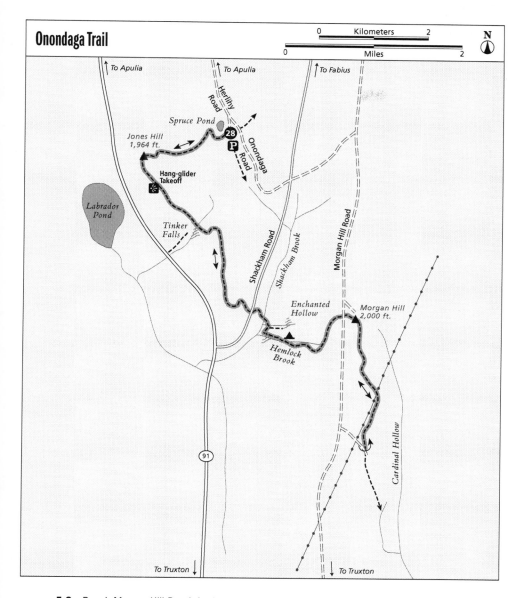

| 0 | Kilometers | 2 |
| 0 | Miles | 2 |

To Apulia
To Apulia
To Fabius
Herlihy Road
Spruce Pond
Jones Hill 1,964 ft.
28
Onondaga Road
Hang-glider Takeoff
Labrador Pond
Tinker Falls
Shackham Road
Shackham Brook
Morgan Hill Road
Enchanted Hollow
Morgan Hill 2,000 ft.
Hemlock Brook
Cardinal Hollow
91
To Truxton
To Truxton

5.8 Reach Morgan Hill Road. Angle across the road, picking up the trail as it ascends.

7.1 Cross an open utility corridor.

7.8 Reach Chickadee Hollow Road, a lightly used truck trail, and turn around, backtracking to Spruce Pond and the trailhead. **Option:** The Onondaga Trail continues traversing private lands, when the fall hunting closure is not in effect, to Cuyler/NY 13 and beyond to state forests and the main FLT. (Carry and follow the FLT Onondaga Trail Sheet O1 map.)

15.6 End at the Spruce Pond trailhead.

Hike Information

Local Information

Visit Syracuse, 109 S.Warren St.,Suite 10,Syracuse;(315) 470-1910;www.visitsyracuse .com.

Cortland County Convention and Visitors Bureau, 42 Main St., Cortland; (607) 753-8463; www.experiencecortland.com

Local Events/Attractions

Cortland County is agricultural, and its agribusinesses lead you on a country drive that is both tasty and educational.You can visit research facilities, farmstands, Christmas tree farms, stables, cideries, dairies, nature centers, and more. Learn more about agribusinesses to visit online at https://experiencecortland.com, or you can contact the Cortland County Convention and Visitors Bureau.

Organizations

Finger Lakes Trail Conference helps maintain and map the trail. FLTC, 6111 Visitor Center Rd., Mount Morris; (585) 658-9320; www.fingerlakestrail.org.

29 Watkins Glen State Park

This park houses one of the premier gorge and waterfall settings in the Finger Lakes Region—and in the nation. Charged with excitement, the hike brings together majestic 200-foot cliffs and the nineteen waterfalls, turbulent chutes, and deep plunge pools that punctuate a 545-foot drop on Glen Creek. A loop fashioned by the Gorge and Indian Trails shows off the canyon spectacle. Scenic bridges, tunnels, and twisting staircases make the trails an attraction as well.

Start: At the concession area (lower) trailhead
Distance: 2.8-mile lollipop
Approximate hiking time: 2 to 2.5 hours
Difficulty: Moderate due to the 832 stairsteps and possibility of slippery wet footing
Elevation change: The hike has about a 500-foot elevation change.
Trail surface: Stone steps and natural surface
Seasons: Best for hiking spring through fall
Other trail users: None
Canine compatibility: Dogs not permitted on Gorge Trail
Land status: New York State Park
Nearest town: Watkins Glen
Fees and permits: Entrance parking fee
Schedule: Park, year-round; Gorge Trail, mid-May through early Nov; sunrise to sunset

Map: https://parks.ny.gov/documents/parks/WatkinsGlenWatkinsGlenTrailMap.pdf
Trail contact: Watkins Glen State Park, 1009 N. Franklin St., Watkins Glen; (607) 535-4511; https://parks.ny.gov/parks/142/
Special considerations: The parking lot can fill at peak times. A fee shuttle bus runs between the lower concession and upper entrance for those who have time for just one-way travel, or who prefer to descend rather than ascend the trail's 832 steps. Watch your footing, because natural springs and the mist from the waterfalls can dampen the walks and steps, making them dangerous. Icy conditions close down the trail. Outside the gorge the park allows the bow hunting of deer in season.

Finding the trailhead: In Watkins Glen find the park entrance west off Franklin Avenue/NY 14, south of Fourth Street. GPS: 42.375272, -76.873102

The Hike

If you love falling water, here's your hiking bonanza: nineteen waterfalls in the space of a mile, tumbling down through a gorge with 200-foot walls on either side. Top this off with a trail that stands as one of the greatest achievements of the venerable Civilian Conservation Corps, and you have a hike to which no other New York State outing can compare.

The bustle at the park entry echoes the site's roots as a private resort in the late 1800s. Off-hour, off-season, and rainy-day visits allow for a quieter, unhurried communion with the grandeur of the gorge. Be sure to bring your camera because snapshots come as fast as blinks.

Stunning historic stairways contribute to the waterfall beauty of Watkins Glen.

For an upstream hike, start at the west end of the parking lot. The stone arch of Sentry Bridge combines with the bulging canyon walls to shape a keyhole view of a waterfall recessed in the shadows, the first in a lineup of great waterfall views. Ascend the first of three tunnels bored into the rock, emerging at Sentry Bridge, which presents an up-canyon view of the pinched gorge, distant views of Watkins Glen village, and close looks at the jointed, layered rock. The Gorge Trail crisscrosses Glen Creek four times but bypasses both High and Mile Point Bridges.

Across Sentry Bridge, look for the Finger Lakes Trail (FLT) to head left; it travels along the south rim. Remain in the gorge, continuing up Watkins Glen. As the Gorge Trail ascends the stairs to Cavern Cascade, look down to a heart-shaped plunge pool. Now pass behind the droplet curtain for a unique perspective. Ahead stretches the Spiral Tunnel staircase, which opens to a view of the site's suspension bridge (High Bridge). Keep to the gorge, passing under the bridge.

As the canyon walls cup and divide, each bend holds a new discovery. A leafy bower claims the Narrows, while a dry, concave bowing of the gorge characterizes the Cathedral. A tiered upstream cascade feeds the 60-foot plunge of Central Cascade, the tallest waterfall in the park. Rainbow Falls showers over the south rim. Beyond it, come to a bridge and Spiral Gorge, a dark, more brooding passage.

The trail emerges into the light at Mile Point Bridge. Continue west along the north wall, bypassing both the bridge and a trail to the right. In the calm above the lower-canyon storm, ascend the stairs dubbed Jacob's Ladder. This stairway leads both to Indian Trail (the loop's return) and the upper entrance. Look for the Indian Trail to head right just past a midway bench on Jacob's Ladder.

A low rock wall or mesh fence edges the Indian Trail as it travels the north rim and slope. Evergreens, dogwood, oak, maple, beech, sassafras, and black cherry contribute to a forest roster that now conceals Glen Creek. The spur from Mile Point Bridge arrives on your right, and before long you again overlook Rainbow Falls.

Staying along the rim, you find a Central Cascade overlook, which provides a totally new perspective. The trail then skirts a cemetery and descends sharply past a lean-to to reach the suspension bridge. Lovers Lane arrives on the right; continue straight ahead (east) to Point Lookout and the park entrance. A detour out onto the bridge, however, provides a grand look 85 feet down to the creek and out the canyon. At Point Lookout you obtain a fine cross-gorge view. Descend the stairs, meeting the Gorge Trail at Spiral Tunnel. Here you retrace the hike back to the trailhead.

Miles and Directions

0.0 Start from the lower (concession area) trailhead and hike upstream.

0.1 Cross Sentry Bridge, meeting the FLT. Continue upstream on the Gorge Trail.

0.3 Reach Spiral Tunnel and the loop junction. Remain on the Gorge Trail.

0.7 View Rainbow Falls.

1.0 Pass Mile Point Bridge, staying on the north side of the gorge.

Watkins Glen State Park

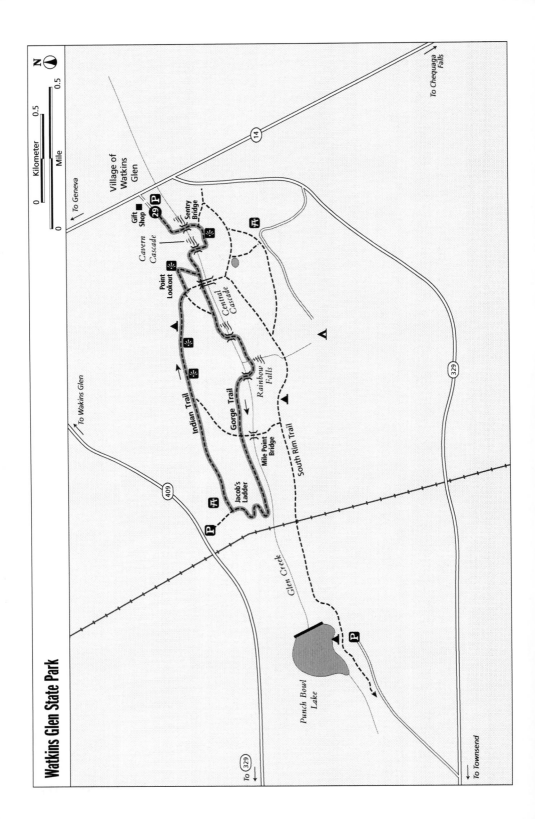

1.5 Ascend Jacob's Ladder to the midway bench, and follow Indian Trail as it heads right (downstream).

1.8 Pass the spur to Mile Point Bridge.

2.0 Overlook Rainbow Falls.

2.3 Reach the suspension bridge and a junction and continue straight. *Note:* A detour onto the bridge offers a plunging view to the creek as well as looks beyond the canyon.

2.4 Reach Point Lookout.

2.5 Close the loop at Spiral Tunnel and backtrack to the lower trailhead.

2.8 End at the concession area.

Options

Another hiking option while at the park is the **FLT.** The park's section of the FLT travels the wooded south rim 3.5 miles out and back to an upstream artificial lake. It shares the first 0.1 mile with the Gorge Trail. After crossing Sentry Bridge, veer left on the FLT, ascend some one hundred steps to the south rim, and turn right on the service road. Spurs branch to the south entrance, campground, and gorge; keep to the white-blazed FLT. Much of the way, appreciation of the gorge is auditory rather than visual. Pass beneath a scenic railroad bridge and view a ragged vertical outcrop. The trail then rounds the nose of a hemlock-shaded point and descends in spurts to Punch Bowl Lake, where you overlook the dam and its vertical falls, and then dip to where beaver gnawings dot the lakeshore. Bullfrogs, cedar waxwings, and red-winged blackbirds animate the site. Marsh grasses claim the upper lake, while cattail peninsulas extend into the open water. This hike's return is as you came, but the FLT does continue upstream.

Hike Information

Local Information

Watkins Glen Area Chamber of Commerce, 214 N. Franklin St., NY Route 14, Watkins Glen; (607) 535-4300 or (800) 607-4552; www.explorewatkinsglen.com

Local Events/Attractions

Watkins Glen International celebrates car racing with everything from NASCAR to vintage motorsport racing. From May through October, you, too, can take three paced laps around the course. For schedules, fees, and details, contact Watkins Glen International, 2790 County Road 16, Watkins Glen; (607) 535-2486; www.theglen.com.

Accommodations

Watkins Glen State Park campground, open early May to mid-October, has 288 sites. Reservations: (800) 456-2267 or www.reserveamerica.com.

30 Buttermilk Falls State Park

Buttermilk Falls caps a dramatic 500-foot free fall on Buttermilk Creek that occurs over a distance of 0.75 mile. Cascades, rapids, bedrock slides, emerald pools, platy cliffs, and a 40-foot rock spire help write the canyon drama. The upper glen holds a more soothing woods-water union. Easy interlocking park trails explore the Buttermilk Creek gorge, its upstream glen, and Treman Lake.

Start: At the lower gorge trailhead, in the park's main area

Distance: 5.2-mile barbell-shaped hike

Approximate hiking time: 3 to 3.5 hours

Difficulty: Moderate

Elevation change: The hike has a 650-foot elevation change: 500 feet on the lower Gorge-Rim Trail loop, and 150 feet on the upper Bear Trail-Treman Lake Loop.

Trail surface: Earthen and paved path

Seasons: Open May through Nov, best for hiking spring through fall

Other trail users: None

Canine compatibility: Leashed dogs permitted but not in bathing areas. (You must present proof of pet's rabies inoculation upon entering park.)

Land status: New York State Park

Nearest town: Ithaca

Fees and permits: Park entrance fee

Schedule: Year-round, gorge trails close early Nov; daylight hours

Map: https://parks.ny.gov/documents/parks/ButtermilkFallsTrailMap.pdf

Trail contact: Buttermilk Falls State Park, 112 East Buttermilk Falls Rd., Ithaca; (607) 273-5761 (summer) or (607) 273-3340; https://parks.ny.gov/parks/buttermilkfalls/details.aspx

Special considerations: Insect repellent is needed in the park's meadow areas.

Finding the trailhead: From the junction of NY 79 and NY 13/34 (the corner of Seneca and Meadow Streets) in southwest Ithaca, go south on NY 13/34 for 1.8 miles and turn left to enter the main area of Buttermilk Falls State Park. GPS: 42.417351, -76.520934

For the upper area, continue 0.1 mile farther south on NY 13/34 and turn left (east) onto Sandbank Road. Go 2.2 miles and turn left onto West King Road. In 1.2 miles turn right onto the park road to reach the upper day-use area in 0.8 mile. GPS: 42.401841, -76.513847

The Hike

This get-to-know Buttermilk Creek hike stitches together four of the park trails: Gorge, Rim, Bear, and Treman Lake, showcasing waterfalls, creek, and the lake. Some ten falls greet you along this hike.

Starting near the swimming hole below Buttermilk Falls, cross the dam to ascend the Gorge Trail, which travels the west wall. Broad Buttermilk Falls sheets over a magnificent canted cliff, sloping to the artificial pool. Cross-beds accent the light-colored rock, and small ledges fold the racing waters into cascades. A steep stairway ascends alongside the falls, isolating aspects of the watery spectacle.

Buttermilk Falls

SAPONY INDIAN VILLAGE

Until 1779 and the Revolutionary War, the park's Larch Meadows held a Sapony Indian village of log cabins. In that year, advance word of the approaching Sullivan Campaign forced the tribe to flee. Although flight spared their lives, the arriving troops torched all the cabins, ending an era.

Beech, hemlock, and a burst of understory greenery complement the canyon water. Upstream a three-tier, three-dimensional falls graces the creek. One level spills through a grotto where the gorge walls pinch together.

Cascades, historic plunge pools, eroded cliff scallops, and hemlock coves build on the canyon's fascination. The trail affords perspectives from below, alongside, and atop the cascades. You will spy a lean-to uphill to the right before arriving at a crescent footbridge over Buttermilk Creek. This leads to the Rim Trail on the east wall, allowing you to shorten the hike. Stay along the west wall.

A ribbony side falls washes over the cliff as a split-level hourglass falls punctuates Buttermilk Creek. Next find Pinnacle Rock, a 40-foot chiseled gray spire isolated from the cliff. Delicate ferns decorate the erosion-resistant ledges. Maple, ash, and basswood shade the way to West King Road.

Cross West King Road and follow the Bear Trail, which continues upstream on the west shore. This trail travels the broad wooded glen, passing some 40 feet from the stream. Hemlock, basswood, maple, oak, and beech shade a plush, green understory. Side trails descend to the bank, while skunk cabbage claims the moist slopes. Where the trail emerges at a picnic area, you can either continue upstream along the creek or follow the road to the site's comfort station, where the Treman Lake Loop starts.

For counterclockwise travel, stay along the west shore, bypassing the dam and spillway feeding to the picnic area falls to travel in forest. Cross-lake views find an attractive cliff scallop and cove. Geese often occupy a small island. Cross a side-drainage footbridge to round the marshy head of Treman Lake, bypassing an orange-blazed trail near a lean-to. Afterward cross the scenic stone bridge over Buttermilk Creek to travel the east shore. Steps top a couple of knolls for overlooks of the lake's cattail waters and the dam's curvature. From shore, you might see sunfish guarding their cleared nests or the snout of a snapping turtle. Beware of poison ivy along the shore and trail. Cross the stone dam and outcrop to complete the loop. Now backtrack the trail to the comfort station and then to West King Road.

Back at West King Road, cross the road bridge to the east shore to hike the Rim Trail downstream. Past an overlook of Pinnacle Rock, the trail gently descends. The views are few and short-lived. As the descent steepens, the trail shows a paved surface, and the corridor becomes more open. Beyond Buttermilk Falls Overlook (a filtered view), the trail descends and contours the slope above the campground road to exit at the refreshment stand.

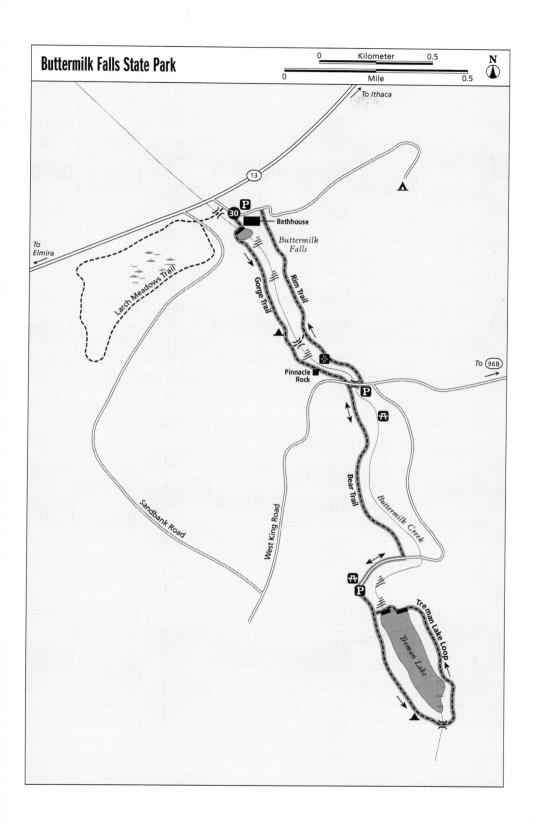

Buttermilk Falls State Park

0   Kilometer   0.5

0   Mile   0.5

N

To Ithaca

To Elmira

13

30

Bathhouse

Buttermilk Falls

Larch Meadows Trail

Gorge Trail

Rim Trail

Pinnacle Rock

To 96B

P

Bear Trail

Buttermilk Creek

Sandbank Road

West King Road

Treman Lake Loop

Treman Lake

Miles and Directions

0.0 Start from the falls swimming hole. Cross the dam to the west wall and hike up-canyon on the Gorge Trail.

0.5 Reach a bridge and continue forward on the Gorge Trail. **Bailout:** You may cross this bridge to the Rim Trail and turn left (downstream) for a 1.1-mile loop.

0.6 Reach Pinnacle Rock.

0.8 Reach West King Road. Follow the Bear Trail upstream along the west bank of Buttermilk Creek. **Bailout:** You can cross the West King Road bridge to reach the Rim Trail and follow it downstream for a 1.7-mile loop.

1.5 Reach a picnic area.

1.7 Reach Treman Lake Loop. Hike it counterclockwise starting along the west shore.

3.4 Close the loop. Backtrack downstream to West King Road.

4.3 Reach West King Road. Cross the bridge and follow the Rim Trail left downstream.

4.9 Reach Buttermilk Falls Overlook.

5.2 End near the refreshment stand.

Options

The park's **Larch Meadows Trail,** a 1-mile interpretive loop, examines a unique marsh, part of ancient Cayuga Lake. Start next to the ballfield restroom, 0.1 mile south of the main entrance, off Sandbank Road. Hike along the southern edge of the ballfield and bear left before the end of the field on a wide mowed swath. Although short, the trail traverses a variety of habitats: mixed woods, skunk cabbage wetland, willow stands, clusters of spreading black walnut, and waist-high ferns, grasses, and wildflowers. Past a 4-foot-diameter sycamore, the trail meets and briefly follows a service road to the right. The trail then resumes to the right, returning to the ballfield.

Hike Information

Local Information

Ithaca/Tompkins County Convention and Visitors Bureau, 904 East Shore Dr., Ithaca; (607) 272-1313 or (800) 28-ITHACA; www.visitithaca.com

Local Events/Attractions

The **Greater Ithaca Art Trail** takes you on a tour of fifty artist studios in the Ithaca area. The media is varied: clay, paint, fiber, film, computer-generation, wood, and more; www.arttrail.com.

Accommodations

Buttermilk Falls State Park campground, open mid-May to mid-October, has twenty-seven campsites and eighteen cabins. Reservations: (800) 456-2267 or www.reserveamerica.com.

31 Robert H. Treman State Park

Tied up in the attractive woodland package of glacier-scoured Enfield Glen, this park unites a narrowed gorge; platy cliffs; the stepped waters, cascades, and waterfalls of Enfield Creek, including the 115-foot Lucifer Falls; a historic mill; and the stunningly beautiful and awesome stone constructions of the Civilian Conservation Corps. The park is named for the benefactor who presented the lands to New York State in 1920, Ithaca merchant and parks commissioner Robert H. Treman. The park's Gorge and South Rim Trails together shape a fine discovery loop.

Start: At the lower gorge trailhead, near park headquarters
Distance: 4.2-mile loop
Approximate hiking time: 2.5 to 3.5 hours
Difficulty: Moderate
Elevation change: There is a 400-foot elevation change between the park's lower and upper sections. A decided climb leads from the lower parking lot into the canyon proper, and stone steps and the Cliff Staircase add to the workout.
Trail surface: Earthen and paved path and stone stairs
Seasons: Best for hiking spring through fall
Other trail users: None
Canine compatibility: Leashed dogs permitted but not in bathing area (You must present proof of your pet's rabies inoculation upon entering park.)
Land status: New York State Park
Nearest town: Ithaca
Fees and permits: Park entrance fee
Schedule: Year-round during daylight hours; all gorge trails close early Nov
Map: https://parks.ny.gov/documents/parks/RobertHTremanTrailMap.pdf
Trail contact: Robert H. Treman State Park, 105 Enfield Falls Rd., Ithaca; (607) 273-3440; https://parks.ny.gov/parks/135/
Special considerations: Be careful during wet conditions, when leaves and walks can be slippery.

Finding the trailhead: From the junction of NY 13 and NY 327, 5 miles south of Ithaca, turn west on NY 327 and proceed 0.1 mile to enter the lower park on the left. An upper entrance sits farther west off NY 327; follow signs. GPS: 42.397701, -76.557559

The Hike

From the lower trailhead, the Gorge Trail jump-starts the heart with a cardiovascular workout, taking you up slope and up canyon on a steep set of stairs. The trail rolls, staying mainly in woods, keeping Enfield Creek a secret save for a distant whisper. Beech, birch, oak, and hemlock provide the overhead shade.

After a half mile the trail overlooks the creek, which presents different personae depending on season and water year. Here it sheets over bedrock shelves, spilling in glistening slides and stepped cascades. The water's movement over time has shaped smooth contours and ledge breaks. The creek's steep banks keep it pristine despite the trail's popularity.

Civilian Conservation Corps construction opened up the gorge to hiking and sightseeing.

The trail takes you to and from the waterway before settling in alongside the creek at a mile. Platy shale cliffs and the bending creek define the trail's course. Cliffs draw eyes skyward with their bulges, incised breakages, and precariously hanging trees.

Beyond the junction with the Red Pine Trail, a waterfall spans the width of the creek. The water plunges over the initial ledge, strikes the sloped base rock, and glides into a pool, where the splash point draws a line of white bubbles.

Hiking past an Enfield Creek bridge, you come to Lucifer Falls, the tallest of the Enfield waterfalls and a showstopper, gracefully dropping and curving over yellowish cliffs in a magnificent high-walled amphitheater of shale and steep flowing greenery. The trail's stairway, balcony, and railing built by the Civilian Conservation Corps (CCC) seamlessly blend into the character of the natural cliff—a remarkable engineering and architectural feat. The masterful work of the CCC is as much a reason to hike this trail as are the waterfalls and cliffs.

Ahead, an upper falls sits snug in a corner. Cross Enfield Creek again at the next bridge, following the left bank as it overlooks a skinny channel marked by potholes and waterfalls. This is a younger gorge, where a natural reroute of Enfield Creek has cut a new course through bedrock. The lower gorge scours out a historic trench that filled with glacial debris at the end of the last ice age. Views from the bridge reveal the lower canyon.

Where the South Rim Trail (the loop's return) heads left, cross the stone bridge over Fish Kill Creek to reach the upper developed park, historic mill, and a waterfall on the creek. The gristmill, on the national and state historic registers, serves as a museum and also houses a restroom. Exhibits are devoted to mill operation, the hamlet of Enfield Falls that preceded the park, and the history of the CCC.

Following the South Rim Trail back down-canyon, ascend the slope, turning left on a service road and then left on the crescent spur to an Enfield Creek overlook. This is one of two dramatic canyon overviews that present the steep shale canyon, the stylish stone stairways, and the tiny hikers tracing the paths below. The second overlook adds Lucifer Falls. More splendid CCC construction follows as you descend the Cliff Staircase. Uphill travelers repeat a common complaint: "More stairs!"

At the base of the stairs, the South Rim Trail turns right and soon returns back upslope, but it never actually traces the rim. Tulip trees enter the mix, and drumming woodpeckers announce their presence. Moisture can bring out red-phase eastern newts. Continue on the wide grade for wooded glen travel. After the trail enters its descent, watch for the rim trail to fork left, leaving the primary contouring grade. You will overlook the Lower Falls summer swimming area before emerging at the cabin area. Angle left through the cabin area to the park road. To return to headquarters parking, take the pedestrian bridge where Enfield Creek flows over the park road.

Miles and Directions

0.0 Start from the lower gorge trailhead, near park headquarters, and ascend the rock stairway.

1.4 Reach the Red Pine Trail junction. Continue forward to the upper gorge.

1.5 Reach an Enfield Creek bridge. Continue forward to the upper gorge. **Bailout:** You can cross here, turning left on the South Rim Trail for a 3.2-mile loop, but you will miss viewing Lucifer Falls and the Old Mill.

1.6 Reach Lucifer Falls Overlook.

1.8 Cross a bridge over Enfield Creek and follow the left bank upstream.

1.9 Reach South Rim Trail (on your left). Delay your loop return, instead crossing the bridge over Fish Kill Creek to reach the upper park and mill museum.

2.0 Reach the Old Mill. Backtrack downstream over the Fish Kill Creek bridge and follow the South Rim Trail (now a right).

2.2 Arrive at a service road. Turn left.

2.3 Follow the crescent spur left to an Enfield Creek overlook.

2.4 Overlook Lucifer Falls and descend the Cliff Staircase.

2.5 At the junction, turn right, continuing on the South Rim Trail. *Note:* Straight leads to the bridge over Enfield Creek first mentioned at 1.5 miles and the Gorge Trail.

3.5 The trail begins to descend.

3.7 Turn left at the fork.

3.9 Overlook the Lower Falls Swim Area.

4.0 Emerge at the cabin-area trailhead. Angle left toward the park road.

4.1 Cross the pedestrian bridge where Enfield Creek flows over the roadway.

4.2 End the loop back at headquarters parking.

Robert H. Treman State Park

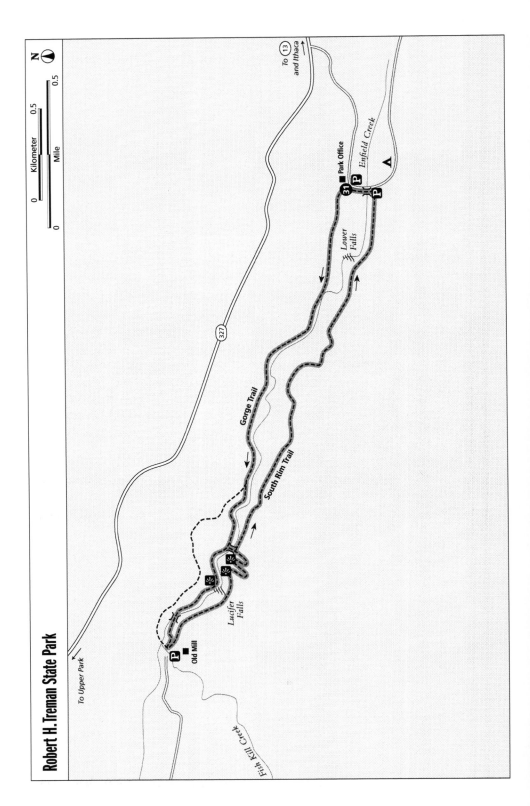

A PARK WITH A PAST

In the early 1800s, before this land became Robert H. Treman State Park, it housed the thriving mill community of Enfield Falls. Although few clues remain today, the hamlet existed for fifty years and had as many as fifteen permanent structures: homes and outbuildings, shops, and businesses. The first gristmill was built in 1817 by Isaac Rumsey. After fire claimed that mill in the 1830s, Jared Treman (Robert's grandfather) built the current mill. The glen's attractive cliff, woods, and falling-water features have long been a lure and helped fill the rooms and stable of the hamlet's Enfield Falls Hotel. Youngsters collected a charge of 10 cents to see the waterfalls. The hotel was also the hamlet's social center, hosting dances. Within the Old Mill today, exhibits and historic maps further flesh out the story of this park predecessor.

During the Great Depression, the Civilian Conservation Corps, Company 1265, had an established camp in what is now the upper park. The men, mostly from urban centers and as many as one hundred in number, lived first in tents and then in more durable wooden barracks and structures. The corps completed critical construction jobs here and in neighboring parks in the Finger Lakes Region, and they were key in this park's recovery from the flood of 1935. You'll witness their legacy in the quality masonry along trails and at campgrounds. If you look closely at the park's cliff walls, you may spy the workers' carved initials or names, "CCC," or "1265"—a proud and fragile link to the past.

Hike Information

Local Information

Ithaca/Tompkins County Convention and Visitors Bureau, 904 East Shore Dr., Ithaca; (607) 272-1313 or (800) 28-ITHACA; www.visitithaca.com

Local Events/Attractions

Adjacent to the Cornell University campus, **Cornell Botanic Gardens** celebrates growing things and the changing of the seasons within its 50 acres of botanical gardens, vast natural areas, and a 150-acre arboretum. The Botanic Gardens is open daily free of charge from sunrise to sunset; peak season is May through mid-October. Cornell Botanic Gardens, 124 Comstock Knoll Dr., Ithaca; (607) 255-2400; www.cornellbotanicgardens.org.

Accommodations

Robert H. Treman State Park campground, open mid-May through November, has eighty-seven campsites (cabin sites are only available through early Nov). Reservations: (800) 456-2267 or www.reserveamerica.com.

Honorable Mentions

N Howland Island Unit, Northern Montezuma Wildlife Management Area

In Cayuga County, north of Cayuga Lake and about 25 miles west of Syracuse, the Barge Canal and Seneca River isolate this 3,100-acre interior island, where eighteen dikes create an extensive network of ponds that attract thousands of migrating waterfowl. Low, rolling hills (drumlins deposited by glacial action 10,000 years ago), planted floodplain, unkempt fields, and hardwood stands complete the island mosaic. The habitats sustain 200 bird species, as well as deer, fox, various small mammals, turtles, frogs, fish, and newts. The site's management roads and dikes lay out easy loop strolls. Bring insect repellent and mosquito netting for more enjoyable visits. You may choose to avoid the area during hunting season (be sure to wear blaze orange if you do venture in). Heed waterfowl nesting closures in April and May.

From I-90, take exit 40 at Weedsport. Go south from the exit on NY 34; in 0.2 mile turn west onto NY 31. Passing through the village of Port Byron, reach Savannah in 13.5 miles, and turn north onto NY 89. Go 0.3 mile and, at the north edge of town, turn east onto NY 274 (Savannah–Spring Lake Road). Proceed 2.3 miles and turn right onto Carncross Road to reach trail parking in another 1.4 miles. GPS: 43.078762, -76.689797. Contact New York State Department of Environmental Conservation, Region 8, 6274 East Avon-Lima Rd., Avon; (585) 226-2466; www.dec.ny.gov.

Wetland ponds create habitat at Howland Island Wildlife Management Area.

O Fillmore Glen State Park

Rarely do hikers find the magical combination of elements that make Fillmore Glen one of the best short hikes in New York State: striking geological formations, glistening gorge walls that weep with spring runoff, a storybook forest, and no fewer than five waterfalls—including one that plummets from a creek tributary at the top of the gorge. Tie all of this with an ingenious system of eight bridges that cross and recross the gorge, laced together by a pathway reinforced with natural stone guard walls, and you have the kind of hiking experience that makes the Finger Lakes region famous.

While this hike is fairly easy in dry weather, the gorge creates a microclimate in which the humidity remains high. Stone steps and earthen pathways can be slippery, and water often drips (or cascades) from the porous shale walls, especially after a heavy rain. Wear footwear that will grip in wet situations.

The street address for this park is 1686 NY Route 38, Moravia. From Syracuse, take NY 5 West about 22 miles to the junction with NY 38 in Auburn. Turn south onto NY 38 and continue 17 miles to the park entrance in Moravia. Park at the main pavilion. The trailhead is behind the building and up the paved path. GPS: 42.69206, -76.39001. Contact Fillmore Glen State Park, 1686 NY Route 38, Moravia; (315) 497-0130; parks.ny.gov/parks/fillmoreglen/.

P High Tor Wildlife Management Area

South of Canandaigua Lake, three separate land parcels compose High Tor Wildlife Management Area (WMA). In the southernmost and largest of the three (3,400 acres), service road,

Ancient trees earn homage along forest trails.

mowed tracks, and foot trail explore wetland, gully, field, and woods. The closed management road running straight through the WMA is the most logical path; it begins off Bassett Road. Side tracks off the management road add visits to area ponds. The Bristol Hills Branch of the Finger Lakes Trail (FLT) also traverses the WMA; look for its orange blazes.

Sightings of common yellowthroat, muskrat, turkey vulture, and ruffed grouse, as well as white-tailed deer bounding through the tall grass, can halt your steps. Tiger and black swallowtail, monarch, and red admiral butterflies seasonally flutter about your ankles and the wildflowers that spangle the road shoulders. Hiking the management road is ideal for being alone with your thoughts or sharing an outing with your dog (which must be leashed or under voice control, because this is a wildlife area). The WMA is open daylight hours only. Carry drinking water.

From the junction of NY 53 and NY 21 in Naples, go south on NY 53 for 0.8 mile and turn left (east) toward Italy Valley on NY 21. In 1.9 miles turn left onto Bassett Road. Find trailhead parking 0.3 mile ahead on the left. GPS: 42.60608, -77.34571. Contact New York State Department of Environmental Conservation, Region 8, 6274 East Avon–Lima Rd., Avon; (585) 226-2466; www.dec.ny.gov.

Central Region

Squeezed by the Adirondacks, the Catskills, and the Finger Lakes, this region represents the central bridging piece in the state puzzle. This cluster of counties has been known as Leatherstocking country, celebrating the works of early American novelist James Fenimore Cooper. It also contains the extraordinarily fertile Cherry Valley, where agriculture still holds sway. Here you will find shining "glimmerglass" lakes, forested ridges, open fields, and shadowy caverns. Beyond the natural areas, tranquil pastoral settings claim the backroads. Rome and Utica are the primary cities to the north; Binghamton is the southernmost city in the region.

Much of New York State's agricultural bounty still comes from this region: more than 600,000 cows produce 12 billion pounds of milk every year; twenty-four apple varieties that make New York the third-largest producer of the fruit in the country; unimaginable amounts of corn for feedstock, fuel, and food; and New York's legendary grapes, most of which are fermented into dozens of varieties of wine.

The Old Erie Canal passes through a rural setting of woods, wetlands, and field.

While today this region features many wide-open vistas of rolling farmland with hills rising in the distance, it also contains a great deal of history. The dream that began as "Clinton's Ditch," the folly of a governor who could see a future of commerce for his state, resulted in the Erie Canal—opening a water route across this land and carrying its bountiful harvests to enterprises far to the west. With prosperity came larger villages, performing arts centers, museums, and eventually the National Baseball Hall of Fame, putting the tiny village of Cooperstown on the map and bringing tourism to the heart of the state.

For hikers, the central region offers long trails through fairly easy terrain, with plenty of wildflowers and occasional ponds hidden away in wetlands and forests. This is a land of gentle slopes and tranquil vistas, and while the hikes may not challenge the quadriceps, their rewards are in the peace and solitude attained with only a bit of effort.

32 Old Erie Canal Heritage Trail

Between DeWitt and Rome, east of Syracuse, this linear New York State park salutes a 36-mile vestige of the historic 363-mile Erie Canal, which links the Hudson River to the Great Lakes. One of the great engineering feats of its day, the canal opened the West to transportation and commerce—a boon to nineteenth-century New York State. Barge-towing mules plodded the towpath throughout the nineteenth century, until motors became commonplace for barges and other watercraft. Today the towpath is a multiuse National Recreation Trail that provides access to parks, museums, and historic structures that tell more about the canal's history.

Start: At the western (Ryder Park) trailhead
Distance: 31.6 miles point-to-point between DeWitt and Lock 21, including 2.2 miles on road between Durhamville and NY 31, or 22.4 miles from DeWitt to Durhamville to limit road travel
Approximate hiking time: Depending on the length you choose to take on, you may spend an hour or several days covering this entire trail segment.
Difficulty: Easy
Elevation change: The flat trail travels at an elevation of 425 feet.
Trail surface: Stone dust or earthen towpath, with brief road links
Seasons: Open year-round, best for hiking spring through fall
Other trail users: Cyclists, horse riders, joggers, anglers, snowmobilers, snowshoers, cross-country skiers
Canine compatibility: Leashed dogs permitted (Keep your canine closely reined because this is a shared-use trail and dogs pose a risk to riders. Bring drinking water for your dog.)
Land status: Old Erie Canal State Historic Park

Nearest town: DeWitt or Rome
Fees and permits: No fees or permits for trail; admission charges for trailside museums
Schedule: Open year-round, dawn to dusk
Map: https://parks.ny.gov/documents/parks/OldErieCanalTrailMap-Overview.pdf
Trail contact: Old Erie Canal State Historic Park, c/o Green Lakes State Park, 7900 Green Lakes Rd., Fayetteville; (315) 637-6111; https://parks.ny.gov/parks/olderiecanal/
Special considerations: A 2.2-mile road interruption occurs between Durhamville and State Bridge (at NY 46 and NY 31), and a handful of shorter road links occur elsewhere on the trail. On the towpath's western end, footbridges at Cedar Bay and Poolsbrook Picnic Areas, at Green Lakes State Park, and at the Fayetteville side canal allow for passage between the north and south shore attractions. Road bridges serve the eastern end. You will find restrooms and drinking water at Cedar Bay and Poolsbrook Picnic Areas, at Green Lakes State Park, at Lock 21, and in communities along the canalway.

Finding the trailhead: From I-481 in East Syracuse, take exit 3E for NY 5/NY 92 and go east toward Fayetteville. In 0.8 mile, where NY 5 and NY 92 split, go left (north) on Lyndon Road for 0.8 mile, bearing left onto Kinne Road. Go 0.4 mile and turn right onto Butternut Drive to find Ryder Park and the western trail terminus on the right in 0.1 mile. GPS: 43.044572, -76.050600

Find the Lock 21 terminus (our eastern terminus) west of Rome, off NY 46, turning north on Lock Road. GPS: 43.208504, -75.618398

Durhamville, the preferred ending for long-distance hikers, is on NY 46 north of Oneida. GPS: 43.117467, -75.670319

Towpaths, once trod by mules, now carry hikers.

The Hike

The Erie Canalway corridor remains largely undeveloped, with a few residential yards backing up to the trail. Parallel roadways can add noise, but mostly this hike brings relaxation, hugging the canal straightaways and gentle bends. Corridor inhabitants including woodchucks, painted and snapping turtles, northern rough-winged swallows (which nest in the unmortared stonework), warblers, and fish like bluegills and carp can lend comedy and surprise. Virginia creeper and wild grape entangle the towpath's diverse tree border, which features maple, box elder, and ash. As you proceed east, the trail initially has mileage markers and crossroad labels, but later such aids wane.

At Butternut Creek in Dewitt, the 1856 Butternut Creek Aqueduct remains in place, an 80-foot-long stone structure with three spans and a concrete channel to direct water into the canal. The route crosses under the relocated Cooper's Tubular Arch Bridge, moved here from the town of Canajoharie to commemorate the work of William B. Cooper, a nineteenth-century civil engineer employed on the New York State Canals. Pass under the bridge to enter Cedar Bay Park.

The tour slips into character with areas of intermittent to full shade and uninterrupted canal viewing. Where the Erie Canal widens into a pond beyond Burdick Road, a side canal paired with its own towpath trail arrives from Fayetteville. A footbridge stitches this spur to the National Recreation Trail.

After Manlius Center the route opens up and the setting becomes more rural. The footbridge to Green Lakes State Park may suggest a side trip. Here an old-growth

CLINTON'S FOLLY

In the beginning, Governor DeWitt Clinton's concept for a canal linking the Hudson River to the Great Lakes met with a wall of skepticism. But by its completion in 1825, "Clinton's Folly" was hailed as the engineering marvel of its day. The finished canal measured 363 miles long and incorporated eighty-three locks to smooth out an elevation gain of 568 feet. Eighteen aqueducts spanned the side waters. The Erie Canal brought construction jobs, a new working class of canallers, and ultimately prosperity for the communities along its length, spurring economic growth for cities including Albany, Syracuse, Rochester, Buffalo, and plenty of smaller port towns. Its acclaim spread across the Atlantic Ocean, and before long, grand tours of the Erie Canal became a must-see American attraction for visiting Europeans, right along with Niagara Falls.

The Erie Canal legacy continues to grow as it contributes top-notch recreation to tour companies, leisure boaters, cyclists, and pedestrians. Two segments, the 70-mile Erie Heritage Canal in western New York and the 36-mile Old Erie Canal at the center of the state, offer snapshots of the corridor's engineering, natural and cultural offerings, and history.

forest surrounds two deep turquoise lakes, which got their vibrant color about 15,000 years ago when a massive glacier meltwater waterfall sculpted these deep lakes. This caused the lakes to become meromictic: While most lakes experience a turnover of their waters with the temperature changes of spring and fall, Green and Round Lakes do not turn over. The result is the lakes' highly unusual clarity, making them transparent all the way to the bottom, and the resulting light penetration produces the saturated green shades.

At Kirkville Road a couple of picnic tables and a small lawn suggest a stop. When the canal widens to a pond, cross-canal views broaden to scenic Poolsbrook Picnic Area, with its benches, tables, shade willows, and apple trees. The park access comes later, where a footbridge spans the again-narrowed canal.

At Lakeport Road cross the road bridge to the Chittenango Landing Canal Boat Museum. (See local attractions below.) Indoor and outdoor exhibits include historic dry-dock bays rebuilt in their original stone, replica sawmill and blacksmith buildings, a mule-drawn steamboat, and fine pictorial history.

The towpath narrows at Canaseraga Road, touring hayfields and cornfields as it alternates between northern and southern towpaths from West Shore Railroad to Bebee Bridge Road. You'll parallel State Street into Canastota to Buck Street, and then follow Canal Street east 0.25 mile before resuming on the towpath. On Canal Street you'll find canal artifacts and photos in the Canastota Canal Town Museum, housed in a circa-1874 building that's on the National Register of Historic Places.

At North Court Road, angle left across the road to resume northern towpath travel at the edge of a cornfield. Canal Street maintains a parallel course. By Cobb Street, leafy trees lace over the route for scenic strolling.

After the detour to the I-90 overpass, towpath travel continues to Durhamville. For hiking, it's best to end at Durhamville because a breach in the towpath here requires you to walk 2.2 miles on road. If you choose, though, you can restart towpath travel on the north side of NY 31 at State Bridge. Extending before you is another 7 miles of trail, taking you through the rural countryside, first on the southern towpath, then on road to the northern towpath at Lock 21, which marks this hike's end. Eastbound from the lock another 4.4 miles of trail continue, initially taking you beside the modern New York State Erie Canal before resuming along the heritage canal.

Miles and Directions

0.0 Start from the western (Ryder Park) trailhead and hike the northern towpath east.

0.8 Cross under the footbridge to Cedar Bay Park.

1.6 Cross Burdick Road.

3.0 Reach Manlius Center.

4.6 Reach the footbridge to Green Lakes State Park and continue east on towpath. **Side trip:** From the footbridge crossing, a 0.2-mile service road ascends to the I-290 crossing to the park. Restrooms are found at the park office. The park's two deep lakes require a longer detour.

6.1 Cross Kirkville Road.

7.3 Cross Poolsbrook Road, later coming to the footbridge crossing to Poolsbrook Picnic Area. The hike continues east.

8.6 Reach the White Bridge Road trailhead with limited parking. **Option:** This site offers an alternative start or a place to park a shuttle vehicle.

11.0 Reach Chittenango Landing Canal Boat Museum.

12.5 Cross Canaseraga Road.

14.9 At West Shore Railroad, cross from the northern towpath to the south shore and continue east.

15.7 Reach Bebee Bridge Road. Turn left (north), cross the road bridge to the northern towpath, and continue east.

16.4 Reach Canastota and follow Canal Street east. **Note:** Here you pass the Canastota Canal Town Museum.

19.5 The towpath halts at North Court Road. Angle across the road to pick up the northern towpath at the edge of a field.

22.0 Cross the I-90 overpass and follow the towpath east to Durhamville.

22.4 Reach Durhamville and a breach in towpath travel. **Option:** End here or continue north along Canal Road to NY 31 at State Bridge.

24.6 Towpath resumes on the north side of NY 31 at State Bridge. Continue east.

31.0 Follow arrows along Lock Road to Lock 21. End here at Lock 21.

36.0 This is the official eastern terminus of the Old Erie Canal towpath.

Old Erie Canal Heritage Trail

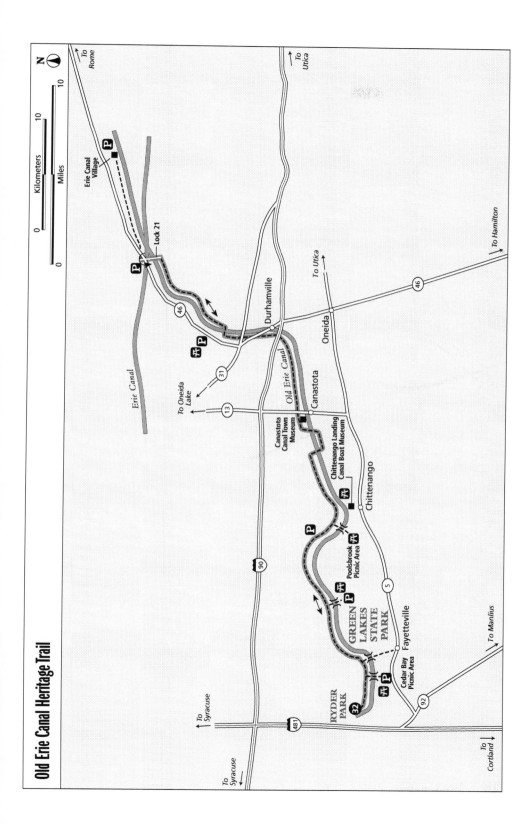

Hike Information

Local Information

Visit Syracuse, 109 S. Warren St., Suite 10, Syracuse; (315) 470-1910; www.visit syracuse.com. **Madison County Tourism,** 3215 Seneca Turnpike, Canastota; (315) 815-5002; www.madisontourism.com.

Local Events / Attractions

The **Canastota Canal Town Museum,** open May through October, occupies an original 1873 canal-era bakery and residence and holds canal and town memorabilia. Canastota Canal Town Museum, 122 Canal St., Canastota; (315) 697-5002; www .canastota-canal.com.

The **Chittenango Landing Canal Boat Museum** is open Wednesday through Sunday from 10 a.m. to 3 p.m. mid-May to mid-October. Museum exhibits and historic structures including a blacksmith shop, a boat shop, and a general store are clustered around three bays. Chittenango Landing Canal Boat Museum, 717 Lakeport Rd., Chittenango; (315) 687-3801; www.chittenangolanding.com.

Accommodations

Green Lakes State Park campground, closed in winter, has 147 sites. Reservations: (800) 456-2267 or www.reserveamerica.com.

Organizations

Parks & Trails New York helps promote, expand, and protect trails, parks, and open spaces statewide and prints and sells a cycling guide to the Erie Canal. Parks & Trails New York, 33 Elk St., Albany; (518) 434-1583; www.ptny.org.

33 Beaver Creek Swamp Loop

In southeast Madison County, this loop in Beaver Creek State Forest travels the wooded and meadow outskirts of Beaver Creek Swamp. The well-marked circuit is part of the extensive 130-mile Brookfield Trail System serving foot, horse, and snowmobile travelers. Although the rolling trail rarely comes in contact with its centerpiece, Beaver Creek Swamp, the surrounding hemlock-hardwood forest, conifer plantations, spring and summer wildflowers, and wildlife encourage exploration. Only horseflies can jar the otherwise tranquil spell.

Start: At the southern Fairground Road trailhead
Distance: 9.5-mile loop
Approximate hiking time: 5.5 to 6.5 hours
Difficulty: Moderate due to terrain
Elevation change: The trail has a 200-foot elevation change.
Trail surface: Gravel and earthen trail, mowed track, woods road, and brief truck-trail segments
Seasons: Open year-round, best for hiking spring through fall
Other trail users: Horse riders, hunters, snowmobilers, snowshoers, cross-country skiers
Canine compatibility: Leashed dogs permitted
Land status: New York State Department of Environmental Conservation (DEC)

Nearest town: Waterville/Sangerfield area
Fees and permits: None
Schedule: No time restrictions
Map: www.dec.ny.gov/docs/regions_pdf/mapbeavercr.pdf
Trail contact: New York State DEC, Region 7, 2715 Highway 80, Sherburne; (607) 674-4017; www.dec.ny.gov
Special considerations: The hike incorporates two short truck-trail segments that are open to vehicles, maximum speed 25 miles per hour. Timbering can occur as part of forest management. Because travel can be hot, carry plenty of water. A bandana for the head and insect repellent can bring some tranquility during bug season (July–Sept).

Finding the trailhead: From the junction of Fairground Road and Main Street (Skaneateles Turnpike) in Brookfield (east of Hamilton), go north on Fairground Road for 1 mile to find trailhead parking on the left. When arriving from US 20, turn south on Bliven Road between Bridgewater and Sangerfield, coming to a Y junction in 1.4 miles. Bear left on Fairground Road and continue 3 miles to find the trailhead on the right, with parking for five vehicles. GPS: 42.825768, -75.307085

The Hike

You'll hike the gravel track west from the parking lot for a clockwise tour. Yellow DEC markers indicate the hiker/horse trail; in some places you may see old orange snowmobile markers. Scarlet tanager, woodchuck, and eastern cottontail may number among the early wildlife sightings. Birch, alder, and shrubs frame the open trail. Keep to the gravel path, crossing the horse bridge over Beaver Creek, where high railings protect horse and rider.

TRAIL ETIQUETTE

Strive for zero impact. Always leave an area just like you found it—if not better than you found it.

- Avoid camping in fragile, alpine meadows and along the banks of streams and lakes.
- Use a camp stove instead of building a wood fire.
- Pack up all of your trash and extra food. Bears live in this region, so take extra precautions with your food and waste.
- Bury human waste at least 100 feet from water sources under 6 to 8 inches of topsoil.
- Don't bathe with soap in a lake or stream—use prepackaged moistened towels to wipe off sweat and dirt, or bathe in the water without soap.
- Stay on the trail. It's true, a path anywhere leads nowhere new, but paths serve an important purpose: They limit impact on natural areas. Straying from a designated trail may seem innocent, but it can cause damage to sensitive areas that may take years to recover, if it can recover at all. Even simple shortcuts can be destructive.

Be sure to pause on the bridge because it serves up the best view of Beaver Creek Swamp. Wide views north and a more restricted view south introduce the attractive marsh. Dark-flowing Beaver Creek meanders through the broad swamp bottom, framed in turn by bog grass, wetland shrubs, and trees. Lilies and other aquatic plants decorate the shallow edge, and dragonflies buzz the surface.

A mowed swath continues the tour, with a scenic row of maple and black-cherry trees toward the swamp, a tidy pine plantation to the left. Rock walls sometimes border the route, while wild strawberries offer tasty bites in June.

At the initial junction, turn right to traverse a low hemlock-clad ridge for a cool, shady passage. Oxalis and mayapple decorate the floor. Descending the ridge, cross a small drainage dotted with false hellebore in late May and dame's rocket later in the summer. An aspen stand and spruce plantation now vary the walk. Within the long grassy meadows dotted by pine and aspen, keep an eye out for wild turkeys.

Occasional engine sounds precede the crossing of Beaver Creek Road and the start of a truck-trail segment. Travel the semishaded dirt road uphill, hiking past a connector to the greater Brookfield Trail System on the left. Before long, the loop turns left, entering the woods and passing a small rock-lined pond built in the 1930s for fire protection. Descend and cross a side brook below the rock ruins of an old dam, where you'll follow the levee to the right (downstream) along a ditch.

Crossing back over Beaver Creek Road, you follow the Glenn Bacon Trail, a mowed swath touring an open meadow corridor with full-skirted spruce, woody shrubs, hawkweed, daisy, buttercup, and floral stalks. Before long, the trail ascends sharply and steadily through mixed forest, then levels to traverse another long meadow, coming to a tribute to Glenn Bacon, a horseman who advanced the recreational

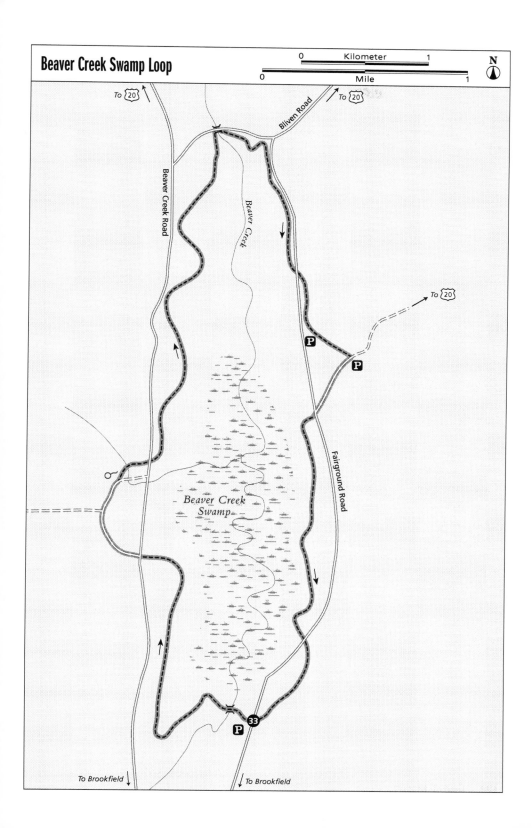

Beaver Creek Swamp Loop

Kilometer

Mile

N

To 20

Bliven Road

To 20

Beaver Creek Road

Beaver Creek

To 20

P

P

Fairground Road

Beaver Creek Swamp

P **33**

To Brookfield

To Brookfield

opportunities in this area. A bench and picnic table overlook Beaver Creek Swamp and the wooded east ridge—a textured tapestry of mottled wetland, shrubs, leafy trees, and sharp plantation outlines.

Stay on the mowed track, alternately touring open field and spruce corridor. The trail rolls as it approaches Bliven Road for a road-bridge crossing of Beaver Creek. A few rural homes come into view. On the opposite shore, the trail passes between meadow and plantation. Soon the trail crosses Fairground Road, touring in meadow and tamarack and traveling past the primary trailhead for equestrian users.

Keep to the east side of Fairground Road, ascending a grassy doubletrack in a cedar-hardwood forest. Where the trail tops out, a truck trail crosses. Turn right on it, descending to and angling left across Fairground Road. Descend farther via foot trail, passing through meadow and crossing over drainages. Past the tamarack seed orchard and spruce corridor, cross Fairground Road again for a brief swing along the wooded east slope before coming out on Fairground Road across from the trail parking.

Miles and Directions

- **0.0** Start from the southern Fairground Road trailhead. Hike the gravel path west for clockwise travel.
- **0.8** Reach a junction and head right.
- **2.2** Cross Beaver Creek Road. Follow a truck trail, still ascending.
- **2.4** Continue forward, past a connector to the greater Brookfield Trail System on the left.
- **2.7** Turn left, entering the woods, bypassing a small rock-lined pond.
- **3.1** Cross Beaver Creek Road to follow the Glenn Bacon Trail.
- **5.2** Cross the Bliven Road bridge over Beaver Creek.
- **6.1** Reach the first crossing of Fairground Road.
- **6.4** Pass a parking area for equestrian users. Continue along the east side of Fairground Road, ascending via grassy two-tracks.
- **6.9** Meet a truck trail and turn right on it, descending to Fairground Road.
- **7.5** Cross Fairground Road. Descend via footpath.
- **9.0** Again cross Fairground Road to travel the wooded east slope.
- **9.5** Emerge at Fairground Road opposite the trailhead. Cross the road, closing the loop.

Hike Information

Local Information

Madison County Tourism, 3215 Seneca Turnpike, Canastota; (315) 815-5002; www.madisontourism.com

Local Events/Attractions

The **National Baseball Hall of Fame and Museum** holds the golden story of baseball. 25 Main St., Cooperstown; (888) 425-5633; www.baseballhall.org.

Honorable Mentions

Q Glimmerglass State Park

In the heart of James Fenimore Cooper country, the wooded flank of Mount Wellington and the field, shrub, and woodland habitats of this state park compose the understated setting of Hyde Bay on Otsego Lake—the liquid jewel of the area. Because of the lake's sparkle, Cooper dubbed it "Glimmerglass" in his popular tales about a frontier hero, the Leatherstocking. In this soothing backdrop, you can enjoy short outings and subtle discoveries.

Historic Hyde Hall marks the launch for a pleasant 3.5-mile hike that combines two loops: the short Otsego Lake loop on the service road that serves up filtered lake views, and the longer blazed loop up Mount Wellington. On the latter, travel the forested slope of evergreens and restless deciduous trees to the upper reaches of Mount Wellington, where you obtain a restricted overlook of the lake and park. Deer sometimes share the view. The route then descends through forest and fern habitat to the mansion area. Follow the road between the twin gate cottages and beneath the domed arch of Tin Top, crossing the grounds to close the loop. Hyde Hall, a dignified stone-block manor formerly owned by Lieutenant George Clarke (a New York State governor from 1736 to 1744), is open daily in summer for guided tours. Other trails in the park visit beaver ponds, woodlands, and fields.

From US 20 in East Springfield, turn south on NY 31, following the signs to Glimmerglass State Park. In 3.9 miles turn right (west) to enter the park. From Cooperstown, go 8 miles north on CR 31 to reach the turn for the park entrance. GPS: 42.792306, -74.875354. An admission is charged. Contact Glimmerglass State Park, 1527 CR 31, Cooperstown; (607) 547-8662; https://parks.ny.gov/parks/glimmer glass/details.aspx.

R Bowman Lake State Park

A quiet wooded setting, gentle terrain, and 35-acre Bowman Lake are the hallmarks of this state park northwest of Oxford and west of Norwich. Bordered by 11,000 acres of state forest land, the park contributes to a broad, open space for wildlife and a tranquil arena for hikers. The long-distance Finger Lakes Trail (FLT) passes through the park and offers a 5.5-mile hike out and back to Berry Hill Fire Tower. The park's Nature Trail rolls out an easy 1.3-mile lake loop.

From the northernmost beach parking, the FLT strings north through woods and tidy pine plantation, tracing brooks and crossing quiet gravel roads, before following Tower Road 0.6 mile to the fire tower. A rustic cabin shares the grassy hilltop with the six-story tower on the National Historic Lookout Register. The tower holds law enforcement radios and is closed to the public. The south-central New York neighborhood reveals low ridges, rolling fields, and wooded hills.

The red-marked Nature Trail starts at the nature center and heads north through the mixed forest of the developed park for a counter-clockwise tour, thrice crossing park roads. Expect rocks, roots, and soggy drainages. Midway you reach a cat-tail shore, later finding a length-of-the-lake view. After contouring the wooded west slope, pass closer to shore to cross the levee dam. Skirt the picnic area to end at the nature center.

From the junction of NY 12 and NY 220 at the village green in Oxford, go 6 miles west on NY 220 and turn right (north) onto Steere Road. In 1.4 miles find the park entrance on the left. GPS: 42.521441, -75.686028. An admission fee is charged. Contact Bowman Lake State Park, 745 Bliven Sherman Rd., Oxford; (607) 334-2718; https://parks.ny.gov/parks/76/.

An ancient maple stands proud at Glimmerglass State Park.

Berry Hill Fire Tower still draws visitors, but no access is allowed.

Capital-Saratoga Region

Five major rivers—the Hudson, Mohawk, Sacandaga, Schoharie, and Hoosick—thread through this east-central New York region, with the tri-city capital complex of Albany, Schenectady, and Troy at its core. This strategic hub belonged originally to the Mohawk Nation, an inconvenience to the Dutch settlers who arrived here in 1624 and to the many European colonists who followed them. The fertile river lands for farming, water-powered industry, routes to the fur harvest, and general trade spurred a struggle for control that continued for centuries. The French and Indian Wars and the American Revolution finally resulted in the land ceding to the new US government, with some areas remaining as Native American reservations.

But despite the natural water routes here, transportation was difficult until the construction of the Erie Canal in 1825. The canal solved the problems of differences in elevation, uneven flows, and waterways wide enough to accommodate barges, introducing a series of locks, aqueducts, and other architectural features. Almost all commerce heading west flowed up the Hudson River from the ports of New York City through Albany, seated at the eastern end of the canal. Railroads replaced the canals and took over most of the cargo transport by the early twentieth century, so today only bills and legislation flow through the city.

In addition to government, tourism helps feed the Capital-Saratoga economy of today, with battlefields and the history and bustle of the nineteenth century central to travel themes. Museums, historic homes, and colonial cemeteries capture the history, while mineral springs, performing arts, and artist colonies likewise attract interest. Harkening to the region's Dutch roots, Albany has hosted an annual tulip festival for more than half a century.

When you hike in the Capital-Saratoga region, you can retrace the march of the British army in 1777 at Saratoga National Historical Park; explore the Helderberg Escarpment; visit field, forest, and wetland habitats; and venture to and along the Taconic Crest. Vistas sweep across the Mohawk and Hudson Valleys and toward the Adirondacks and drift across state borders to Massachusetts and Vermont. The region offers quiet nature strolls and vigorous hikes, with a range of country and urban walks in between.

34 Wilkinson National Recreation Trail

The two Battles of Saratoga fought in the fall of 1777 marked the turning point of the American Revolutionary War. Colonist victories over the British in this key area along the Hudson River convinced the French that the Americans could prevail. When France responded by declaring war on Great Britain, the tide turned toward American independence. This National Recreation Trail (NRT), an interpretive loop through fields and woods, retraces the doomed British march and visits sites where fortifications stood and key battles raged.

Start: At the visitor center trailhead
Distance: 4.8 miles out-and-back, including Breymann's Redoubt detour and Freeman Loop
Approximate hiking time: 2.5 to 3.5 hours
Difficulty: Easy
Elevation change: The trail has about a 200-foot elevation change.
Trail surface: Mowed, earthen, and paved path
Seasons: Open year-round, best for hiking spring through fall
Other trail users: Snowshoers, cross-country skiers
Canine compatibility: Leashed dogs permitted on trails (cleanup required), no dogs in buildings except service dogs
Land status: Saratoga National Historical Park
Nearest town: Stillwater
Fees and permits: None

Schedule: Grounds, sunrise to sunset; visitor center, 9 a.m. to 5 p.m. daily except major holidays; auto-tour road, early Apr through Nov weather permitting
Maps: www.nps.gov/sara/planyourvisit/upload/Wilkinson-Trail-Hiking-Guide-1042022_Stop-6-Detour.pdf
Trail contact: Saratoga National Historical Park, 648 Route 32, Stillwater; (518) 670-2985; www.nps.gov/sara
Special considerations: Well-signed with station posts, the NRT occasionally crosses a horse trail, and it slips across the auto-tour route four times. Because ticks do occur here, take the necessary precautions and check yourself and your pet for ticks. Trails can be slippery in spring. Carry drinking water for yourself and your pet.

Finding the trailhead: From Troy, go 17.5 miles north on US 4 and turn left (west) to reach the Saratoga National Historical Park access road. Go 2.3 miles to the visitor center. From New York State Thruway I-87 south of Saratoga Springs, take exit 12 and follow the well-marked route to the park. It travels NY 67 east, US 9 north, Highway 9P east, NY 423 east, and NY 32 north to enter the park in 12 miles. Be alert for the frequent turns. GPS: 43.012771, -73.649292

The Hike

Exit the back door of the visitor center and turn right, following the trimmed grass and cinder path past cannons and memorials to reach both the trail kiosk and the initial junction at interpretive station A. Bear left for the trail. The wide mowed track passes through a shrubby transition habitat; woods of planted pine, maple, oak, aspen, and fruit trees; and rolling untamed fields of thigh-high grasses and wildflowers. Islands of trees dot the fields. The National Park Service (NPS) purposely manages the property to maintain the look of the land during the campaign of 1777. Only a few neighborhood rooftops break the spell.

Downy, hairy, red-bellied, and pileated woodpeckers telegraph their locations in the woods, while bobolinks, eastern meadowlarks, song sparrows, eastern bluebirds, and eastern towhees spread cheer in the field. White-tailed deer may cross your path.

Before long, a spur to the left leads to Auto Tour Stop 7, Breymann's Redoubt. Here you converge on a paved walk to find interpretive displays, a pair of cannons, and posts outlining the site of the German breastwork. The crude log barrier 200 yards long and 7 feet high was intended to protect the British right flank, but on October 7, 1777, General John Burgoyne of the British Regulars led his 1,500 men into the neighboring farm field, and American general Horatio Gates ordered his forces to advance against them. The

Artillery pieces hint at the Revolutionary War actions that played out along the Wilkinson Trail.

battle raged until the Americans captured Breymann's Redoubt, and Burgoyne found himself out of options. He retreated with 1,200 fewer men than he had when he started, leaving Saratoga under cover of darkness, and the entire Revolutionary War turned in America's favor.

From the redoubt, bear right on a paved lane to the Boot Monument, a tribute to Benedict Arnold, who received a leg wound while distinguishing himself in the fray.

Return to the Wilkinson Trail and turn left, quickly reaching the loop junction at station C; go left (clockwise). New York aster, common and swamp milkweed, Queen Anne's lace, butterfly weed, and several kinds of goldenrod interweave the summer and autumn fields. Cross the tour road for the first time and pass through a pine corridor, reaching the Liaison Trail at station N. Follow the Wilkinson Trail through mixed woods.

The battle of Saratoga turned the tide of the Revolutionary War in the Patriots' favor.

The second road crossing follows. The trail now travels a wooded plateau between the Mill Creek and Great Ravine drainages. When the British marched along this route in 1777, old-growth trees 6 feet in diameter cloaked the highland. A couple of plank crossings precede the footbridge at station L. Cross the bridge and bear right. This open field would have been cultivated in the eighteenth century. Cross over the auto-tour road and continue through the field, accompanied by the buzzing of pollinators.

The Wilkinson Trail then dips through a ravine to tour a low ridge clad in pine. Beyond station H stretches another long, open field. At the base of a rise, cross over a horse trail before ascending to meet a paved walk. Here the Wilkinson Trail bisects the 0.6-mile Freeman Loop. Go left, adding a clockwise tour of this side trail.

This circuit and its spurs visit the John Freeman Farm and Balcarres Redoubt, key locations in the battles of September 19 and October 7, 1777. Interpretive signs, some with recorded messages, describe a British fortification that withstood a fiery American onslaught; a monument to a fallen American captain; Bloody Knoll, named for the many casualties on October 7, 1777; and an obelisk and exquisitely crafted cannons. The Liaison Trail, which you encountered earlier, also meets up at Freeman Loop.

After completing Freeman Loop, turn right, resuming the Wilkinson Trail. Pass through field and pine stand to make one last crossing of the tour road. At station D, cross over a horse trail, coming to a T junction with a mowed path. Go right toward the visitor center. Close the loop at station C and bear left, returning to the visitor center.

Miles and Directions

0.0 Start at the visitor center trailhead. Exit the center's back door and turn right to reach the trail kiosk and station A in 500 feet. Bear left for the Wilkinson Trail (WT).

0.6 Reach a junction and take the left spur to Auto Tour Stop 7, Breymann's Redoubt.

0.7 Reach Breymann's Redoubt and the Benedict Arnold site. Backtrack to the WT.

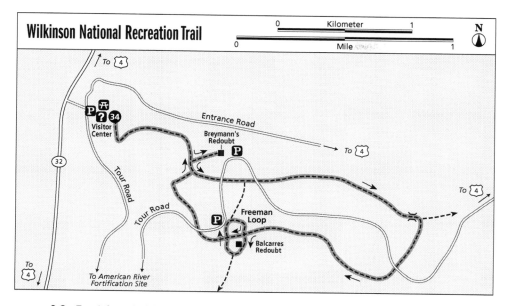

Wilkinson National Recreation Trail

0   Kilometer   1

0   Mile   1

N

0.8   Turn left on the WT, quickly reaching the loop junction at station C. Go left (clockwise).

1.1   Cross the auto-tour route.

1.2   Reach the Liaison Trail at station N. Proceed forward on the WT. **Ballout:** Turn right on the Liaison Trail to shorten the loop by 2 miles.

2.0   Reach the junction at station L. Bear right upon crossing the footbridge.

2.2   Cross the auto-tour route.

3.2   Where the WT bisects Freeman Loop, head left (clockwise) on the 0.6-mile loop.

3.8   Close Freeman Loop. Turn right to resume on the WT.

4.0   Cross the auto-tour route.

4.1   Past station D, reach a T junction with a mowed path. Head right toward the visitor center.

4.2   Close the loop back at station C. Bear left toward the visitor center.

4.8   End at the visitor center.

Hike Information

Local Information

Saratoga Convention and Tourism Bureau, 60 Railroad Place, Suite 301, Saratoga Springs; (518) 584-1531; www.discoversaratoga.org

Local Events/Attractions

Saratoga Spa State Park, noted for its mineral waters and classic architecture, is a National Historic Landmark. It is home to the Saratoga Performing Arts Center, the Spa Little Theater, the Saratoga Automobile Museum, and a wide range of recreation opportunities. Saratoga Spa State Park, 19 Roosevelt Dr., Saratoga Springs; (518) 584-2535; https://parks.ny.gov/parks/saratogaspa.

35 Taconic Crest Trail

The nearly 40-mile-long Taconic Crest Trail strings from southwest Vermont through New York to Pittsfield State Forest in Massachusetts. Hiking the New York section of the trail north from Petersburg Pass (on NY 2) to the NY 346 trailhead at the Hoosic River showcases the trail's finest attributes. This segment travels hardwood forests, serves up multistate views, and visits a geologic oddity—a snow hole.

Start: At the Petersburg Pass/NY 2 trailhead

Distance: 8.8-mile shuttle

Approximate hiking time: 5 to 6.5 hours

Difficulty: Strenuous

Elevation change: From Petersburg Pass (elevation 2,100 feet), the trail climbs to the hike's high point at White Rock (elevation 2,500 feet). Where the hike ends at NY 346 is the low point (500 feet).

Trail surface: Earthen path, woods road

Seasons: Open year-round, best for hiking spring through fall

Other trail users: Snowshoers, cross-country skiers

Canine compatibility: Leashed dogs permitted (Carry water for your animal and dispose of animal waste away from trails and water.)

Land status: New York State Department of Environmental Conservation (DEC), Williams College, and private land

Nearest town: Berlin

Fees and permits: None

Schedule: Daylight hours on Williams College Land; no restrictions on DEC land

Map: https://taconichikingclub.org/taconic-crest-trail

Trail contact: New York State DEC, Region 4, 1130 North Westcott Rd., Schenectady; (518) 357-2234; www.dec.ny.gov

Special considerations: There is no camping in the Williams College Hopkins Memorial Forest or on any private land. Use care when crossing NY 2. Be sure to leash dogs to protect research sites, wildlife, and other trail users. Bring water for you and your pet.

Finding the trailhead: From the NY 2–NY 22 junction at Petersburg (or Petersburgh), go 5.3 miles east on NY 2 to reach the large, open parking lot for Petersburg Pass Scenic Area on the right. The northbound trail starts across the highway. GPS: 42.723187, -73.277823

Reach the trail's northern terminus off NY 346, 2.5 miles east of North Petersburg. The small developed trailhead is on the south side of the highway just before the Hoosic River bridge and the route's crossing into Vermont. GPS: 42.809597, -73.288821

The Hike

Ascend north on a steep footpath behind the sign that says "Petersburg" to meet up with the white-blazed Taconic Crest Trail. Over-the-shoulder views present Petersburg Pass and Mount Raimer. A spur presents a western perspective of the valley below and the Adirondacks beyond.

In 2,600-acre Hopkins Memorial Forest, the rolling trail alternately traverses the west flank and the Taconic crest. From full-canopy forests of birch, beech, maple, oak, and black cherry, you enter areas of low-stature trees with shrubby understories.

Leaf litter can mask trails but brightens the forest floor.

Heralds of June-blooming azaleas can grab attention. As you proceed forward past the marked Shepard's Well Trail, candelabra-trunked trees dip low in their shades of autumn. Elsewhere silver snags (victims of the pear thrip infestation of the late 1980s) may draw your eyes skyward.

Where the Birch Brook Trail heads right, hip-high fountains of ferns claim the trail's left side. The crest trail steadily climbs, slipping into southwest Vermont before returning to New York at White Rock, a signed landmark. This site owes its US

Geological Survey designation to the milky-white quartz scattered throughout the woods. Open berry fields present vistas of the rolling New York terrain.

From White Rock the trail drifts east, dipping into beech forest. At the marked Y junction, detour right for a short descent to the Snow Hole. This ground cavity shows jagged, mossy walls that meet in an ill-fitting bite. Enter the chasm for a big surprise—the chill air from the snow and ice that linger into summer. The chill supports a boreal understory of hobblebush, club moss, and oxalis. Area rocks bear some names and dates from visitors of more than a century ago, but the genuine etchings must be sorted from modern pranksters' markings. A path overlooks the cavity and its cavelike end. Backtrack and resume northbound crest travel.

Where the trail flattens, puddles may require evasion; as the trail ascends again, you'll find trail markers that lead to a little-tracked crescent along the eastern slope, which soon returns to the main grade. There's not much to see up there, so you might just skip it.

After a measured descent, proceed forward at the next woods road junction. The trail rises farther as it leads you past some showy black-cherry trees. A steeper descent follows, where loose rock and downward-pointed roots can steal footing. Catch glimpses down the east and west flank as the ridgetop narrows, but no open views. Where the ridge regains its height, enjoy a pretty grass-and-fern passage. The trail then dips west, returning to the crest at a junction. Keep right.

Blue DEC trail markers join the familiar white diamond markers. At the Prosser Hollow Junction, yellow disks lead left (west) to Prosser Hollow trailhead. Continue north, tracing the crest on a woods road. Where you descend into a big horseshoe bend, keep alert for the multiple markers showing where you abandon the woods road to follow a lightly tracked footpath through the woods proper.

The trail rolls over a huckleberry-clad hill to cross an old grade and start the biggest descent of the hike. The steepness, brushing grasses, and muddy spots complicate travel, and insects can be persistent here. But superior trail markings, birdsong, and sightings of fox, deer, grouse, and woodpecker help erase hard feelings.

Another set of multiple markers sends you left across and down the slope to where the trail crosses a gravel road. The trail later zigs right, through a meadow of knee-high vegetation with milkweed and oxeye daisy, returning to forest to continue the descent. A brook crossing on stones leads to the NY 346 trailhead.

Miles and Directions

- **0.0** Start from the Petersburg Pass trailhead and head north on the crest trail.
- **0.7** Proceed forward past the Shepard's Well Trail.
- **1.5** Proceed forward past the Birch Brook Trail.
- **2.5** Reach White Rock. Continue on the crest trail, which drifts east here.
- **2.9** Reach a marked Y junction; detour right for a 250-foot descent to the Snow Hole. **Ballout:** The Snow Hole makes a satisfactory turnaround site for out-and-back travel.
- **3.0** Return to the Taconic Crest Trail and turn right (north).

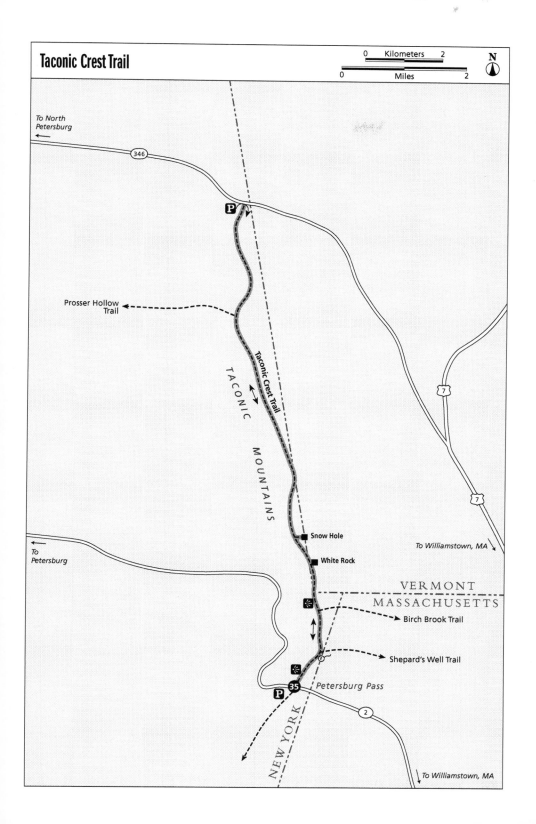

3.5 Markers indicate a little-tracked 0.2-mile crescent spur along the eastern edge of the slope. Because of its limited view, continue ahead on the main wide grade.

4.0 Reach a woods road junction; proceed forward, ignoring the route that angles in on the right.

4.9 Reach a junction. Keep right, avoiding the unmarked woods road that heads left.

6.1 Reach Prosser Hollow Junction. Proceed north on the crest trail to NY 346. **Option:** The yellow disks to the left lead west to the Prosser Hollow trailhead for an alternative 7.5-mile shuttle. (Study area maps for how to get to this trailhead to locate a shuttle vehicle.)

6.6 Reach a junction. Continue forward (northbound), ignoring a trail angling back to the right.

6.9 Leave the woods road as it descends into a big horseshoe bend, following markers and foot trail left into woods.

7.5 Reach a set of multiple markers. Head left across and down the slope to cross a gravel road.

8.0 Trail zigs right, passing through a transitioning meadow of knee-high vegetation.

8.2 Reenter forest, still descending as the crest drops to the Hoosic River Valley.

8.8 Cross a brook to end at the NY 346 trailhead.

Hike Information

Local Information
Discover Albany, 25 Quackenbush Sq., Albany; (518) 434-1217 or (800) 258-3582; www.albany.org

Local Events/Attractions
Bennington Battlefield State Historic Site in Walloomsac and the visitor center at **Barnett Homestead** recap a moment in Revolutionary War history. On this battlefield in 1777, the militiamen from several states, under the command of General Stark, defeated the British, who were attempting to raid the American storehouses and stables at Bennington. Bennington Battlefield State Historic Park, 5231 Route 67, Walloomsac; (518) 860-9094; https://parks.ny.gov/historic-sites/benningtonbattlefield/details.aspx.

Accommodations
Cherry Plain State Park, 10 State Park Rd. in Petersburg, off NY 22, is open Memorial Day to Labor Day and has twenty campsites and ten additional hike-in sites. Reservations: (800) 456-2267; www.reserveamerica.com.

Organizations
Taconic Hiking Club helps maintain the trail; http://taconichikingclub.org.

Honorable Mentions

S Five Rivers Environmental Education Center

At this nationally recognized environmental education center, just west of Delmar, you can examine habitat interrelationships while touring field, forest, meadow, and pond. The center takes its name from the five major rivers flowing into the greater area: the Hudson, Mohawk, Sacandaga, Schoharie, and Hoosick. Six easy self-guided nature trails explore the center grounds, ranging from a fragment of a mile to 2 miles long. Bird-watching, spring and summer wildflowers, and sightings of beavers, deer, turtles, and frogs engage nature trail hikers. Take the necessary precautions for ticks, and carry insect repellent. The site is open year-round (weather permitting) from sunrise to sunset; interpretive center: 9 a.m. to 4:30 p.m. Monday through Saturday (closed Sun and state holidays).

From the junction of NY 52 (Elm Avenue) and NY 443 (Delaware Avenue) in west Delmar, go 1.4 miles west on NY 443 and turn right (north) on Orchard Street at a sign for the center. Go 0.4 mile and turn left on Game Farm Road, reaching the center entrance and parking lot on the right in 0.3 mile. GPS: 42.609760, -73.889648. Contact Five Rivers Environmental Education Center (EEC), New York State Department of Environmental Education, 56 Game Farm Rd., Delmar; (518) 475-0291; www.dec.ny.gov/education/1835.html

Geese find Five Rivers suitable for raising a family.

T John Boyd Thacher State Park

This 2,300-acre state park west of Albany boasts 6 miles of the famous Helderberg Escarpment—one of the richest fossil-bearing formations in the world—as well as Mohawk–Hudson Valley panoramas, a historic Indian trade route, echoes of Tory spies, and a Revolution-era paint mine. Waterfalls and mixed woods complement the limestone cliff landscape. Red-tailed and red-shouldered hawk, rabbits, deer, and fox find habitat here. Short trails throw open the park pages: the 1-mile out-and-back Indian Ladder Trail, the 2.5-mile Escarpment Trail, and a 1-mile nature loop.

Between Indian Ladder and LaGrange Bush Picnic Areas, the park's premier Indian Ladder Trail wraps below the 100- to 200-foot-high light-colored cliffs of the Helderberg Escarpment. Millions of years ago, an uplift of limestone, sandstone, and shale, followed by ages of weathering and erosion, brought about the site's vertical fracturing. Here the Mohawk Schoharie built a shortcut to the valley, placing a sturdy notched trunk against the cliff for descending and scaling. Today stonework steps pull that duty, making this one of the most popular trails in the region. The cliffs pull eyes skyward with their overhangs, flutes, fissures, clefts, and hollows, but it's the high waterfalls along this trail that really command respect.

The thin footpath of the Escarpment Trail hugs the fenced escarpment rim as it skirts the developed park. Views sweep the Mohawk–Hudson Valley and the escarpment arc. Clear days reveal the distant ragged outline of the Adirondack High Peaks and Vermont Green Mountains as common ravens, red-tailed hawks, and turkey vultures soar below the rim.

The Nature Trail (or Forest Trail) travels textured woods of maple, hickory, oak, hemlock, white pine, aspen, and paper birch. Lady's slipper, violet, clintonia, and mayapple sprinkle the forest floor.

The least complicated approach to the park is to take NY 85 west from Albany (NY 85 is exit 4 off I-90) and follow it to NY 157 (about 10 miles). Go right on NY 157 and continue 4 miles into the park. A vehicle entrance fee is collected May through October; gates close promptly at sunset. Plan to be off the trails accordingly. GPS: 42.656522, -74.018107. Contact Thacher State Park, 830 Thacher Park Rd., Voorheesville; (518) 872-1237; https://parks.ny.gov/parks/128/.

Ferns dress the cliff ledges of the Indian Ladder Trail.

The Catskills

C laiming a big chunk of the southern heel of this boot-shaped state, this region brings together the chiseled beauty and lore of the Catskill Mountains, the blinding white cliff-and-crag realm of the Shawangunks, and the outlying wooded ridges parted by thin valleys. This is a countryside of kill (Dutch for river) and clove (split in the landscape), the land of Rip Van Winkle and Sleepy Hollow. Naturalist John Burroughs walked its reaches and drew from its inspiration.

At the emotional and geographic heart of this region is Catskill Park, a marriage of both private and public forest preserve lands set aside as "forever wild." Since its foresighted start in 1885, the park has swelled to 300,000 acres with ninety-eight mountain peaks topping 3,000 feet, high enough to show alpine characteristics.

Mary Glen Falls accents a wooded scenic grotto.

Quarries pulled bluestone and other treasures from the mountains for paving and building, and early industrialists harvested hemlock bark here for tanning. In the nineteenth and twentieth centuries, these mountains represented an idyllic summer retreat for well-to-do New York City dwellers as they escaped from the dirt, noise, congestion, and heat of the city—as well as one of the few places Jewish families were welcomed, as their landsmen from eastern Europe settled here and built resorts just for them. Popular mountain hotels sprang up as well and competed for moneyed clientele with luxury accommodations.

The grand Catskills views attracted and inspired the Hudson River School of landscape painters, and they continue to draw artists today. From fields of wildflowers in spring to the inviting coolness of mountaintop and hollow in summer, from autumn's kaleidoscopic explosion to winter's snowy elegance, the Catskills provide nonstop riches.

Carriageways that led to mountain house retreats provide ideal hiking routes today. Foot trails explore forest, field, pond, lakes, and escarpment rims, taking hikers to sweeping vistas of the Catskills, Mohonks, and the Hudson Valley. As if that weren't enough, this region boasts the largest freshwater wetland in southern New York, at Bashakill Wildlife Management Area.

36 North–South Lake Loop

This Catskill Mountains loop, one of the best in the region, travels the escarpment and wooded outskirts of North–South Lake, snapping up cherished views and passing cultural sites. Waterfalls, azalea and mountain laurel, and fall foliage complement the woodland sojourn.

Start: At the North Lake beach area trailhead
Distance: 9.3-mile loop
Approximate hiking time: 5 to 7 hours
Difficulty: Moderate
Elevation change: The rolling trail has about a 600-foot elevation change.
Trail surface: Earthen and rocky path
Seasons: Open year-round, best for hiking spring through fall
Other trail users: Horse riders (on marked shared routes only), mountain bikers (where appropriate), hunters, snowshoers, cross-country skiers
Canine compatibility: Dogs permitted but must be controlled at owner's side by leash or voice command
Land status: New York State Department of Environmental Conservation (DEC)

Nearest town: Haines Falls
Fees and permits: Seasonal day-use fees or campground fees
Schedule: No time restrictions
Map: https://andyarthur.org/data/map_013258_d.pdf or New York–New Jersey Trail Conference Trail Map 40, North Lake Area Catskill Trails, for purchase at www.nynjtc.org
Trail contact: New York State DEC, Region 4, Stamford Office, 65561 Highway 10, Suite 1, Stamford; (607) 652-7365; www.dec.ny.gov
Special considerations: Avoid the escarpment edge during icy conditions and be careful there under wet conditions. Where sections of the loop are open to joint hiker-horse usage, yield right-of-way to horse riders and control dogs.

Finding the trailhead: From New York State Thruway I-87, take exit 20 at Saugerties and go north on NY 32 to its junction with NY 32A (6 miles from the I-87 exit). Bear left on NY 32A, staying on it for 1.8 miles; there turn west onto NY 23A. In 4.8 miles in Haines Falls, turn right onto NY 18 (Haines Falls Road) for North–South Lake Campground, reaching the entrance station in 2.2 miles. Find the trailhead at the upper end of North Lake beach parking in another 1.6 miles; look for blue blazes and a sign for Artists Rock. GPS: 42.198086, -74.034991

The Hike

Follow the blue trail left (north), rounding and ascending to Artists Rock, avoiding a yellow spur just ahead. Black oak, maple, pine, azalea, and mountain laurel decorate the escarpment brink. The broad sandstone ledges lay out a natural avenue. The jut of Artists Rock provides a fine vantage point for a 180-degree Hudson Valley panorama; turkey vultures soar below the point. Ascend to the next ledge tier for a peek at North–South Lake (formerly two lakes) and then round below an immense conglomerate outcrop eroding from the cliff.

The Escarpment Trail delivers spiritual views of Catskill Park.

At a mile, detour right to Sunset Rock for one of the finest vistas in the Catskills; the loop continues straight. This detour takes you to the escarpment edge of Lookout Point for northeast views before continuing to a series of plane-topped outcrops composing Sunset Rock. Fissures a foot wide and 20 feet deep isolate the rock islands. Views sweep across North–South Lake and its wooded basin to the swaybacked ridge of High Peak and Roundtop Mountain.

Resume the counterclockwise loop toward Newmans Ledge. Ascend along a thin edge with a disturbing drop. Vistas span Rip Van Winkle Hollow to Rip's Rock—this is, after all, Knickerbocker and literature's Washington Irving country. The trail then wraps and ascends to a junction below Badman Cave, shaped by an overhang and reached by a rock scramble. The loop continues straight on the yellow Rock Shelter Trail for a steady forest descent. Footing grows rocky along the brook that drains to Mary's Glen.

At the trail junction near a weeping overhang, bear right, staying on the yellow trail. Spring peepers can bring noisy vitality to the glen. Where the yellow trail draws even with the top of this 10-foot waterfall, veer left for the loop. Rocks and roots trouble the descent, while old-growth maple trees grace the woods.

At Haines Falls Road, angle left to walk along Schutt Road, from which you quickly turn left, following the blue Escarpment Trail. Descend along the wide lane, touring the hemlock-birch forest, passing colonial rock walls, and crossing an old railroad grade.

After crossing Lake Creek, turn right on the woods road and bear left soon after on an earthen lane paralleling the creek. Scenic rockwork comes into view downstream. A bench surrounded by forget-me-nots in spring separates the trail from the stream. After the trail turns away, floral shrubs fill the midstory with color and fragrance in late spring. At a rocky drainage, a rock obelisk with a boulder crown honors firefighter Frank Layman, who lost his life in the fire of 1900. Round the monument to the left, and in a few steps take a sharp left back uphill to the escarpment. View the Kaaterskill drainage and the wooded ridge of High Peak and Roundtop Mountain.

Pass through a rock channel for a wrapping ascent of the wooded escarpment, and proceed forward to Inspiration Point, hiking past a second Sunset Rock. Beyond Inspiration Point, the "V" of Kaaterskill Canyon opens to a Hudson Valley view. After turning right on a woods road, follow the blue trail left at the upcoming junction.

Azalea, laurel, and oak frame this rocky woods-road ascent to the next junction, where the blue trail heads right on a narrowed forest lane. Ahead, follow signs to the right for Boulder Rock. Beyond Split Rock, where massive blocks have pulled apart from the escarpment face, you'll find Boulder Rock, a naturally transported boulder that came to rest on the escarpment ledge. Bear left and meet the red trail.

Here you turn right, coming to a clearing and sign that together recall Catskill Mountain House, a grand hotel that hosted presidents and dignitaries in the nineteenth century. Round left, away from the sign, and ahead bear right to end back at beach parking.

Miles and Directions

0.0 Start from the upper end of North Lake beach parking. Follow the blue trail left (north) for a counterclockwise loop.

0.4 Reach Artists Rock.

1.0 Reach a junction and detour right to Sunset Rock. The loop continues forward.

1.2 Reach Sunset Rock. Backtrack to the loop and turn right (1.4).

2.2 Reach Badman Cave and the Rock Shelter Trail. Follow the yellow Rock Shelter Trail straight ahead for a steady descent.

2.8 At a junction near a weeping waterfall, bear right, staying on the yellow trail. **Option:** The red trail here descends to Ashley (or Mary's Glen) Falls, a beaver meadow, and the campground.

4.1 Meet Haines Falls Road. Angle left to reach and briefly walk Schutt Road.

4.2 Follow the blue Escarpment Trail, turning left off Schutt Road.

4.7 Cross the Lake Creek footbridge, coming to a junction. Turn right on a woods road, and soon after bear left on an earthen lane paralleling Lake Creek downstream.

5.4 At the Frank Layman firefighter monument, round the obelisk to the left, and in a few steps take a sharp left uphill.

5.8 Reach the escarpment and continue following the blue Escarpment Trail.

6.2 Reach Inspiration Point.

7.0 Turn right on a woods road, reaching a junction. There turn left, still on the blue trail.

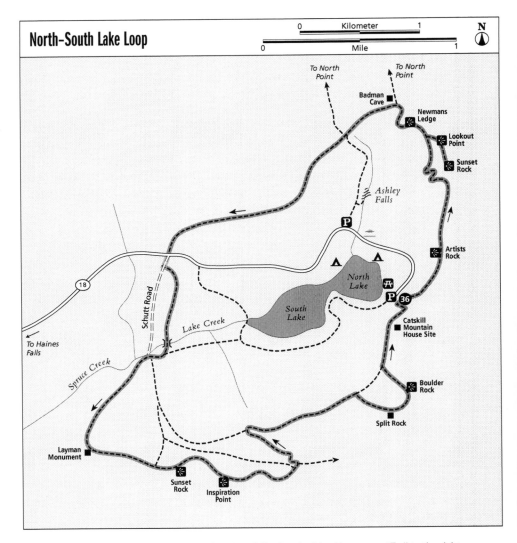

7.5 Reach a junction with a red trail. Continue following the blue Escarpment Trail to the right.

8.2 Follow the Escarpment Trail heading right to Boulder Rock. **Option:** The red trail bypasses Boulder Rock.

8.4 Reach Boulder Rock and bear left.

8.5 Meet the red trail and turn right, continuing on the Escarpment Trail.

9.0 Reach the Catskill Mountain House site. Round to the left, away from the sign.

9.1 Bear right.

9.3 End at the parking area back at North Lake beach.

Hike Information

Local Information

Greene County Tourism, 700 Route 23B, Leeds; (518) 943-3223 or (800) 355-CATS (2287); www.greatnortherncatskills.com

Local Events/Attractions

Together, the **Thomas Cole National Historic Site** and **Hudson River School Art Trail** introduce nineteenth-century artist Thomas Cole and his creative contemporaries and direct you to the sites that inspired their great landscape paintings. The Thomas Cole National Historic Site, 218 Spring St., Catskill; (518) 943-7465; www.thomascole.org.

Accommodations

North–South Lake Campground, open early May through late October, has 219 sites. DEC office: (607) 652-2032; campground phone: (518) 589-5058.

Organizations

New York–New Jersey Trail Conference helps maintain, mark, and map trails. NY–NJ Trail Conference, 600 Ramapo Valley Rd., Mahwah, NJ 07430; (201) 512-9348; info@nynjtc.org; www.nynjtc.org.

37 Indian Head Mountain Loop

West of Saugerties, this loop rewards with a classic Catskill setting, vistas, and challenge. Central to this hike are the 500-foot cliffs of Indian Head. Wildflowers, fall foliage, and wildlife sightings lend to the attraction. Above the 3,000-foot elevation, a rare spruce-fir complex claims part of the journey.

Start: At the Prediger Road trailhead
Distance: 6.9-mile loop
Approximate hiking time: 4 to 5 hours
Difficulty: Strenuous
Elevation change: The trail travels between 1,890 and 3,573 feet in elevation, with the high point found at Indian Head summit.
Trail surface: Earthen or rocky path, rocky woods road
Seasons: Open year-round, best for hiking spring through fall
Other trail users: Hunters, skilled snowshoers
Canine compatibility: Dogs permitted but must be controlled at owner's side by leash or voice command (Keep your animal leashed when crossing private land.)
Land status: New York State Department of Environmental Conservation (DEC) land, private land at start

Nearest town: Tannersville
Fees and permits: None
Schedule: No time restrictions
Maps: www.dec.ny.gov/docs/lands_forests _pdf/recmapihw.pdf or for purchase from New York–New Jersey Trail Conference, Trail Map 41, Northeastern Catskill Trails (www.nynjtc.org)
Trail contact: New York State DEC, Region 4, Stamford Office, 65561 Highway 10, Suite 1, Stamford; (607) 652-7365; www.dec.ny.gov
Special considerations: Both the parking and the start of the trail occur on private land. Respect all posted notices to preserve the access privilege. Use caution on rocky climbs and descents. There is no camping and there are no campfires allowed above the 3,500-foot elevation.

Finding the trailhead: From the junction of NY 23A and County Road 16 in Tannersville, head south on CR 16 (Depot Street) for 5.5 miles; the road name changes several times. Turn right onto Prediger Road. Go 0.5 mile, finding trail parking along the right shoulder only. Do not clog the road or block the private residence either by parking on the left or too close to the trailhead. Leave enough space between parked vehicles for returning hikers to pull out safely. GPS: 42.133986, -74.104424 (See hike's Options for an alternative start.)

The Hike

From Prediger Road, follow the red markers of the Devil's Path, passing through a stile and crossing a footbridge to enter hemlock-deciduous woodland. Travel is on a woods road with a modest incline. At the upcoming loop junction, proceed forward on the red trail toward the Devil's Kitchen lean-to and Indian Head summit; the loop's return is via the blue Jimmy Dolan Notch Trail on your right.

Soon the old road tapers to trail width. Big maples and birch compose the canopy above the boulder-studded forest floor. Porcupine, deer, eastern newt, mouse, and toad can divert attention. After crossing a thin creek, turn right on a woods road (the Long Path). At the signed junction ahead, continue following the red markers, turning right to climb toward Indian Head Mountain and destinations west.

The trail, at times root-bound and rock-studded, crosses muddy drainages. Hemlocks return to the mix, and some birch trees display impressive root systems. Steep spurts interrupt the trail's otherwise comfortable ascent. Mossy rocks and ledges contribute to the mountain visuals.

After a sharp climb, you obtain an outcrop ledge overlooking the steep wooded slope for an exciting view of Roundtop Mountain, High Peak, Plattekill Mountain, Platte Clove, and the Hudson River Valley beyond the clove. Autumn blends colorful leaves with evergreen boughs.

Trillium announces spring on Indian Head Mountain.

As the thin trail contours the slope, it next extends views toward Overlook Mountain. Tackling the rocky climb ahead may require you to use your hands. A corridor of spruce and fir precedes an opening extending views toward Overlook, Slide, and Plateau Mountains; Ashokan Reservoir; Cooper Lake; Mount Tobias; and postcard-pretty serial peaks.

Cross a small saddle for the final assault on Indian Head Mountain, which again requires some high-stepping and hand assists. Be careful here, especially under wet conditions or when burdened by a heavy pack. Vistas can suggest breathers. Past the 3,500-foot elevation mark, top the summit ridge. The trail then rolls along the top; log walks span marshy sites.

For this hike, the views are gathered on the way to the summit. The summit's reward is its fragile spruce-fir complex, a rarity for this part of the country, limited to the very high reaches. No camping is allowed here. After the summit stroll the trail descends with a bold start, and it is again rugged. Glimpses of Twin Mountain accompany the descent. Birch is now the primary tree.

At Jimmy Dolan Notch you'll find a trail junction. For the loop, follow the blue trail heading right toward Platte Clove Road (CR 16). The red trail continues west to other Catskill destinations. Before heading down off the mountain, a detour left (south) to the edge of the Notch offers a farewell view toward Ashokan Reservoir and Slide Mountain Ridge looking out through the natural "V" shaped by Twin and Indian Head Mountains.

The descent from the Notch remains steep, rocky, and at times sun exposed. Gradually the woods become more mixed and the trees bigger. Entering a drainage area, the descent eases and the trail arcs right. Hemlocks fashion a deeper woods. On the woods road the trail then contours the slope. Cross the creek to close the loop back at the initial junction, and turn left, retracing your steps to the trailhead.

Miles and Directions

0.0 Start from the Prediger Road trailhead. Follow the red markers.

0.5 Reach the loop junction. Proceed straight ahead on the red trail.

1.2 Cross over a thin creek.

1.8 Turn right on a woods road (the Long Path).

1.9 Reach a signed junction; follow the red trail to the right. *Note:* The blue markers straight ahead lead to Overlook Mountain.

3.2 Reach a vista outcrop ledge.

3.7 Reach a manicured view.

4.0 Cross a small saddle on the way to Indian Head Mountain.

4.3 Reach the summit of Indian Head Mountain.

4.7 Descend from the summit.

4.9 Reach Jimmy Dolan Notch and a junction; follow the blue trail right toward Platte Clove Road (CR 16). **Option:** The red trail continues west to other Catskill mountains.

6.4 Cross a creek to close the loop. Backtrack left to the trailhead.

6.9 End at the Prediger Road trailhead.

Options

For a dry-weather alternative start to this trail, reducing pressure on the Prediger Road trailhead, try taking the **Long Path** through Platte Clove Preserve. Look for the Long Path's aqua blazes to descend south off Platte Clove Road (CR 16), 0.7 mile east of the Prediger Road–Platte Clove Road intersection. Trailhead parking is on the north side of Platte Clove Road 0.2 mile farther east. GPS: 42.133749, -74.081983

The Long Path dips to cross Plattekill Clove on a Kingpost footbridge, and then ascends on or beside the historic Overlook Mountain House Road, touring in mixed woods and crossing upper drainages. Interpretive panels introduce features along the way, including old bluestone quarry sites. At 0.9 mile the Long Path intersects the red-blazed Devil's Path at the 1.8-mile junction. Straight ahead leads to Indian Head Mountain, the Devil's Kitchen lean-to, Echo Lake, and Overlook Mountain. The trail to the right leads to Jimmy Dolan Notch Trail and the Prediger Road trailhead. When starting from the preserve, you shave 0.9 mile off the hike's distance each way, but you increase the overall elevation gain.

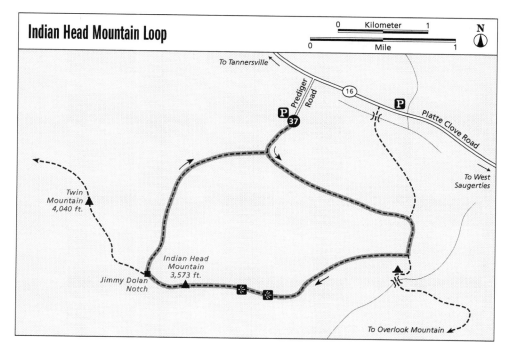

Kilometer

Mile

N

To Tannersville

Prediger Road

16

Platte Clove Road

To West Saugerties

Twin Mountain 4,040 ft.

Indian Head Mountain 3,573 ft.

Jimmy Dolan Notch

To Overlook Mountain

Hike Information

Local Information

Greene County Tourism, 700 Route 23B, Leeds; (518) 943-3223 or (800) 355-CATS (2287); www.greatnortherncatskills.com

Local Events/Attractions

Mountain Top Arboretum, a nonprofit garden preserve in the northern Catskills, is a living museum with native and introduced trees, plants, and shrubs. Reach it off NY 23C, 2 miles north of Tannersville on Maude Adams Road. Donation requested. Mountain Top Arboretum, PO Box 379, 4 Maude Adams Rd., Tannersville 12485; (518) 589-3903; www.mtarboretum.org.

Accommodations

North–South Lake (DEC) Campground, east of Tannersville via NY 23A and County Road 18, is open early May through late October and has 219 sites. DEC office: (607) 652-2032; campground phone: (518) 589-5058.

Organizations

New York–New Jersey Trail Conference helps maintain, mark, and map trails. NY–NJ Trail Conference, 600 Ramapo Valley Rd., Mahwah, NJ 07430; (201) 512-9348; info@nynjtc.org; www.nynjtc.org.

38 Overlook Mountain Hike

While the southern approach to Overlook Mountain is perhaps the most popular peak climb in the entire Catskills, this hike offers an alternative approach, arriving from the north. The route is indeed longer, but it offers a comfortable grade, pleasant backdrop, points of interest, and fewer travelers. A detour finds charming Echo Lake, another endorsement. But however you choose to reach the mountaintop, the lookout tower, now in its second life thanks to dedicated volunteers, caps the journey with grand overlooks of the Catskill neighborhood.

Start: At the Prediger Road trailhead
Distance: 13.8 miles out-and-back, including spur to Echo Lake
Approximate hiking time: 8 to 9.5 hours
Difficulty: Moderate
Elevation change: The trail has a 1,250-foot elevation change, with the high point at Overlook Mountain, elevation 3,140 feet.
Trail surface: Earthen path, woods road
Seasons: Best for hiking spring through fall
Other trail users: Hunters, snowshoers, cross-country skiers
Canine compatibility: Dogs permitted but must be controlled at owner's side by leash or voice command. (Keep your animal leashed when crossing private land.)
Land status: New York State Department of Environmental Conservation (DEC) land, private land at start
Nearest town: Tannersville

Fees and permits: None
Schedule: No time restrictions
Maps: www.dec.ny.gov/docs/lands_forests _pdf/mapoverlook.pdf or New York–New Jersey Trail Conference Trail Map 41, Northeastern Catskill Trails, for purchase: www.nynjtc.org
Trail contacts: New York State DEC, Region 3, 21 South Putt Corners Rd., New Paltz; (845) 256-3000; www.dec.ny.gov. New York State DEC, Region 4, Stamford Office, 65561 State Highway 10, Suite 1, Stamford; (607) 652-7365; www.dec.ny.gov.
Special considerations: Because both the parking and the start of the trail occur on private land, respect all posted notices to preserve the access privilege. Heed the posted camping closure at the fire tower. Be attentive and mind your pets atop Overlook Mountain and near the ruins, because timber rattlesnakes dwell there.

Finding the trailhead: From the junction of NY 23A and CR 16 in Tannersville, head south on CR 16 (Depot Street) for 5.5 miles; the road name changes several times. Turn right on Prediger Road. Go 0.5 mile, finding trail parking along the right shoulder only. Do not clog the road or block the private residence either by parking on the left or too close to the trailhead. Leave enough space between parked vehicles for returning hikers to pull out safely. GPS: 42.133986, -74.104424

The Hike

This hike shares its first 1.9 miles with Indian Head Mountain Loop (the preceding hike). Begin by following the red Devil's Path markers, passing through a stile and

Echo Lake affords a quiet spot on the way to Overlook Mountain.

crossing a footbridge to enter hemlock-deciduous woodland, traveling on a woods road. Proceed straight ahead, past the blue Jimmy Dolan Notch Trail. The old road tapers.

Big maples and birch weave the canopy above a boulder-studded forest floor. Wildlife can add surprise. You cross a thin creek and turn right on a woods road. Then at the signed junction, you begin following blue markers toward Overlook Mountain.

Next up is the Devil's Kitchen lean-to, with its privy and reliable creek source. One weekday in June, the lone occupant was a porcupine. Pass through the lean-to camp and cross the creek footbridge for a steady ascent. Nettles, trillium, clintonia, starflower, and Canada mayflower announce springtime, giving way to daisy fleabane, oxeye daisy, yarrow, birds-foot trefoil, and butter-and-eggs in summer.

Rounding the slope of Plattekill Mountain, you hike past a low stone bench and travel the semishaded brink of an excavation with stone foundations. Here a thin footpath divides the vegetation of the old road, azalea brings its fragrant pink signature, and oaks join the mix.

At the Echo Lake Trail junction, detour right, descending sharply along the former carriage road to the lake and its lean-to, which looks out on a grassy shore. A path rings the lake; above it looms the ridge of Overlook Mountain. In spring thousands of polliwogs can blacken the shallows, while small toads seemingly cause the roadbed to percolate. Summer and fall bring their own nuances to the lake setting. The destination ideally suits novice backpackers.

Resume the southbound trek to Overlook Mountain, ascending along an escarpment edge for the next while. Mountain laurel, azalea, and pockets of beech trees adorn the way. A fuller forest follows. Pass an unusual balanced rock on the right where rock ledges and overhangs characterize the forest. Filtered views stretch to Indian Head and Twin Mountains. Beyond, you may find piped water for wetting the brow.

NEW YORK'S HISTORIC FIRE LOOKOUTS

In 1912 New York State authorized the construction of lookout towers across this forested state for the purpose of spotting forest fires. More than one hundred fire towers were erected and staffed atop the state's tallest peaks. Nearly a quarter of these watched over the Catskills region; nine were in Catskill Park. The building, staffing, and supplying of these steely "watchmen" prompted the blazing of trails into the state's isolated reaches. These trails serve recreational users today.

Fire lookouts served the state for nearly a century. The last fire spotter in the Catskills descended the ladder in 1990, surrendering watch at Red Hill Fire Tower in Claryville. Modern surveillance supplanted the usefulness of human spotters, and a wholesale abandonment of the fire towers followed, often accompanied by the dismantling or razing of the towers for safety. With the abandonment of the towers, a romantic hero, the dutiful and individualistic fire observer, was lost to future generations as well.

The 1990s, though, marked a reversal in trend. Preservation raised a call to arms, and dedicated volunteers and state personnel answered. Now fire towers lift the public into the clouds for great views and a taste of history. Interpretation and education keep this noble chapter in state and forest history alive.

The Overlook Mountain fire tower is one of five fire towers still standing in Catskill Park. The other four are the Red Hill, Balsam Lake Mountain, Tremper Mountain, and Hunter Mountain towers. The fire tower atop Slide Mountain, the tallest peak in the Catskills, sadly was dismantled before this restoration movement took wing.

The tower at Overlook Mountain (elevation 3,140 feet) has been in place since 1950, although the tower itself boasts an earlier history, dating to 1927. It was originally built on Gallis Hill, west of Kingston, before finding its way to Overlook Mountain. This tower's working life came to an end in 1988. In the late 1990s, committed volunteers began the task of restoring it, replacing its landings and rebuilding stairs. Now on the National Historic Lookout Register, this tower reopened on National Trails Day, June 5, 1999, to once again offer Catskill Park–Hudson River Valley views from 60 feet above the summit. The tower's cab is open to the public when volunteer interpreters staff the tower and the summit cabin information station on weekends from Memorial Day weekend through Indigenous Peoples' Day in October.

A comfortable ascent on a woods road leads to the fire tower. Spurs to the right deliver ledge views stretched south-southeast to the Hudson River, peering down and out of Lewis Hollow. The creased rocks shaping the road's left shoulder likewise may beckon for a closer look. You may climb the nine-story steel-framed lookout tower—just heed the posted number allowed up at any one time (six when we last climbed it). The tower cab, though, is only open weekends from Memorial Day weekend through Indigenous Peoples' Day, when volunteers are present.

Ruins hearken to the glory days of Catskill Mountain resorts.

Southern views sweep Ashokan Reservoir, the Slide Mountain area, Cooper Lake, and Mount Tobias. The western vantage rounds up the Saw Kill drainage to Plateau, Sugarloaf, and Twin Mountains, with Hunter Mountain rising beyond Stony Clove Notch. The forest sweep above the 3,000-foot elevation reveals the tattered legacy of the top-lopping so-called Tax Day Storm of 2007, which hit the forest preserve conifers hard. But the event plays a role in nature's cycles, opening the forest for warblers.

A picnic table welcomes a stay for lunch, but camping is prohibited. When ready, backtrack to the trailhead.

Miles and Directions

0.0   Start from the Prediger Road (northern) trailhead. Follow the red Devil's Path.

0.5   Reach a trail junction and continue straight on the red trail. *Note:* Right is the blue Jimmy Dolan Notch Trail.

1.2   Cross over a thin creek.

1.8   Turn right on a woods road (the Long Path).

1.9   At the marked Indian Head Mountain junction, follow the blue markers straight ahead toward Overlook Mountain.

2.1   Reach the Devil's Kitchen lean-to.

4.2   Reach the Echo Lake Trail junction. Descend right, following the yellow trail along a former carriage road to the lake.

4.9   Reach Echo Lake. Return uphill. **Option:** A 0.5-mile trail rings the lake for additional discovery.

5.6   Reach the Overlook Mountain Trail. Turn right.

6.2   Pass an unusual balanced rock on the right.

7.0   Reach a signed junction near a signal tower and the Overlook Mountain House ruins. Follow red markers left to the Overlook Mountain summit. **FYI:** From the ruins, the carriage

OVERLOOK MOUNTAIN HOUSE

Overlook Mountain, a subject for the Hudson River School of painters in the nineteenth century, has long been a calling card for the Woodstock area. It looms above the 590-acre Overlook Mountain Wild Forest and offers rewarding views. Two unusual woodland occurrences lend singularity to the mountain: red oaks, a lowland species uncommon at 3,100 feet of elevation, find an unexpected niche on the Overlook Mountain summit. Not only that, these oaks stand shoulder to shoulder with red spruce and balsam fir, trees that typically withhold their presence until 3,300 feet in elevation.

On a plateau below the Overlook Mountain fire tower sit the ruins of Overlook Mountain House. This mountain luxury hotel opened for business in the early 1870s, offering a pleasant retreat from the dirt and noise of New York City. Although one of several mountain hotels tucked in the Catskill Mountains, it held the distinction of being the highest mountain hotel, at an elevation of 2,920 feet. The original hotel could accommodate 300 guests, but it met with tragedy: When the owner's son, a known practical joker, reported that the hotel was on fire on April 1, 1875, no one took him seriously, and the building burned to the ground. New owners rebuilt it three years later, but it burned once again in 1923, and its third iteration could not regain its original glory. The stock market crash during its third building was a hurdle the hotel could not conquer. It never again opened to guests, and looting and time stole its grandeur. Trees now grow in the hotel lobby and halls, and the ruins only whisper of a time long past.

road continues south downhill 2 miles to Meads, suggesting either an alternative start or a spotting site for a shuttle vehicle. Be mindful in parking to avoid being ticketed.

7.6 Reach the Overlook Mountain fire tower. Return north to the trailhead, forgoing side trips.

13.8 End at the Prediger Road trailhead.

Options

If time is limited, the summit hike from the **Overlook Mountain** trailhead in Meads (north of Woodstock) ascends steadily on road grade, reaching the Overlook House ruins in 2 miles and the summit fire tower in 2.6 miles (a 1,500-foot elevation gain). From the common on NY 212 in Woodstock, turn north toward Meads on County Road 33/Rock City Road. In 0.6 mile continue straight on twisting, paved Meads Mountain Road to reach the trailhead parking in another 2 miles. The lot quickly fills on weekends and in summer. GPS: 42.071006, -74.122612. However, a new trailhead and parking area on McDaniel Road should relieve some of the pressure on this site. Its connector trail, though, adds distance.

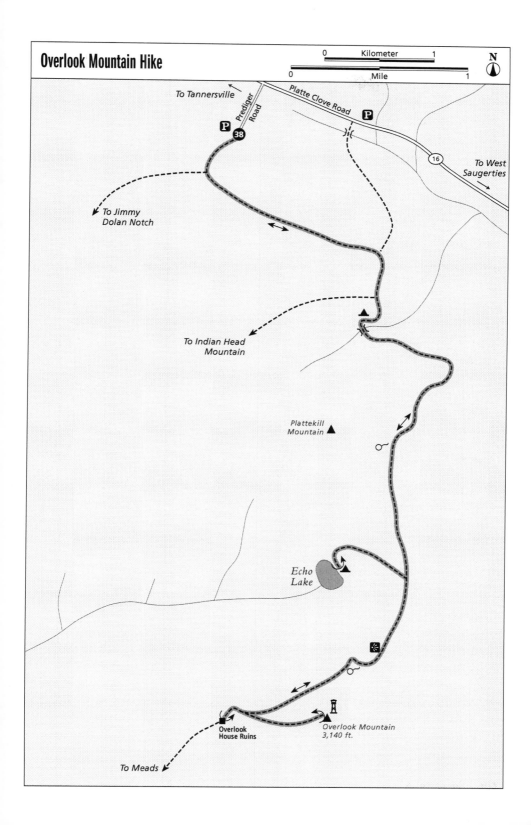

Overlook Mountain Hike

0 —————— Kilometer —————— 1

0 —————— Mile —————— 1

N

To Tannersville

Platte Clove Road

Prediger Road

🅿 38

🅿

16

To West Saugerties

To Jimmy Dolan Notch

To Indian Head Mountain

Plattekill Mountain ▲

Echo Lake

Overlook House Ruins

Overlook Mountain 3,140 ft.

To Meads

DEHYDRATION

Have you ever hiked in hot weather and had a roaring headache and felt fatigued after only a few miles? More than likely you were dehydrated. Symptoms of dehydration include fatigue, headache, and decreased coordination and judgment. When you are hiking, your body's rate of fluid loss depends on the outside temperature, humidity, altitude, and your activity level. On average, a hiker walking in warm weather will lose four liters of fluid (roughly a gallon) a day. That fluid loss is easily replaced by normal consumption of liquids and food. However, if a hiker is walking briskly in hot, dry weather and hauling a heavy pack, he or she can lose one to three liters (three quarts) of water an hour. It's important to always carry plenty of water and to stop often and drink fluids regularly, even if you aren't thirsty.

Hike Information

Local Information
Greene County Tourism, 700 Route 23B, Leeds; (518) 943-3223 or (800) 355-CATS (2287); www.greatnortherncatskills.com. **Woodstock Chamber of Commerce** and Arts, 10 Rock City Rd., Woodstock; (845) 679-6234; www.woodstock chamber.com.

Local Events/Attractions
Woodstock's appeal to artistic senses has attracted a thriving and eclectic artist colony to its midst, and each fall the community hosts an **Artist Studio Tour.** Various galleries welcome you year-round, and art classes are offered. Contact the Woodstock Chamber of Commerce and Arts (see above).

Accommodations
North–South Lake (DEC) Campground, east of Tannersville via Highway 23A and County Road 18, is open early May through late October and has 219 sites. DEC office: (518) 457-2500; campground phone: (518) 589-5058.

Organizations
New York–New Jersey Trail Conference helps maintain, mark, and map trails. NY–NJ Trail Conference, 600 Ramapo Valley Rd., Mahwah, NJ 07430; (201) 512-9348; info@nynjtc.org; www.nynjtc.org.

39 Slide Mountain Loop

Southwest of Woodstock, this hike strings together the yellow Phoenicia–East Branch Trail, the red Wittenberg-Cornell-Slide Trail, and the blue Curtis-Ormsbee Trail for a rolling exploration at the western extent of the Burroughs Range. Traversing hemlock-deciduous woodland and lofty conifer-birch forest, this popular trail tops the highest point in the Catskills and visits the Burroughs Plaque and Curtis-Ormsbee Monument. The loop dishes up vistas and strings past rock features.

Start: At the Slide Mountain trailhead
Distance: 7.2 miles out-and-back, with a midway loop
Approximate hiking time: 4 to 5 hours
Difficulty: Moderate (but with some difficult rocky and wet stretches)
Elevation change: The elevation change is about 1,800 feet, with the summit high point at 4,180 feet.
Trail surface: Earthen or rocky path and woods road
Seasons: Best for hiking spring through fall
Other trail users: Hunters, snowshoers
Canine compatibility: Dogs permitted but must be controlled at owner's side by leash or voice command
Land status: New York State Department of Environmental Conservation (DEC)
Nearest town: Pine Hill
Fees and permits: None
Schedule: No time restrictions

Maps: www.dec.ny.gov/docs/lands_forests _pdf/recmapsmwa.pdf; New York–New Jersey Trail Conference Trail Map 43, Southern Catskill Trails, for purchase at www.nynjtc.org
Trail contact: New York State DEC, Region 3, 21 South Putt Corners Rd., New Paltz; (845) 256-3083; www.dec.ny.gov
Special considerations: The sensitive nature of this popular peak requires respect. Because the site cannot sustain heavy foot traffic, do not make this an annual trek, and keep your hiking party small. Avoid travel during and immediately following a rainstorm. If trails are wet, you should avoid the Curtis-Ormsbee Trail and keep to the red Wittenberg-Cornell-Slide Trail, a carriage road that can better handle foot traffic. Plan a day hike versus an overnight stay. But if you do choose to camp, remember to protect this area's sensitive fir complex. There is no camping and there are no fires allowed above the 3,500-foot elevation.

Finding the trailhead: From the junction of NY 214 and NY 28 in Phoenicia, go west on NY 28 for 7.9 miles, reaching Big Indian. There turn south on NY 47, go 9 miles, and turn left to enter the off-road parking area for the Slide Mountain trailhead. GPS: 42.008856, -74.427463

The Hike

Rock-hop across the brook-sized West Branch Neversink River and follow the yellow markers for a rocky ascent. An open forest of maple, birch, and beech clads the slope. Where the trail reaches a woods road, follow it right for contouring travel. Past a pipe providing water (treat trail sources), reach the initial loop junction. Turn left on the red trail, a rocky woods road—be careful not to turn an ankle.

Essayist John Burroughs, honored by this plaque, made Slide Mountain famous.

Leafy branches lace over the ascending trail, offering a fragile shade, while seasonal runoffs race across the route. The trail narrows and steepens, soon pulling above the 3,500-foot elevation. Fir, birch, and snags compose the skyline. Where the trail next contours the slope, tightly spaced firs squeeze the passage. Winds assail the ridge, and weather-watchers can delight in the rapid cloud changes. At the second loop junction, proceed on the red trail to Slide Mountain. The blue Curtis-Ormsbee Trail to the right puts the loop on the hike's return.

On the way to Slide Mountain, climb steadily along the north edge of the ridge, remaining in tightly clustered firs. Canada mayflower, clintonia, and moss touch green to the forest floor. A ledge to the left offers a view toward Giant Ledge–Panther Mountain. Just ahead, the trail tops Slide Mountain.

Beyond the summit, reach a vista ledge with the John Burroughs plaque just below it. This early-day environmental essayist introduced Slide Mountain to the world. He camped where the plaque now rests. Ledge views span the spire-topped firs to an all-star lineup of Catskill peaks, including Wittenberg, Plateau, Twin, Indian Head, and Overlook Mountains. Cornell and Friday Mountains frame a view of Ashokan Reservoir. As you continue along Slide Mountain, you will come to another viewpoint located at the so-called Ladders, a steep descent off the mountain via braced steps. The top of the ladder offers a view of the Woodland Valley bowl.

LIVING IN SYMPATHY WITH NATURE

John Burroughs (1837-1921), the Roxbury, New York-born environmentalist and writer, introduced Slide Mountain to the world through his nature essays. He grew up in the Catskills and, in the reflective veins of Emerson, Thoreau, and Whitman, wrote more than thirty books. According to biographer Edward J. Renehan Jr., Burroughs "urged simple living in sympathy with nature." Today the dramatic range arcing from Slide Mountain to Wittenberg Mountain wears the Burroughs name. On his celebrated trek to Slide Mountain, he traveled cross-country from Woodland Valley, coming out just north of the summit. On reaching the mountain, he ascended the 1820s rock slide that gave the peak its name. Forest has since reclaimed the scar. On his sojourns he slept beneath the overhang next to which the Burroughs memorial plaque now hangs. During his lifetime he traveled with the likes of Theodore Roosevelt and John Muir.

Turn around at the Ladders viewpoint and backtrack to the blue Curtis-Ormsbee foot trail to add the midway loop, which leads into a fir forest laced with birch and hobblebush. The April 2007 ice and snow event snapped the tops off most of the balsam fir and spruce trees, leaving behind an unusual forest skyline that has mostly recovered. Before long, steep downhill spurts replace the mild descent, and the forest becomes shrubby with a meadow floor. Where stones aid crossing at marshy sites, the soft ground often records the tracks of deer.

At Paul's Lookout, taking a few strides off trail brings you to a ledge for a Table Mountain vista. The trail resumes with a couple more plunges, and views span the East Branch Neversink River. You may have to use your hands on the sharp descents that follow. Shortly after you see a rock island pulled away from the slope, descend to skirt the massive rock. At its base, you can view the road-sized gap at the split and see where cross-beds have eroded clean through.

The trail now flattens for a comfortable shady-woods stroll to the next junction, site of the 3-foot-tall marble tribute to trail builders William Curtis and Allen Ormsbee, who designed the scenic trail you have just traveled. You now turn right on woods road, following yellow blazes back to the trailhead. While less rocky than the previous woods roads, springs can muddy boots.

After passing a small woods road on the left, cross a log bridge over the seasonally babbling headwater of the West Branch Neversink. Rocks can prove invaluable for hopscotch travel ahead on the soggy road. Close the loop, turn left, and then take the rocky descent to the trailhead.

Slide Mountain Loop

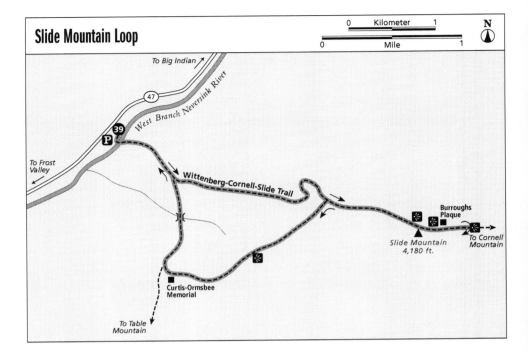

Miles and Directions

0.0   Start from the Slide Mountain trailhead. Cross the brook-sized river on stones, or wade.

0.4   Reach a woods road and follow it right. ***Note:*** Take a moment to note the junction here for your return trek.

0.7   Reach the initial loop junction. Turn left on the rocky woods road of the red trail.

2.0   Reach the second loop junction. Remain on the red trail to Slide Mountain. ***Note:*** The blue trail on the right adds the return's loop.

2.5   A ledge to your left offers a northern view.

2.7   Top Slide Mountain, and just beyond it, find the ledge view with the Burroughs plaque below it. Resume your hike east.

2.9   Reach the Ladders and a final view. Backtrack to the 2-mile junction.

3.8   At the 2-mile junction, follow the blue trail left, adding the loop.

4.6   Reach Paul's Lookout for a view out to Table Mountain.

5.5   Reach the junction at the trail-builder monument. Turn right on the woods road, following yellow blazes.

6.2   Pass a small woods road to your left and then cross a log bridge over the babbling headwater of the West Branch Neversink River.

6.5   Close the loop at the 0.7-mile junction. Turn left on the woods road.

6.8   Descend left on footpath, backtracking to the trailhead.

7.2   End at the trailhead.

Hike Information

Local Information

Visit the **Catskills,** visitcatskills.com

Local Events/Attractions

The **Delaware and Ulster Railroad,** on NY 28 in Arkville, serves up yesteryear relaxation and nostalgia aboard its historic excursion train. It travels through pastoral and Catskill Mountain settings, traveling along the East Branch of the Delaware between Arkville and Roxbury. Trains run weekends late May through October, with additional runs on Thursday and Friday in July and August. Delaware and Ulster Railroad, 43510 State Highway 28, Arkville; (845) 586-3877; https://durr.org.

Accommodations

Woodland Valley (DEC) Campground, south of Woodland (reached south off NY 28 west of Phoenicia), is open mid-May through Indigenous Peoples' Day in October and has sixty-five campsites. Reservations: (800) 456-2267; www.reserve america.com.

Organizations

New York–New Jersey Trail Conference helps maintain, mark, and map trails. NY–NJ Trail Conference, 600 Ramapo Valley Rd., Mahwah, NJ 07430; (201) 512-9348; info@nynjtc.org; www.nynjtc.org.

40 Minnewaska State Park Preserve

A former resort and a onetime battleground between developers and environmentalists, this state park preserve unfurls a welcoming and tranquil natural realm. The site boasts white-cliff escarpments, indigo waters, and soothing forests—images to delight poet and photographer alike. Comfortable carriageways and foot trails travel the preserve. The selected carriageway circuit travels from Lake Minnewaska, around Lake Awosting, and across a Shawangunk escarpment rim for a visually rich experience.

Start: At the picnic area trailhead
Distance: 11.8-mile out-and-back lasso-shaped hike that includes spur to Rainbow Falls
Approximate hiking time: 6.5 to 8 hours
Difficulty: Moderate due to distance
Elevation change: The trail has about a 500-foot elevation change.
Trail surface: Slate or earthen carriageways and foot trails
Seasons: Best for hiking spring through fall
Other trail users: Cyclists, horse riders (permit required), cross-country skiers
Canine compatibility: Leashed dogs permitted (Dogs, however, are not allowed in buildings, on walkways, or in picnic or bathing areas.)
Land status: New York State Preserve
Nearest town: New Paltz

Fees and permits: Fee site
Schedule: 9 a.m. to dusk
Map: https://parks.ny.gov/documents/inside-our-agency/MasterPlans/MinnewaskaStatePark/MinnewaskaStateParkFinalTrailsPlan.pdf; New York–New Jersey Trail Conference Trail Map 104, Shawangunk Trails–South: for purchase at www.nynjtc.org
Trail contact: Minnewaska State Park Preserve, 5281 Route 44-55, Kerhonkson; (845) 255-0752; https://parks.ny.gov/parks/minnewaska
Special considerations: Deer hunting (season runs Oct into Dec) is allowed in sections of the park, but it is generally away from the carriageways. Be cautious along the cliffs and know that rattlesnakes and copperheads find habitat in the park.

Finding the trailhead: From New York State Thruway I-87, take exit 18 for New Paltz and go west on NY 299 for 7.2 miles. At the junction with US 44/NY 55, go west on US 44/NY 55 for 4.4 miles and turn left for the park. The trail starts from the picnic area at the end of the park road. GPS: 41.728699, -74.237443

The Hike

Descend following the red trail to the Minnewaska lakeshore. At the northwest corner of the lake (opposite the swimming area), take the green Upper Awosting Carriageway west. The fine-grade slate offers a smooth walking surface. Hemlock, maple, oak, beautiful white birch, and mountain laurel compose the woods. The mild uphill grade is more apparent to the eye than the body. The carefree stroll allows eyes and thoughts to roam. A deer crossing your path may shake you from your reverie.

At an old orchard, the snarled trees still flower in spring, and rusted pieces of farm equipment blend into the meadow. Side brooks sheet over the outcrops, draining to

Kempton Ledge extends overlooks of Minnewaska State Park Preserve.

Peters Kill below, and color-coded foot trails branch away. Pass beneath a power line, traveling among scenic rock ledges with vegetated shelves. The aqua-blazed Long Path emerges from a break in Litchfield Ledge and crosses the carriageway.

Detour right on the Long Path to visit Rainbow Falls. Descend through deep woods of mature hemlock and beech, crossing a side drainage and then Huntington Ravine. Rainbow Falls plunges into a side stream. The waterfall's rivulets pour from an overhang, embellishing a color-streaked cliff and a growing streamer of algae.

Continuing west on the Upper Awosting Carriageway, the terrain gradually flattens. At the junction approaching Lake Awosting, turn right onto a black-blazed earthen carriageway for a counterclockwise tour of the lake. The dam presents an open lake view. Pinched at its middle, this huge lake shows scalloped coves, evergreen and deciduous shores, and slopes and ledges of white quartzite. Sweet pepperbush, azalea, and mountain and sheep laurel braid a showy understory.

You pass a ranger's cabin, staying above shore for overlooks and cross-lake views, but no lake access. At an open flat, an old foundation, broken bricks, and glass hint at a bygone time. At junctions, keep to the black carriageway. Closer to shore, pass monstrous hemlocks, scenic pines, and lakeside outcrops; side paths visit small peninsulas. Past the foot trail to Spruce Glen and Murray Hill, the swimming area opens out, its lakeward white outcrop bumpy with quartz.

Stay on the black carriageway, drifting into woods before reaching one final lakeside spur for farewell lake viewing. At the upcoming junction, head right for the Hamilton and Castle Point Carriageways. The trail alternately tours mixed woods and stands of small, bizarrely shaped pines. Glimpses of the white-gray cliff of Castle Point precede the next junction. Here, go left on the shale-surfaced Castle Point Carriageway, following blue markers.

Pass beneath jutting overhangs and ledges for views toward Battlement Terrace. Ahead, top Castle Point Terrace, reaching Castle Point for a spectacular 180-degree vista sweeping west and south to Hamilton Point, Gertrude's Nose, Lake Awosting, the wooded rims and swells of the park, and the distant Hudson Valley. On descent, perspectives shift east, adding views of Sky Tower in the nearby Mohonks.

Pass under a power line. From Kempton Ledge, overlook Palmaghatt Kill, the Hudson Valley, and an isolated outcrop of fluted cliffs. Pale-green lichens blotch the smooth white stone, and deep fissures invade the terrace. Stick with the descending blue carriageway. When you reach Lakeshore Drive (the red carriageway rounding Lake Minnewaska), turn left to close the loop at the swimming area and return uphill to the picnic area.

Half the size of Lake Awosting, stunning blue-green Lake Minnewaska reflects a partial shoreline of abrupt white cliffs with talus skirts. Atop the terrace sits the attractive stone park office building. Hemlocks and pines interweave the leafy trees of shore. Autumn's paintbrush amplifies the beauty of this closing image.

Miles and Directions

0.0   Start from the picnic area trailhead and descend via the red trail.

0.1   Reach Lake Minnewaska. From the lake's northwest corner, hike west on the green Upper Awosting Carriageway.

2.6   Meet the aqua-blazed Long Path. Detour right on the Long Path to Rainbow Falls.

2.9   Reach Rainbow Falls, then return to the carriageway tour.

3.2   Continue right (west) on Upper Awosting Carriageway.

3.7   Reach the Lake Awosting junction. Turn right, following a black-blazed earthen carriageway for counterclockwise lake travel.

4.1   Pass a ranger's cabin.

6.4   The carriageway drifts into woods.

6.7   A spur leads to a ledge overlook of Lake Awosting. Follow the carriageway as it turns away from the lake for good.

6.8   Reach a junction. Go right for Hamilton and Castle Point Carriageways.

7.5   Reach a junction. Go left on the shale-surfaced Castle Point Carriageway, following blue markers.

8.2   Reach Castle Point.

10.5   Reach Kempton Ledge. Follow the blue carriageway downhill, avoiding a spur turning right to Hamilton Carriageway.

11.4   Reach red-blazed Lakeshore Drive (the Lake Minnewaska Carriageway) and turn left on it.

11.7   Close the loop and ascend to the picnic area.

11.8   End at the picnic area trailhead.

Minnewaska State Park Preserve

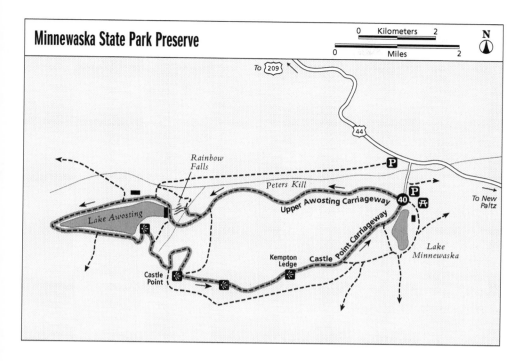

Hike Information

Local Information

New Paltz Regional Chamber of Commerce, 257 Main St., New Paltz; (845) 255-0243; www.nyconnects.ny.gov/providersnew-paltz-regional-chamber-of -commerce-sofa-ag-410990

Local Events/Attractions

Flowing past the town of New Paltz, the **Wallkill River** is popular for canoeing and kayaking. The 12.2-mile cinder- or gravel-surfaced Wallkill Valley Rail Trail travels parallel to but away from the river, offering hiking and mountain-biking opportunities. The rail trail reveals river views in town and again where it crosses the Wallkill. If you need still greater adventure, rock climbing and ice climbing in the Shawangunks are world-renowned, with popular routes in Mohonk Preserve west of New Paltz. Climbing guides and clinics operate in the New Paltz area. Contact the New Paltz Regional Chamber of Commerce.

Organizations

New York–New Jersey Trail Conference helps maintain 30 miles of hiking trail in the park. NY–NJ Trail Conference, 600 Ramapo Valley Rd., Mahwah, NJ 07430; (201) 512-9348; info@nynjtc.org; www.nynjtc.org.

41 Bashakill Wildlife Management Area

At this 2,200-acre wildlife management and bird conservation area—more than half of it freshwater wetland—a former railroad grade rolls out an avenue to relaxation and nature discovery. Part of the greater Long Path, this rail-to-trail travels at the eastern edge of Bashakill Marsh, which is the largest freshwater marsh in southeastern New York. A premier bird-watching site, birders delight in spring-nesting warblers and waterfowl, brooding summer birds, and fall migrants. Both daylight and evening watches are possible. Six trailheads access the rail trail, readily allowing hopscotch or car-shuttle travel.

Start: At the southern trailhead
Distance: 13.0 miles out-and-back, including side trails
Approximate hiking time: 6.5 to 8.5 hours
Difficulty: Easy
Elevation change: The trail is virtually flat.
Trail surface: Earthen or grassy railroad grade or path
Seasons: Best for hiking spring through fall
Other trail users: Birders, hunters, mountain bikers, snowshoers, cross-country skiers
Canine compatibility: Dogs permitted but must be controlled at owner's side by leash or voice command
Land status: New York State Department of Environmental Conservation (DEC)

Nearest town: Wurtsboro
Fees and permits: None
Schedule: Year-round, 24 hours (In winter, snow and unplowed lots can limit access.)
Map: www.dec.ny.gov/docs/wildlife_pdf/bashakillwma.pdf
Trail contact: New York State DEC, Region 3, 21 South Putt Corners Rd., New Paltz; (845) 256-3060; www.dec.ny.gov
Special considerations: You will find no amenities other than parking; bring water. Expect some soggy stretches, and avoid this trail during hunting season. Although the WMA prohibits camping and campfires, night fishing, owl watching, and stargazing are acceptable nighttime activities here.

Finding the trailhead: From NY 17/I-86, take exit 113 and go south on US 209 for 5.2 miles, turning left onto NY 163/NY 61 for Otisville. Go 0.4 mile and turn left to round the WMA's east shore on South Road. In 0.1 mile find a fishing access; in 0.2 mile find the southern trailhead for the WMA's rail trail. GPS: 41.502474, -74.549015. You'll find the trail's northern terminus at the southeast outskirts of Wurtsboro.

The Hike

Northbound, follow the rail trail at the edge of the marsh. Woody vines sag between the trees, shaping a thin border between the trail and the wetland flat. Soggy reaches can claim both sides of the levee. Crossbeams and footbridges ease drainage crossings. In some places the old rail ties ripple the trail bed or lie discarded to its side. Duckweed, lily pads, clumps of arrowhead, algae, and flooded stumps and snags vary viewing.

Columbine, wild geranium, and violet sprinkle color trailside. Open sites offer fine marsh vantages and fishing access. Baltimore oriole, common yellowthroat,

The vast freshwater marsh of Bashakill WMA attracts birds and birders.

marsh wren, scarlet tanager, eastern bluebird, green heron, ruffed grouse, Virginia rail, American bittern, sora, osprey, and a wide variety of waterfowl can quickly add sightings to a birder's list. Woodchuck, muskrat, beaver, and white-tailed deer are among the possible mammal sightings.

At the junction near the second trailhead parking lot, veer left off the railroad grade to follow a nature trail before continuing forward. The nature trail takes you closer to the wetland as it swings a loop, with short, dead-end side spurs branching to fishing or viewing spots. Viewpoints take in the open water, treed islands, pickerelweed, and lily pads. Canada geese may navigate faint channels through the aquatic vegetation or disappear into the marsh upon riotous landings. White pines and oaks contrast with marsh views.

Northbound, back on the grade, travel a scenic aisle of white birch to a boardwalk. Cross this and an area of embedded ties to reach the next parking area and a boat launch. Red-winged blackbirds may fiercely distract you from their nests and sometimes bomb geese and other predators that swim past. Pickerelweed, smartweed, rushes, and sedges dominate the main marsh.

Woods travel then follows, with the occasional gnarled maple and pockets of poison ivy tucked in the deeper grass. Where you cross a bridge, skunk cabbage and false hellebore line the brook and riddle the wetland woods as the trail alternates between woods and marsh.

After crossing Haven Road, walk the gravel access road through the parking lot and round the gate to the north, returning to rail trail passage. This is the most popular WMA access and it often overflows with birders' vehicles, especially during the spring warbler season. Past a scenic multi-trunked pine, keep an eye out for a side trail ascending the steep incline on the left to a viewing tower that overlooks the meandering course of Bashakill and the wetland mosaic. Continue on the side spur as it hooks past the tower to return to the rail trail. Back on the grade, pass the next parking area.

THE DELAWARE AND HUDSON CANAL

On the west side of Bashakill Marsh, snatches of the historic Delaware and Hudson Canal (1828–1898) offer additional exploration. A blockade halting soft-coal shipments from England gave rise to this 108-mile canal linking the domestic coal fields of Pennsylvania with the Hudson River ports.

Swampy passages ahead can interrupt woods travel. Footbridges over the split flow of Bashakill mark off distance. Sounds of NY 17/I-86 precede the highway underpass, where Virginia creeper scales the tunnel's concrete walls. The rail corridor opens overhead, and alert turtles plop into the water from the banks as you pass. The hike ends opposite Walker Lane in southeast Wurtsboro; return south. The Long Path continues north.

Miles and Directions

0.0 Start from the southern trailhead and hike the rail trail north. ***Note:*** The rail trail heading south from here dead-ends in 0.2 mile.

0.5 Reach a junction. Turn left and add a clockwise tour of the nature trail loop before resuming northbound. ***Note:*** The footbridge to the right leads to a trailhead parking lot.

1.2 Return to the rail trail and turn left (north).

1.6 Reach the third parking area and a boat launch.

3.7 Cross Haven Road to the fourth trail parking area. Hike the gravel access road through the parking lot and round the gate to the north.

4.4 Head left up the bank to add the viewing tower side loop.

4.6 Turn left (north) upon returning to the rail trail.

4.7 Pass the fifth parking area. **Bailout:** This site makes a good turnaround point or spotting location for a shuttle vehicle because the rail trail ahead encounters more human intrusions.

6.0 Reach the NY 17/I-86 underpass.

6.5 Reach Walker Lane in southeast Wurtsboro (the sixth access). Backtrack south.

13.0 End at the southern trailhead.

Hike Information

Local Information

Sullivan County Visitors Association, 15 Sullivan Ave., Liberty; (845) 747-4449 or (800) 882-2287; https://sullivancatskills.com

Local Events/Attractions

The **Upper Delaware Scenic Byway** (NY 97) parallels the Delaware River from Port Jervis to Hancock, traversing an area of southern New York rich in natural beauty and history. The river has national park status, designated the Upper Delaware

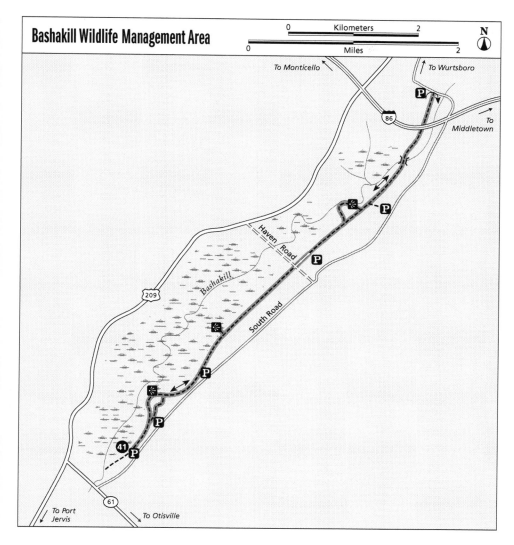

Scenic and Recreational River. Cross-river views find Pennsylvania. Superintendent, 274 River Rd., Beach Lake, PA 18405; (570) 685-4871; River Hotline Information: (845) 252-7100; www.nps.gov/upde.

Organizations

The **Basha Kill Area Association** leads hikes, conducts birding field trips, and performs cleanups and other projects at Bashakill WMA and publishes and markets a field guide to the wetlands. The Basha Kill Area Association, PO Box 1121, Wurtsboro, NY 12790; info@thebashakill.org; https://thebashakill.org.

Honorable Mentions

⋃ Little Pond Loop

This moderately difficult hike travels 5.3 miles, exploring the gentle western relief of the Catskill Mountains and swinging between Little Pond and Touchmenot Mountain, with a spur to Cabot Mountain. Travel mixed forest, conifer plantation, beaver-modified waters, and meadow habitats. Little Pond, a long lake with a small dam at its developed end, sits in between low wooded ridges and holds stocks of pan-sized fish. Because this site bustles in summer, you will likely find the pond area more enjoyable before or after the summer vacation season.

Big trees always cause a double-take.

On Cabot Mountain expect to use your hands when climbing among the ledges and overhangs. Below the summit the open ledge of Beaver Kill Vista offers a leaf-edited view of Touchmenot Mountain, the Catskill ridges beyond Beaver Kill, and the glare of Little Pond. Columbine dresses the rock in spring, drawing hummingbirds to your feet. The summit is wooded but pretty with a lush fern floor.

From NY 30 on the south shore of Pepacton Reservoir, 13.5 miles equidistant from Margaretville and Downsville, turn southeast onto Beech Hill Road; go 6.3 miles and turn left onto Beaver Kill Road (NY 54). In 2 miles turn left on Barkaboom Road, continue for 0.2 mile, and turn left on Little Pond Road. The Little Pond Campground entrance station is in 0.8 mile. The loop starts near the bathhouse and shower facility above the pond. This is a fee area. GPS: 42.037684, -74.743597. Contact New York State Department of Environmental Conservation, Region 4, Stamford Office, 65561 Highway 10, Suite 1, Stamford; (518) 357-2450; www.dec.ny.gov.

⋁ Mohonk Mountain House–Mohonk Preserve

In the northern Shawangunks, west of New Paltz, these adjoining private properties introduce the Mohonk area splendor—inspiring cliffs, grand views, and fragile habitats. Mohonk Mountain House, a National Historic Landmark and commercial resort, has served outdoor recreationists since 1869. Although access to the castle-like house (hotel) is restricted to paying guests, its regal exterior complements the trail-webbed Lake Mohonk setting. Linked by an extensive trail network, Mohonk Preserve extends the realm of hiker possibility with its attractive woods and rock features. It is the largest visitor/membership-supported nature preserve in New York State. The parking and per-person entry fees are steep, but payment for a day's hiking at one site buys same-day hiking privileges at the other, giving you three trails from which to choose.

Carriageways roll out idyllic strolls through Mohonk Preserve.

The 1-mile out-and-back Sky Top Hike (closed in winter) starts at the Mountain House and ascends from a mystical lake, crossing ledges to Hayes Lookout and the Albert K. Smiley Memorial Tower. Views include Lake Mohonk, the Mountain House, the Hudson Valley, and Catskill ridges and peaks.

The 4.2-mile out-and-back Bonticou Crag Hike ascends through the preserve's mixed forest. It passes a clearing dubbed "the million-dollar view," skirts historic farm structures, and travels shared-use carriageways and the Northeast Trail, to top out at the white rock crag. Mountain laurel, low-stature trees, azalea bushes, and humped outcrops lead you to the summit, where you can view wooded Guyot Hill, the Wallkill and Hudson River valleys, and the Catskills.

The Trapps Loop travels 5.25 miles on the preserve's Overcliff and Undercliff Carriageways, leading you to woods with old-growth trees, mountain laurel and rhododendron blooms, cliffs, and breakaway boulders. Along Undercliff Carriageway, climbers scale the 200-foot white quartzite cliffs.

From New York State Thruway I-87, take exit 18 and go west on NY 299, passing through New Paltz and crossing over the Wallkill River bridge. Take the first right onto Springtown Road; bear left at the fork in 0.5 mile to Mountain Rest Road. Follow it 3.4 miles to enter the Mohonk Mountain House gateway. (Hike the Huguenot Trail to access the hike to Sky Top.) GPS: 41.769426, -74.157119

For the Bonticou Crag Hike, remain on Mountain Rest Road, proceeding another 0.9 mile. Turn right onto Upper Knoll Road and drive 0.2 mile to the preserve's Spring Farm trailhead. GPS: 41.779622, -74.125308

For Mohonk Preserve Trapps Gateway Visitor Center and the Trapps Loop, from I-87's exit 18, go 7.2 miles west on NY 299, reaching the junction with US 44/NY 55. Go west on US 44/NY 55 for 0.4 mile to reach the center and its parking on the right. The Trapps Loop can be accessed either from the center or from the West Trapps Entry trailhead. Find its parking on the right 1.3 miles west of the center off US 44/NY 55. GPS: 41.736756, -74.198719

Contact Mohonk Mountain House, 1000 Mountain Rest Rd., New Paltz; (855) 883-3798; www.mohonk.com; and Mohonk Preserve, PO Box 715, New Paltz, NY 12561; (845) 255-0919; www.mohonkpreserve.org.

Hudson River Valley

This New York region celebrates the Hudson River—a vital transportation and recreation corridor, past and present. In 1609, while sailing for the Dutch East India trading company, Henry Hudson entered the New York harbor and sailed the *Half Moon* up what is now known as the Hudson River, covering about 150 miles before realizing this river was not the anticipated passage to China. His exploration revealed the promise of this region for the Dutch, the first Europeans to probe this land, so it wasn't long before the Hudson River began to play a key role in the development of the local colonies, carrying settlers and their goods up the river to form communities to the north. With the growth of New York City as the continent's most productive eastern port, the Hudson River became an important conduit to westward expansion. The Revolutionary War, the Erie Canal, and the Hudson River School of artists all have stories tied to this region.

Since the beginning of European colonization, the river has been the center of a battle to preserve the purity of its waters, the beauty of its low mountains, and the fertility of its verdant hillsides, engaging in many cycles of conflict with the lumber industry, polluting corporations, and commuters seeking refuge from New York City's congestion. Thanks to the foresight of a handful of wealthy families—the Roosevelts, Vanderbilts, and Rockefellers among them—large swaths of mountains, forest, and valley became permanent parks, preserves, and wildlife refuges. The Hudson River flowed at the center of a groundbreaking effort to reclaim it from manufacturers who dumped chemicals and sewage into it, and the movement to save it in the 1960s spurred the creation of the US Environmental Protection Agency (EPA). Today the National Park Service acknowledges the critical role the valley has played in American history by naming it the Hudson River Valley National Heritage Area. In addition, the river is one of only fourteen federally recognized Great American Rivers. The Hudson River Maritime Museum in Kingston documents much of the river's history as a major route for commercial trade.

At its northeastern end, the attractive Taconic skyline separates New York from Massachusetts and Connecticut. In the southern river valley, East and West Hudson Highlands face off across the broad river, striking land forms that rise from sea level to 1,600 feet and extend for 15 miles along the riverbanks. The Palisades, home to the acclaimed Bear Mountain/Harriman State Park complex, adds to the wild bounty, and the Appalachian Trail (AT) spends much of its 95-mile New York sojourn in the land of the Hudson. The AT crosses the Hudson River at Bear Mountain Bridge.

The South Taconic Trail shares its trailhead with this Massachusetts falls, Bash Bish.

42 Taconic State Park

In the southern Taconic Mountain Range, abutting 11 miles of the Massachusetts and Connecticut border, this New York state park blurs state lines. Bash Bish Falls, which annually brings 100,000 visitors to Taconic State Park, actually lies in Massachusetts but is most easily reached by this park's trail. The park's skyline South Taconic Trail meanders in and out of New York and Massachusetts with an equal disregard for borders. The southbound trek to Brace Mountain, featured here, offers tristate views. The park's waterfall trail can put a refreshing exclamation mark on the featured hike, while a mountain trek north can extend exploration.

Start: At the Bash Bish trailhead
Distance: 16.2 miles out-and-back to Brace Mountain
Approximate hiking time: 9 to 11 hours
Difficulty: Strenuous
Elevation change: Southbound, the South Taconic Trail starts at an elevation of 800 feet, tops Alander Mountain at 2,250 feet, and then rolls between 1,500 and 2,300 feet, tagging Brace Mountain at 2,311 feet.
Trail surface: Earthen foot trail and woods road
Seasons: Open year-round, best for hiking spring through fall
Other trail users: Hunters, snowmobilers
Canine compatibility: Leashed dogs permitted (Be sure to clean up after your dog on the waterfall trail.)
Land status: All state lands: New York State Park and Massachusetts state land
Nearest town: Copake Falls
Fees and permits: Entrance fee
Schedule: Sunrise to sunset in New York

Maps: Northern section: https://parks.ny.gov/documents/parks/TaconicCopakeFallsAreaTrailMapNorth.pdf; southern section: https://parks.ny.gov/documents/parks/TaconicCopakeFallsAreaTrailMapSouth.pdf
Trail contact: Taconic State Park, 59 Rudd Pond Rd., Millerton; (518) 789-3059; https://parks.ny.gov/parks/taconiccopake
Special considerations: Although this New York state park prohibits trailside camping within reach of the South Taconic Trail, Massachusetts has a first-come, first-served cabin and 15 backcountry campsites (contact Mount Washington State Forest, 545 East St., Mount Washington, MA 01258; (413) 528-0330; www.mass.gov/locations/mount-washington-state-forest). It is best to avoid the trails during deer-hunting season (Nov–Dec) in both New York and Massachusetts. But if you do hike, wear blaze-orange clothing. Bear and bobcat sightings have been reported, so store food safely and be watchful of your children and pets.

Finding the trailhead: From Copake Falls go 0.7 mile east on NY 344 to reach the park's Bash Bish trailhead on the right. GPS: 42.117095, -73.507811

The Hike

For the featured hike on the South Taconic Trail, follow the signature white markings south along the limited-access road that angles downhill to the cabins, west of the Bash Bish trailhead. Cross the bridge and hike past the cabins before entering

The cairn on Mt. Brace summit signals a fine stopping point on the South Taconic Trail.

the wilds on a foot trail. A contouring ascent through mountain laurel, a sharp climb through a stand of 1- to 3-foot-diameter hemlocks, and passages in high-canopy maple forest and pine-oak woods carry you to the ridge and a junction.

A short detour here on a blue-marked spur leads to a vantage that reveals a 180-degree western perspective, with Washburn Mountain prominent. The white-marked South Taconic Trail continues its southbound ascent in oak woodland and later a hemlock grove, soon bypassing a second blue trail and generally hugging the ridge. Pines appear now and again, and views flip to the east.

Before reaching an old lookout site on Alander Ridge, you may come to a painted blue marker on a flat, exposed outcrop. Depending on when the trail was last blazed, it may be faint, so keep an alert eye. For the South Taconic Trail alone, continue straight ahead, staying with the white blazes. Should you opt instead for an Alander Mountain detour, descend left on the blue trail, coming to a saddle where a rustic cabin sits. The cabin offers a dry overnight wayside on a first-come, first-served basis. Early summer azalea and laurel fancy it up. From the cabin area, the blue trail descending past the structure is the one that leads through Massachusetts's Mount Washington State Forest to the designated backpacker campsites, a considerable hike. The blue-marked route climbing eastward tags the Alander summit in about 0.25 mile for a view.

Before long on the South Taconic Trail, you'll come upon a fine 270-degree view of Massachusetts's Alander Mountain and Mount Frissell, Connecticut's Round Mountain, and New York's Brace Mountain and the westward valley and foothills. An outcrop of wavy-patterned schist provides the viewpoint. The trail, shaded by mixed oaks, maple, and beech, now drops away, sometimes steeply. Where it comes out at a former woods road, follow the woods road left. As you ascend from a drainage dip, pass an overgrown blue trail on the left.

A few white pines tower trailside near the junction with the red Robert Brook Trail. Fragments of rock wall or waist-high ostrich ferns lend decoration to the South Taconic Trail. Where the mountain laurel bushes close ranks, a splendid floral aisle escorts you skyward in early summer.

Look for a foot trail to veer right. It leads you across a ridge outcrop to a western viewpoint before returning once more to the woods road. Hike past the path to the Ashley Hill Trail. After the grade has eased, a red trail descends left toward Mount Frissell and **Tristate Point.** The South Taconic Trail continues on an old woods road toward Brace Mountain.

Where the road trail forks, go right. A shrubby, open complex contains this moderate-grade route. Take the foot trail heading left to top Brace Mountain at an impressive 5-foot-tall cairn. Views sweep the tri-state area. Return now as you came, or continue south to Whitehouse Crossing.

Miles and Directions

0.0   Start west of the Bash Bish trailhead, and descend the limited-access road that angles downhill to the cabins.

1.1   Reach a ridge junction. Follow the 0.1-mile blue spur to a vantage point before continuing on the white-blazed ascent.

3.0   Reach a notch.

3.5   Reach the junction on the Alander Mountain ridge near the former lookout site; continue south. **Option:** For an Alander Mountain detour, descend left on the blue trail, coming to a saddle and a cabin. The blue fork descending past the cabin traverses Massachusetts's Mount Washington State Forest, eventually reaching backpacker campsites. The blue fork ascending east tags Alander summit in 0.3 mile for views.

5.2   Pass the red-blazed Robert Brook Trail.

6.7   Follow the foot trail that veers right for a crescent spur to a western vantage, returning to the woods road.

6.8   Hike past the Ashley Hill Trail (blue).

7.6   Pass the Mount Frissell Trail (the red trail descending left). Option: You can detour along this trail, finding first **Tristate Point** (just a simple border cairn, which happens to be the highest point in Connecticut) and then the oak-crowned summit of Massachusetts's Mount Frissell, but no views.

7.8   At the road fork, go right, continuing on the South Taconic Trail.

8.2   Spur left, topping Brace Mountain. Backtrack on the South Taconic Trail to the trailhead. **Option:** You can continue hiking south on the South Taconic Trail to Whitehouse Crossing.

16.2   End west of the Bash Bish trailhead.

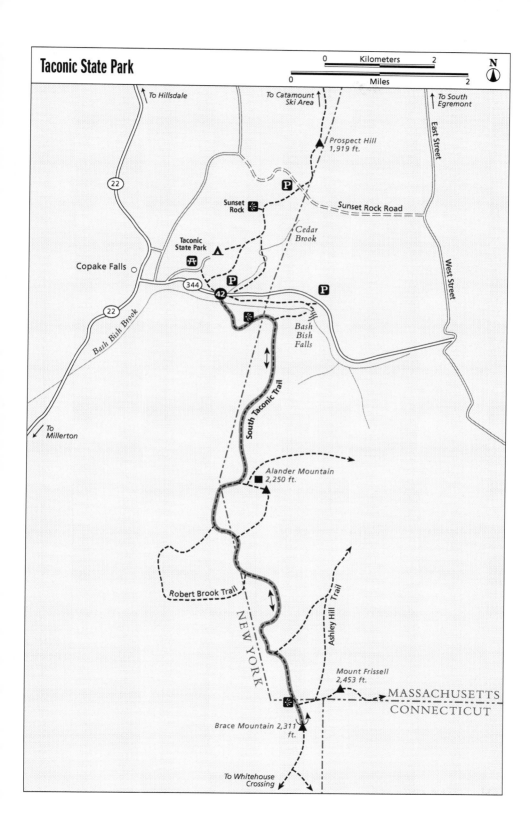

Taconic State Park

0 ——— Kilometers ——— 2
0 ——— Miles ——— 2

N

To Hillsdale

To Catamount
Ski Area

To South
Egremont

▲ Prospect Hill
1,919 ft.

East Street

(22)

🅿

Sunset
Rock 🔾

Sunset Rock Road

*Cedar
Brook*

Taconic
State Park   ▲

🅿

🅿

West Street

Copake Falls ○

(344)

42

🔾

*Bash
Bish
Falls*

(22)

Bash Bish Brook

South Taconic Trail

To
Millerton

■ Alander Mountain
2,250 ft.
▲

Robert Brook Trail

Ashley Hill Trail

NEW YORK

Mount Frissell
2,453 ft.
▲

MASSACHUSETTS
CONNECTICUT

🔾

Brace Mountain 2,311
ft. ▲

To Whitehouse
Crossing

LIGHTNING

Thunderstorms build over the mountains almost every day during the summer. Lightning is generated by thunderheads and can strike without warning, even several miles away from the nearest overhead cloud. The best rule of thumb is to start leaving exposed peaks, ridges, and canyon rims by about noon. This time can vary a little depending on storm buildup. Keep an eye on cloud formation, and don't underestimate how fast a storm can build. The bigger they get, the more likely a thunderstorm will happen.

Lightning takes the path of least resistance, so if you're the high point, it might choose you. Ducking under a rock overhang is dangerous, as you form the shortest path between the rock and ground. If you dash below tree line, avoid standing under the only or the tallest tree. If you are caught above tree line, stay away from anything metal you might be carrying. Move down off the ridge to a low, treeless point and squat until the storm passes. If you have an insulating pad, squat on it. Avoid having both your hands and feet touching the ground at once, and never lay flat. If you hear a buzzing sound or feel your hair standing on end, move quickly, as an electrical charge is building up.

Options

For the 1.5-mile out-and-back hike to **Bash Bish Falls,** follow the closed service road east upstream from the falls trailhead. This overlooks Bash Bish Brook, a sparkling stream coursing over bedrock. Although the deep pools look inviting, swimming is not allowed (though you are likely to see people in the water at the base of the falls). Hemlock and maple lace over the trail. Stairs then descend to the boot-polished schist outcrop that provides unobstructed falls viewing. Bash Bish Falls spills in an energetic rush around a skyward-pointing rock wedge. The right half shows a tiered veil broadening at the base; the left, a showery drop ending in a water slide. An emerald plunge pool cupped in a crescent cliff captures the water.

The **South Taconic Trail** (North) offers a moderate 7.4-mile out-and-back to Prospect Hill or a 4.2-mile shuttle. To position the shuttle vehicle, take Cemetery Road north from Copake Falls to North Mountain Road. Continue north on North Mountain Road for 1.4 miles and turn right onto unmarked Sunset Rock Road, a seasonally maintained single-lane gravel road. Drive 1.1 miles more to trail parking on the right. GPS: 42.138362, -73.490952

Northbound from the falls trailhead, angle west across NY 344, following white blazes up a wooded slope to the left of the Cedar Brook drainage. The marked route travels woods roads through changing forests. Tall pines and maples offer shade, but with each burst of ascent, the trail opens up. At 2.5 miles exit a shrub corridor to find an unmarked 0.1-mile spur leading left to Sunset Rock; the continuation of the South Taconic Trail follows the faint jeep track straight ahead. The bump of westward-facing Sunset Rock (elevation 1,788 feet) overlooks the immediate valley farmland, with the Catskills and Hudson Valley some 50 miles distant.

The South Taconic Trail ahead flattens as it follows the grassy jeep track through an arbor of oak, pine, and mountain laurel. It then dips and angles downhill across Sunset Rock Road (the shuttle parking) at 3.2 miles, setting up the final climb to Prospect Hill. Outcrops on the summit ridge extend western views of farmland, eastern views of Mounts Everett and Darby, and southern views of Bash Bish and Alander Mountains. Before a New York–Massachusetts boundary marker, turn left, topping Prospect Hill (elevation 1,919 feet) at 3.7 miles, for a better view than you found at Sunset Rock. Backtrack to the trailhead or to your shuttle vehicle.

Hike Information

Local Information

Columbia County Tourism Department, 401 State St., Hudson; (518) 828-3375; www.columbiacountytourism.org

Local Events/Attractions

Harlem Valley Rail Trail, built on the old railroad bed that connected New York City, the Harlem Valley, and Chatham, extends a paved discovery route to hikers and cyclists. You'll find accesses in Ancram, Copake, and Copake Falls/Taconic State Park. HVRT Association, (518) 789-9591; www.hvrt.org.

Accommodations

Taconic State Park Campground, open early May through October, has 115 sites (serving both tent and trailer campers) and three cabin areas. Reservations: (800) 456-2267; www.reserveamerica.com.

43 Hudson Highlands State Park Preserve: Cornish Estate/Undercliff

The lush emerald views from the top of this challenging trail make the climb over cobbles and boulders just that much more rewarding.

Start: Little Stony Point Parking area on NY 9D in Beacon, in Hudson Highlands State Park Preserve
Distance: 4.4-mile loop
Approximate hiking time: 4 hours
Difficulty: Strenuous
Elevation change: 1,100 feet
Trail surface: Dirt, lots of loose rocks, large slabs
Seasons: Open year-round, best for hiking spring through fall
Other trail users: Trail runners
Canine compatibility: Leashed dogs permitted

Land status: New York State Park Preserve
Nearest town: Cold Spring
Fees and permits: None
Schedule: Sunrise to sunset
Map: https://parks.ny.gov/documents/parks/HudsonHighlandsTrailMapNorth.pdf
Trail contacts: Hudson Highlands State Park Preserve, Route 9D, Cold Spring; (845) 225-7207; parks.ny.gov/parks/9/
Special considerations: Wear sturdy footwear with good ankle support. Consider a walking stick or ski poles to help with areas of loose cobbles and boulders.

Finding the trailhead: From New York City, take NY 9A North from West 79th Street. In 1 mile take the Saw Mill River Parkway north to NY 100/NY 9A north in Mount Pleasant. Take the NY 100 N/NY 9A N exit from the Taconic State Parkway. Continue to follow NY 9A north 34 miles to US 9 north. Take US 9 north to NY 403 in Philipstown. Take NY 403 N to NY 9D N in Cold Spring. Continue through Cold Spring to the Little Stony Point parking area on NY 9D north (on your left). **Metro North:** Cold Spring Station. **From the north,** take I-84 east to NY 9D south in Philipstown. Turn right on NY 9D south and continue to the Little Stony Point parking area on NY 9D (on your right). **Trailhead GPS:** 41.42678, -73.96603

The Hike

If you've never ventured into Hudson Highlands State Park Preserve, consider this loop trail an overview of the park and the many riches you will find here. The Cornish Estate Trail is an easy walk to the ruins of a once-majestic estate; the Undercliff Trail climbs to a combined scramble and rock-hop over a boulder-strewn trail corridor, finally rewarding you with sprawling views of the river and valley below; and the Washburn Trail features lots of cobbles that roll under your feet with each step. Bring your ski poles or walking stick and brace yourself for a demanding hiking experience—but one with the tangible rewards of satisfying panoramas once you reach the top.

Stretching about 16 miles along the east shore of the Hudson River in a series of detached land parcels, Hudson Highlands includes the Osborn Preserve, Bull Hill,

Explore the ruins of the Cornish estate before heading to the top of the Undercliff Trail. Photo by Nic Minetor

LOVE AMONG THE RUINS

We mentioned at the outset the ruins of the Cornish Estate, the mansion and grounds once known as Northgate. Back in 1917, 56-year-old Edward J. Cornish married Selina Coe Bliss Carter (who was 67), and the newlywed couple bought this 650-acre estate from diamond merchant Sigmund Stern, who had built it for himself and his family in the early 1900s. Here the Cornishes lived in comfort and created a sprawling country home with gardens, a swimming pool, a greenhouse, a barn that housed the family's prizewinning Jersey cows, and many other amenities, bringing in their friends for house parties and enjoying their decision to reject life in the city in their autumn years. Edward Cornish funded this pleasant life through his position as president of National Lead Company.

It seemed that they would share this harmony until the end of their days . . . and they did, as their lives both ended abruptly in 1938 within two weeks of each other. Edward died at his desk at age 77, and Selina passed away shortly thereafter at age 88. The mansion stood empty, the grounds went to seed, and eventually the dilapidated property met destruction by fire in 1956 (though some reports say 1958). Indeed, the ruins, while fascinating to examine, still retain an air of melancholy with the ravages of wind and weather taking their toll on the remaining brickwork. Recently discovered photos of this estate in its heyday reveal that the mansion had a Tudor-revival design with shingle-style architecture. If you're a fan of mysterious places, make a stop here as you round the bend from the Cornish to the Undercliff Trail. (Please don't climb the ruins—save your scrambling for the trail.)

Breakneck Ridge, Sugarloaf Mountain, the south summit of Mount Beacon, and Beacon Reservoir, as well as Bannerman Island and Denning Point. The park's 6,000-plus acres remain almost completely undeveloped, so while the trails are unusually well marked and easy to follow, that's just about all of the obvious human intervention you will find here. Please remain on the trails—with the increased popularity of this preserve, it's imperative that hikers keep to the trails and help this wilderness stay pristine.

What you will witness with every step, however, is the herculean efforts made by the state of New York and groups of concerned citizens to rescue and preserve this land after iron and copper mining, logging, and other industrial pursuits scraped the surrounding mountains nearly bare. Citizens formed an organization called the Hudson River Conservation Society to lead the charge against further industry, working at the grassroots level (literally, in this case) to convince landowners to donate their holdings to the New York State Department of Environmental Conservation. Even

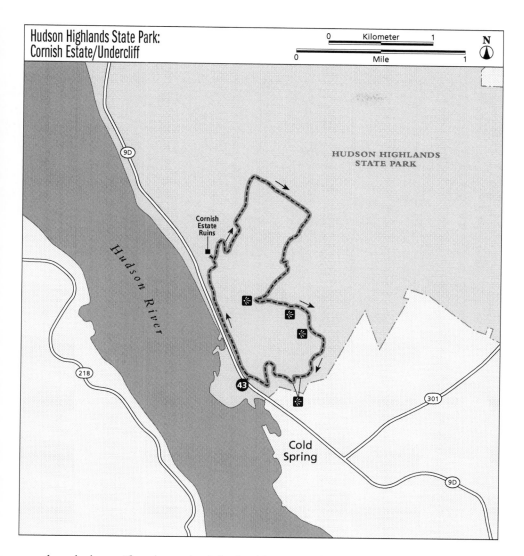

0   Kilometer   1

0   Mile   1

N

HUDSON HIGHLANDS
STATE PARK

Cornish
Estate
Ruins

Hudson River

218

43

301

9D

9D

Cold
Spring

though these efforts began back in the 1930s, it took until the 1960s before the state made significant headway in turning land into parks. When Consolidated Edison proposed a hydroelectric power plant that would dominate Storm King Mountain, the state drew the proverbial line in the sand and redoubled its preservation efforts.

Major headway began when the Rockefeller family gave a deed of trust to the state for land purchases, allowing New York to acquire about 2,500 acres along the river and protect it from development forever. Another 1,033 acres came from landowner and conservation leader William Henry Osborn in 1974, and Scenic Hudson, now a powerful land trust, acquired other parcels to bring the park to its current shape and size.

Note: The Hudson Highlands have seen a surge in popularity recently, with people taking the train up from New York City to the seasonal Breakneck Ridge stop and hiking through the park on a number of trails, completing their day by boarding the train at Cold Spring station at the other end of the park. This has made some of the trails particularly crowded on weekends. If you crave solitude, make your visit to this park on a weekday for the most satisfying experience. If you love seeing hundreds of people enjoying the Hudson Valley wilderness areas as much as you do, however, join the fun and come on a Saturday or Sunday. Just please, please stay on the trails, and help the park maintain the beauty of this special place.

Miles and Directions

0.0 From the parking area at Little Stony Point, cross the road and proceed to the well-marked trailhead. Follow the Cornish Trail (blue markers).

0.3 The blue trail turns right on a paved road. (There's a gate to your left; don't go that way.)

0.8 At the Y, follow the directions on the sign and bear right for the Undercliff Trail. The ruin of the Cornish Estate is to your left—you may want to make a quick side trip for a closer look. In a moment the pavement ends and the trail becomes crushed stone.

1.2 Here is a stone structure that looks like a well—it's more of the Cornish Estate.

1.4 The trail splits. Go right on the blue trail.

1.5 The red trail joins the blue trail from the left. Continue straight, now following the red trail along a stream. The trail is now strewn with rocks.

1.6 The green trail ends here on your left, at the stream crossing. Continue straight.

1.7 The bridge to your left is where the yellow (Undercliff) trail joins. Follow the yellow markers and blazes from here. Watch for arrows painted on rocks on the ground. There will be a lot of rocks. In a moment the yellow trail turns right. From here, it's a climb over a rocky trail with boulders that get larger as you go.

2.4 After an uphill stretch, you reach a high point. (It's not the highest point.) Continue straight on the yellow trail.

2.9 Here is the first great viewpoint. There are big rock slabs here on which you can sit and enjoy the view of the Hudson River looking east.

3.0 This is the second excellent viewpoint.

3.2 The white (Washburn) trail joins here. This is your route down. Turn right on the white trail.

3.3 Here's another nice viewpoint.

3.8 At this viewpoint you can see how far down you've already come (about 700 feet). In about 0.1 mile, there's a last view of the Hudson River before the final descent.

4.0 When you come out of the woods, turn left on the white trail. The big rocks are behind you; the rest of the trail is cobbles and sandy soil.

4.4 You've reached the trailhead. The parking area is across the road.

Hike Information

Local Information

Travel Hudson Valley, (800) 232-4782; www.travelhudsonvalley.com. Dutchess County Tourism, 3 Neptune Rd., Suite A11A, Poughkeepsie; (800) 445-3131; www.dutchesstourism.com.

Local Events/Attractions

Franklin and Eleanor Roosevelt and the Vanderbilt family built sprawling mansions on expansive grounds in Hyde Park, both of which are now National Historic Sites maintained by the National Park Service. The mansions are open year-round for guided and self-guided tours. **Home of Franklin Delano Roosevelt National Historic Site:** www.nps.gov/hofr. **Vanderbilt Mansion National Historic Site:** www.nps.gov/vama.

Organizations

New York–New Jersey Trail Conference maintains many trails in New York. NY–NJ Trail Conference, 600 Ramapo Valley Rd., Mahwah, NJ 07430; (201) 512-9348; info@nynjtc.org; www.nynjtc.org.

44 Breakneck Ridge Trail

On the east side of the Hudson River in Hudson Highlands State Park, this trail makes a rugged ascent from near river level to roll along a knobby ridge to a restored and reopened fire tower. From the highland ridge and the tower, take in views of the Hudson River, the Shawangunks, and the Catskill Mountains. A mixed forest embellished with mountain laurel and spring and summer wildflowers shapes much of the hike.

Start: At the tunnel trailhead
Distance: 9.6 miles out-and-back with a loop return
Approximate hiking time: 5.5 to 7 hours
Difficulty: Strenuous due to the initial rock scramble
Elevation change: The trail has a 1,500-foot elevation change, with the high point atop South Beacon Mountain.
Trail surface: Rocks, earthen path, woods road, along with an elevated connector path and stone steps
Seasons: Open year-round, best for hiking spring through fall
Other trail users: Hunters (during the bow deer hunt and spring shotgun turkey hunt)
Canine compatibility: Leashed dogs permitted (When hiking with your dog, start at the Wilkinson/Breakneck Bypass trailhead, avoiding the initial rock scramble, a danger for your pet.)
Land status: New York State Park Preserve or private easements
Nearest town: Beacon

Fees and permits: None
Schedule: Sunrise to sunset
Maps: https://parks.ny.gov/documents/parks/HudsonHighlandsTrailMapNorth.pdf; New York–New Jersey Trail Conference Trail Map 102, East Hudson Trails (available at traditional and online bookstores or from the Conference: www.nynjtc.org)
Trail contact: Hudson Highlands State Park Preserve, Route 9D, Cold Spring; (845) 225-7207; parks.ny.gov/parks/9/
Special considerations: Expect some rock scrambles, and wear boots that protect ankles. It's best to avoid the rocky ascent during snow and ice. There is no camping and no building fires. The turkey hunt is managed to minimize conflict, with no hunting after 10 a.m. and none on weekends. Look for an elevated connector path linking the train platform, a welcome center (information station where trail stewards answer questions on busy weekends), and the tunnel trailhead, removing foot traffic from NY 9D.

Finding the trailhead: From the NY 301–NY 9D junction in Cold Spring (8.5 miles north of Bear Mountain Bridge), go north on NY 9D for 2.1 miles. Trailhead parking is north of the tunnel, on the west side of the highway. GPS: 41.445779, -73.979449. You'll find the return trail 0.2 mile north on the right.

The Hike

White blazes and Taconic Region state park disks mark the way. Follow the new pedestrian pathway south to the tunnel and the trail's historic rocky start, with some modern enhancements. You'll earn early Hudson River views with the hearty ascent

A rocky climb puts you atop Breakneck Ridge.

of the tunnel embankment and steep west flank of Breakneck Ridge. Sumac, birch, viburnum, and grasses intersperse the rock.

With a few directional changes (pointed out by arrows), attain the rocky shoulder of the ridge for more views of the river, Pollepel Island, Storm King Mountain across the way, and Palisades Interstate Park to the south. The ascent now follows the ridgeline, adding looks at the steep drainage shaped by Breakneck Ridge and Mount Taurus.

At 1 mile in, reach the first vista knoll as the trail rolls from bump to bump, traversing the ridge north. Oak, maple, ash, and birch weave woods passages between the knobs. Where fuller woods crowd the dips, ruffed grouse and deer may spook on your approach.

Before long the red Breakneck Bypass trail descends left. It offers an easier return to the trailhead, but first continue the pursuit north. The next rise holds a 360-degree view of the Hudson River, the valley communities, the I-84 bridge, and South and North Beacon Mountains. On your descent from the rise, a blue trail arrives on the right to share ridge travel. Patches of mountain laurel brighten the forest.

> The South Beacon summit did not support a fire tower until 1931. Before that, spotters sighting a fire had to hike 0.25 mile down the mountain to a tree where the telephone line ended, scale that tree to get to a temporary phone, and then call in the report.

The blue trail departs to the left where the white trail enters a brief forested ascent to tag Sunset Point—a rock outcrop ringed by low oaks. A flatter tour follows before the sharp descent to Squirrel Hollow Brook, which generally carries enough water to dampen a bandana. Cross the brook and briefly merge with the yellow Wilkinson Trail, a woods road. Follow it right for a short distance and then break away left for a demanding ascent via Devil's Ladder. White arrows point the way up this steep, rocky slope. A fire swept the site decades ago; young birch and bigtooth aspen head the list of succession species. The trail then grades into woods before emerging into the open at the Mount Beacon Fire Tower on South Beacon Mountain.

The rehabilitated 1931 steel tower lifts the intrepid 60 feet high and delivers worthy views. Even without the tower's loft, the view from atop the breezy ridge trumps all previous ones. Take in the river, the ridge, and nearby peaks as well as the distant flat skyline of the Shawangunks and more ragged outline of the Catskills. Although the white trail continues north, for this hike retrace your steps to the Breakneck Bypass for the return to your vehicle.

Follow the red-blazed Breakneck Bypass, a foot trail, down the deciduous-wooded west flank. Mountain laurel earns a stronghold, while viburnum and huckleberry weave a complement. At times the descent is markedly steep. After following a thin seasonal drainage, you will reach an outcrop with limited river views and a good look at Sugarloaf Mountain. Where you meet the woods road of the yellow-marked Wilkinson Trail, bear left on it, descending to NY 9D. Big tulip trees and dogwoods decorate the lower slope. The trail comes out on the east side of the highway. Turn left (south) to end back at your vehicle.

Miles and Directions

0.0   Start at the tunnel trailhead. After following the designated pedestrian pathway to the tunnel trailhead, climb the tunnel embankment to the west slope.

1.0   Reach the first vista knob on the ridge.

1.5   Reach Breakneck Bypass (the return) and continue north on the white-blazed ridge trail.
    Bailout: If time is limited, you can shorten the hike, descending left now on the bypass trail and left again where you meet the Wilkinson Trail for a 3.2-mile loop.

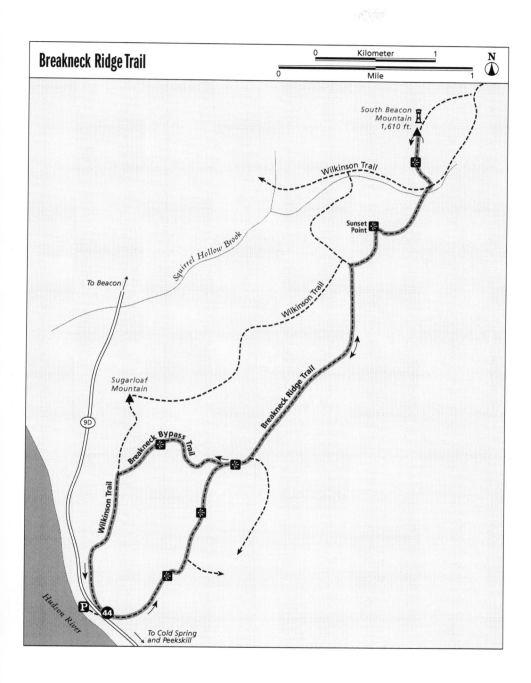

Breakneck Ridge Trail

0 — Kilometer — 1

0 — Mile — 1

N

South Beacon
Mountain
1,610 ft.

Wilkinson Trail

Sunset
Point

Squirrel Hollow Brook

To Beacon

Wilkinson Trail

Sugarloaf
Mountain

9D

Breakneck Ridge Trail

Breakneck Bypass Trail

Wilkinson Trail

Hudson River

P 44

To Cold Spring
and Peekskill

2.0 The ridge trail briefly merges with the blue Notch Trail.

4.1 Cross Squirrel Hollow Brook, coming to the woods road of the yellow Wilkinson Trail. Follow it right for a short distance and then break away left.

4.2 Ascend Devil's Ladder (white arrows point the way up this steep, rocky slope).

4.7 Reach Mount Beacon Tower atop South Beacon Mountain. Backtrack to the Breakneck Bypass trail.

7.9 Reach the red-blazed Breakneck Bypass. Turn right for the descent to NY 9D.

8.9 Meet the Wilkinson Trail and head left on it.

9.4 Emerge on the east side of NY 9D. Turn left (south) to return to your vehicle.

9.6 End at trail parking.

Hike Information

Local Information

Travel Hudson Valley, (800) 232-4782; www.travelhudsonvalley.com. **Dutchess County Tourism,** 3 Neptune Rd., Poughkeepsie; (800) 445-3131; www.dutchess tourism.com.

Local Events/Attractions

The Hudson Valley is home to **Mount Gulian Historic Site,** the colonial homestead of the Verplanck family that served as General von Steuben's headquarters in the Revolutionary War. A Verplanck descendent who trained, led, and fought alongside the US Colored Troops in the Civil War recorded his experiences in fifty-nine letters. An escaped slave served as the property's gardener. These are just some of the stories that permeate this home, shown by guided tour. Mount Gulian Historic Site, 145 Sterling St., Beacon; (845) 831-8172; www.mountgulian.org.

Accommodations

Clarence Fahnestock State Park, off NY 301 east of the trailhead, is open late April through early December and has eighty-one campsites. Reservations: (800) 456-2267; www.reserveamerica.com.

Organizations

New York–New Jersey Trail Conference helps maintain, mark, and map trails. NY–NJ Trail Conference, 600 Ramapo Valley Rd., Mahwah, NJ 07430; (201) 512-9348; info@nynjtc.org; www.nynjtc.org.

45 Harriman State Park: Pine Meadow Lake Loop

Pine Meadow Lake is the anchor to this rolling, circuitous meander through the milder reaches of Harriman State Park. The loop takes you through woodland, atop hills and rock features, and past brook, lake, and swamp. History, birds, and nature's seasonal embellishments justify the physical exertion. The counterclockwise loop unites the area's Pine Meadow, Suffern–Bear Mountain, Tuxedo–Mount Ivy, and Seven Hills Trails.

Start: At the Reeves Meadow trailhead
Distance: 13.2-mile loop
Approximate hiking time: 7 to 9 hours
Difficulty: Strenuous
Elevation change: The trail travels between 500 and 1,200 feet above sea level, with the high point atop Diamond Mountain.
Trail surface: Rocky and earthen trail, woods road
Seasons: Open year-round, best for hiking spring through fall
Other trail users: None
Canine compatibility: Leashed dogs permitted (leash not more than 6 feet long) and must display rabies tag
Land status: New York State Park
Nearest town: Suffern
Fees and permits: None
Schedule: Daylight hours

Maps: https://parks.ny.gov/documents/parks/HarrimanTrailMap.pdf; New York–New Jersey Trail Conference Trail Map 3: Southern Harriman–Bear Mountain Trails, www.nynjtc.org
Trail contact: Harriman State Park, Administration Building, Palisades Interstate Park Commission, Bear Mountain; (845) 947-2444; https://parks.ny.gov/parks/145
Special considerations: Expect muddy passages, especially in early spring and following rains. A precarious rocky descent off Diamond Mountain requires caution and the use of hands. There is no camping, and no fires are allowed along the trail. Rangers caution hikers to wear a watch and carry emergency flashlights, especially when getting a late start, and to be alert to which trails they have followed. Cell service may be spotty, so don't trust your safety to it. Obtain and use a reliable map to ensure a good and safe time. Bring drinking water.

Finding the trailhead: From New York State Thruway I-87, take exit 15 and go north on NY 17 for 2.1 miles, passing through Sloatsburg. Turn right onto Seven Lakes Drive and go 1.5 miles to find Reeves Meadow Visitor Center on the right and additional parking 500 feet past it on the left. GPS: 41.173802, -74.168638

The Hike

From the east side of the visitor center, hike north to locate an old woods road entering the woods on the right. This is the Pine Meadow Trail, marked with red or red-on-white blazing. Follow it upstream along Stony Brook, an attractive boulder-strewn stream accented by cascades and pools. Hemlock, oak, maple, birch, and beech fashion this shady woods, a shelter for white-tailed deer.

Stony Brook offers a picturesque stop along the Pine Meadow Lake Loop.

Bear right uphill, still following red markers on a wide rocky trail threaded by small drainages. On the slope, mountain laurel contributes to the full midstory. After the Hillburn-Torne-Sebago Trail briefly shares the route, bear left at the fork. Tulip trees and box elder appear helter-skelter as you continue upstream along quiet-spilling Pine Meadow Brook, a headwater of Stony Brook. Where the trail grows soggy, rocks become allies instead of obstacles. A small fireplace sits where the blue Seven Hills Trail merges from the right.

Across the Pine Meadow Brook footbridge, the red and blue trails divide. This is the loop junction. Follow the red Pine Meadow Trail upstream (right) to Pine Meadow Lake for counterclockwise travel. You pass a scenic moss-and-fern-dressed boulder before reaching trailside GaNusQuah (Giant Stones) Rock, a room-sized boulder overlooking Pine Meadow Brook. A side loop heads left, passing a stone foundation. Ahead, a remnant pipeline and old holding pond remind us of the days of the Civilian Conservation Corps camps.

At Pine Meadow Lake, detour right to the dam for an open lake vista, the last you will see before thick shrubs block the view. After a while, pass the ruins of Conklin Cabin, which dates to 1778. Before reaching the inlet, the trail swings left, away from Pine Meadow Lake.

With a brook crossing, swampy stretches again suggest hopscotch travel from rock to rock. Azaleas favor the moist reaches. Meet the yellow Suffern–Bear Mountain Trail and follow it left. A steep descent precedes the ascent of Panther Mountain, a scooped hilltop with twin peaks. Outcrops at the first summit provide the lone views east and south. The quiet terrain rolling away offers no clue that New York City lies within 30 miles.

Descend from the second summit into full, rich forest, where you may hear Baltimore oriole, red-eyed vireo, wild turkey, eastern towhee, and scarlet tanager in the woods. The trail rolls from rise to brook, arriving at another fireplace ruin and an overgrown woods road, the red-blazed Tuxedo–Mount Ivy Trail; go left on it.

The trail now skirts Squirrel and Big Green Swamps, with filtered looks at the shrub-filled bottomlands. Where the trail meets a woods road between the two, bear right. Cross a footbridge and continue left through a mountain laurel showcase if it happens to be June; wildflowers may crowd the understory in other seasons. At the white Breakneck Mountain Trail, stay on the red trail as it curves left. After you cross a gravel road and view the lower end of Big Green Swamp, the trail climbs, traversing the flat outcrops of a small rise. There is less foot traffic here, so watch for markers to be sure you're still on the trail.

Beyond a woods road, follow the more defined blue Seven Hills Trail left. With a brief woods road passage, the rolling foot trail traverses woods, overlooks the watery arm of Lake Sebago, and resumes straight ahead at a junction with the yellow trail. Stay on the blue trail, crossing Diamond Mountain with its striated granites.

Brief, complicated descents lead to and from an open outcrop ledge, offering a grand view across the treetops and out the Pine Meadow Brook drainage. Think through each descent, being watchful of thin ledges. Use your hands as needed, but look before you reach, because snakes live here. Where the blue trail comes out at Pine Meadow Brook, turn left (upstream) to close the loop. Cross the footbridge and turn right, retracing your steps to Reeves Meadow Visitor Center.

Miles and Directions

0.0 Start from the Reeves Meadow trailhead. Hike north to pick up the Pine Meadow Trail, here a woods road heading right (red or red-on-white blazing).

1.2 The Hillburn-Torne-Sebago Trail briefly shares the route; 500 feet ahead, bear left at the fork.

1.5 The blue Seven Hills Trail merges from the right.

Pine Meadow Lake Loop

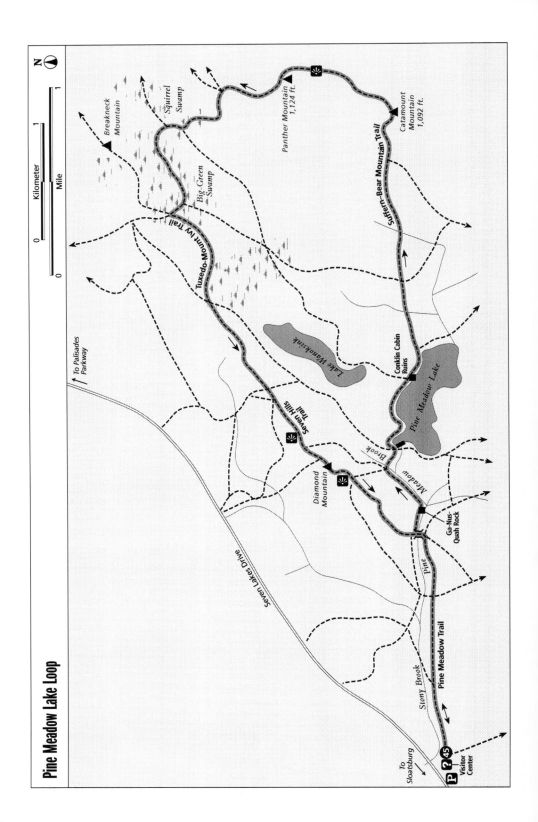

1.6	Cross the Pine Meadow Brook footbridge, reaching the loop junction. Head right (upstream) following red markers.
2.2	A side loop to the left passes a stone foundation.
2.4	Reach the dam and a Pine Meadow Lake vista.
3.0	Pass the ruins of Conklin Cabin.
4.7	Meet the yellow Suffern–Bear Mountain Trail. Follow it left for the loop.
5.4	Reach Panther Mountain.
6.5	Meet the overgrown woods road of the red-blazed Tuxedo–Mount Ivy Trail; go left on it.
8.0	Reach the white Breakneck Mountain Trail; stay on the red trail as it curves left.
9.9	Reach the blue Seven Hills Trail; follow it left.
10.5	Reach a yellow trail. Continue straight ahead on the blue Seven Hills Trail.
10.6	Reach Diamond Mountain. Continue following blue blazes.
11.6	Close the loop. Cross the footbridge and turn right to backtrack the red Pine Meadow Trail to the trailhead.
13.2	End back at the Reeves Meadow Visitor Center.

Hike Information

Local Information

Rockland County Office of Tourism, 50 Sanatorium Rd., Building A, 8th Floor, Pomona; (845) 364-2170; http://explorerocklandny.com

Local Events/Attractions

Stony Point Battlefield State Historic Site, a fee site, brings to life a page of early Hudson River history. During the Revolutionary War, Brigadier General "Mad Anthony" Wayne captured the British fortification here in a midnight bayonet strike, giving the Americans control over the river. The park offers museum military exhibits, a slide program, a grounds interpretive trail, a military encampment, the restored 1826 lighthouse (the oldest remaining light on the Hudson), and weekend camp cooking and musket demonstrations. The park has daily hours mid-April through October and a reduced schedule in winter (call for details). Stony Point Battlefield State Historic Site, 44 Battlefield Rd., Stony Point; (845) 786-2521; https://parks .ny.gov/historic-sites/stonypointbattlefield/maps.aspx.

Accommodations

Harriman State Park's Beaver Pond Campground (open early Apr through Columbus Day weekend) has 128 campsites. Reservations: (800) 456-2267; www .reserveamerica.com.

Organizations

New York–New Jersey Trail Conference helps maintain, mark, and map trails. NY–NJ Trail Conference, 600 Ramapo Valley Rd., Mahwah, NJ 07430; (201) 512-9348; info@nynjtc.org; www.nynjtc.org.

Honorable Mentions

W Bear Mountain Loop

This demanding 9.7-mile loop rolls through the steep wooded terrain of Bear Mountain State Park, topping Bear and West Mountains and offering views of the Lower Hudson River area. Counterclockwise, you travel the Major Welch (red), the Appalachian (white), the Timp-Torne (blue), and the Suffern–Bear Mountain (yellow) Trails.

From the south side of Bear Mountain Inn, hike west to follow the Major Welch Trail north along the west shore

An attractive trail shelter calls hikers aside on Bear Mountain Loop.

of developed Hessian Lake. Ascend the treed north flank of Bear Mountain. Steep spurs and contouring passages give way to the granitic outcrop leading to Perkins Tower (2.2 miles), an attractive five-story 1930s stone tower.

Still following red, descend the outcrop ledges to the southeast below the tower, rolling between granite ledge terraces and tilted outcrops, adding views south and west. At 3 miles cross a road and turn left on the white-blazed Appalachian Trail (AT). The AT descends steeply to cross Seven Lakes Drive (4.2 miles), where you follow the historic 1777 Trail left for 0.1 mile. The 1777 Trail retraces the path taken by the British when they stunned the colonists by overtaking two crucial forts along the Hudson River in the Revolutionary War.

Still tracking white blazes, turn right at a pine plantation to ascend briefly on woods road before continuing on the foot trail. Atop West Mountain, outcrops extend views. The trail then merges with the blue Timp-Torne Trail for rolling travel, tagging the high point at 5.1 miles. Remain on the blue trail, soon merging with the yellow Suffern–Bear Mountain Trail for rolling ridge and forest travel. Keep to the yellow trail, generally descending to cross and parallel Doodletown Brook downstream. Meet the 1777 Trail once again, and continue following the yellow blazes. After crossing Seven Lakes Drive, meet once more with the AT. Continue straight, following the yellow and white blazes to end at the southwest corner of Hessian Lake.

From the Bear Mountain toll bridge over the Hudson River, go south on US 9W for 0.4 mile; turn right to reach the fee parking lot at Bear Mountain Inn. GPS: 41.312518, -73.988859. Contact Bear Mountain State Park, Palisades Parkway or Route 9W North, Bear Mountain; (845) 786-2701; https://parks.ny.gov/parks/bearmountain/details.aspx.

✕ Mianus River Gorge Preserve

In contrast to the drama of the sheer sandstone-shale gorges of the Finger Lakes Region, the steep ravine of Mianus River Gorge southeast of Mount Kisco captivates with dark-woods enchantment. Spared the ax because of its steep character, the preserve boasts one of the few intact stands of old-growth eastern forest. This 960-acre preserve, the very first land project of the Nature Conservancy (TNC), managed by Mianus River Gorge Inc., bears the distinction of being the first National Natural History Landmark in the United States. The 6 miles of interlocking, color-coded trails lead you along gorge and rim, past 350-year-old hemlocks; charming cascades; the peacefully flowing, 20-foot-wide Mianus River; and a historic quartz-feldspar quarry excavated by Native Americans thousands of years ago. The preserve is open April through November from 8:30 a.m. to 5 p.m.; donations welcome (no pets, smoking, picnicking, or wheeled vehicles).

From the Bedford Village green, go 0.8 mile east on NY 172 (Pound Ridge Road) and turn right onto Stamford/Long Ridge Road. In 0.5 mile turn right onto Miller's Mill Road, cross the bridge in 300 feet, and turn left onto Mianus River Road. Find the trailhead on the left in 0.6 mile. Or from the Merritt Parkway (CT 15) in Connecticut, take exit 34 and go north on CT 104 (Long Ridge/Stamford Road) for 7.2 miles, and turn left onto Miller's Mill Road, crossing the bridge and turning into the preserve. GPS: 41.185813, -73.621445. Contact Mianus River Gorge Preserve, 167 Mianus River Rd., Bedford; (914) 234-3455; http://mianus.org.

Y Clarence Fahnestock Memorial State Park

The blue 3.7-mile Three Lakes Trail offers a linear sampling of the lake-woods offering of this 14,000-acre state park in Putnam and Dutchess Counties. The four-season park is noted for its Taconic Outdoor Education Center and great family recreation, including groomed ski trails. Three Lakes Trail strings together Canopus Lake, Hidden Pond, and John Allen Pond. It follows along Canopus Creek, tours tranquil woods and outcrop rises, skirts meadow and marsh, and runs

Water lilies decorate pond edges at Clarence Fahnestock Memorial State Park.

through aisles of mountain laurel. Songbirds, frogs, dragonflies, and deer contribute to the trail's sounds and sights. The diverse canopy is a leaf-peeper's joy, and delicate lilies can adorn ponds. Stone walls hint at long-ago farms, and old iron mines harken to the nineteenth century, when the iron industry flourished here.

From I-84 east of Beacon, take exit 16S, heading south on the Taconic State Parkway toward New York City. Go 5.8 miles on the parkway and take the Cold

Spring–Carmel exit, heading west on NY 301 toward Cold Spring and Clarence Fahnestock Memorial State Park. Go 1.2 miles, passing the park campground and Pelton Lake Picnic Area, to find trail parking on the right (north) side of NY 301 at Canopus Lake. Three Lakes Trail heads south on the opposite side of the road, just east of the Appalachian Trail (AT). Use care in crossing the road. GPS: 41.45483, -73.83368. Contact Clarence Fahnestock State Park, 1498 NY 301, Carmel Hamlet; (845) 225-7207; https://parks.ny.gov/parks/fahnestock/details.aspx.

Z Sterling Forest State Park

Sterling Forest State Park encompasses 21,938 acres in New York State and New Jersey, and it seems incongruous to find such a dense, pristine woodland so close to the nation's most populated metropolis. Here visitors can walk a length of the iconic Appalachian Trail, or visit during the spring migration to see the warbler, vireo, and hawk action at this critical stopover point along the Atlantic Flyway. As an official Bird Conservation Area, Sterling Forest provides one of the largest continuous tracts of wooded habitat in the Hudson Highlands, making it an important and much beloved hotspot for birders from New York City and the surrounding area.

The forest traces its name to Scotland's Fifth Earl of Stirling, who purchased this land from the Iroquois people in 1702 along with a group of colonists from the United Kingdom. Over the course of the next two centuries, its mineral-rich outcrops supported a thriving iron industry, which closed its mines in the 1920s and left the area. A Swedish insurance company bought up the land in the 1990s with plans to develop it with nearly 15,000 residential units and millions of square feet of commercial space. But nearly 30 nonprofit organizations came together to fight the development, and in 1998 the Trust for Public Land and the Open Space Institute prevailed, negotiating the purchase of the land by the Palisades Interstate Park Commission. This cleared the way for it to become a state park, protecting it in perpetuity.

Access the trails in New York from NY 17A and County Roads 5, 19, 84, and 91, among others. GPS: 41.198681, -74.256991. Contact Sterling Forest State Park, 116 Old Forge Rd., Tuxedo; (845) 351-5907; https://parks.ny.gov/parks/74/details.aspx.

Sterling Forest brings together woods and waters, attracting hikers.

Long Island

The keeper of New York State's ocean shores and some of its most inviting beaches, Long Island's 118-mile length provides homes for 7.6 million people and still manages to preserve some significantly pristine wildlands. Since the end of the last ice age, the tidal strait of the East River has separated Long Island from the New York mainland. Features including remnant moraines running along the north shore and the island's spine, kettle lakes, and arable sandy plains of silt speak to Long Island's glacially influenced origins.

The island's earliest inhabitants were peaceful Indigenous peoples, arriving here as much as 12,000 years ago and experiencing many shifts in their way of life, from pursuing big game to hunting smaller animals and gathering most of their food, to the agrarian society they had formed by the time Europeans arrived in the 1500s. Paumanok, the Algonquin name for Long Island, has been translated to mean "a

West Pond Trail is popular for birding and nature study.

place where tribute is brought," referring to the quahog and conch shells the various tribes on the island used to make wampum—the main currency for tributes or taxes between tribes.

The Dutch and English arrived and began to settle this land, but the Revolutionary War drove the Europeans out, and newly minted Americans turned this island into a hub for fishing and agriculture. It wasn't until the soldiers returned home from World War II and the GI Bill boosted homebuilding across the country that Long Island assumed its modern persona: the suburban counterpart to New York City. The Hamptons, legendary first as the location of F. Scott Fitzgerald's classic novel *The Great Gatsby* and later through countless movies and TV series, turned the easternmost seashores into the playground of the very, very wealthy. But there is much more to Long Island: a prized flyfishing river, produce stands, vineyards producing some of America's finest wines, colonial homes, lighthouses, maritime museums, aquariums, campgrounds . . . and hiking trails.

Despite its proximity to Manhattan, the island boasts a surprising wealth of natural discovery and even secluded spots for solitary reverie. Between Gateway National Recreation Area and Montauk Point, Long Island brings together rare pine barrens; seaward, bay, and Long Island Sound shores and beaches; ghost forests; dune habitats; and spring-fed rivers. Endangered piping plovers and least terns choose to nest on the island's barrier and bay beaches. Terrapin; fox; deer; great horned, barred, and eastern screech owl; and osprey are other wild inhabitants. This region is even home to the state's lone federally designated wilderness, the Otis Pike High Dune Wilderness at Fire Island National Seashore.

46 Jamaica Bay Wildlife Refuge: West Pond Trail

At Gateway National Recreation Area, southwest of John F. Kennedy International Airport, this simple interpretive loop within the Jamaica Bay Wildlife Refuge introduces the wildlife and natural habitat of West Pond, Jamaica Bay, and Long Island's outwash plain. The site boasts 330 bird species over the course of a year, with a full calendar of seasonal arrivals: warblers (Apr/May), shorebirds (July/Aug), raptors (Sept–Nov), and winter waterfowl (Mar through early Apr). Terrapins nest here in June and July. What's unexpected is this natural bounty sits within sight of the New York City skyline.

Start: At the back of the visitor center

Distance: 1.8-mile loop

Approximate hiking time: 1 to 2 hours

Difficulty: Easy

Elevation change: The hike is flat.

Trail surface: Gravel walking path

Seasons: Year-round

Other trail users: Birders

Canine compatibility: Dogs not permitted

Land status: Gateway National Recreation Area (National Park Service)

Nearest town: Howard Beach

Fees and permits: No fees but permit required (Regardless of the hour of your visit, you are required to carry a free visitor pass while touring the refuge trails. Acquire your pass at the visitor center. If you are planning an early-morning visit, obtain your pass the preceding day.)

Schedule: Year-round, sunrise to sunset; visitor center, Fri–Mon 10 a.m. to 4 p.m. except major holidays

Map: www.nps.gov/gate/planyourvisit/map _jbu.htm

Trail contact: Gateway National Recreation Area, 210 New York Ave., Staten Island; (718) 354-4606; www.nps.gov/gate

Special considerations: Stay on the trails, be alert for poison ivy, and respect closures for wildlife. Come prepared for mosquitos and ticks. There is no food, no smoking, no pets, and no jogging allowed on the trails.

Finding the trailhead: From the Belt Parkway in New York City (Brooklyn), take exit 17S and go south on Cross Bay Boulevard for Gateway National Recreation Area. In 3.5 miles turn right (west) for the visitor center and trailhead. GPS: 40.616834, -73.824590

The Hike

Protected by Rockaway Peninsula, the islands of Jamaica Bay Wildlife Refuge make up a vital habitat and sanctuary for native and migratory wildlife. West Pond Trail encircles one of the impoundment ponds protected originally as a New York City park, now as part of the national park system. But in 2012 Hurricane Sandy breached the 45-acre pond, mingling its water with Jamaica Bay, thus changing its freshwater dynamics. With its shoreline and trail restored in 2017, visitors now can enjoy a living laboratory as the pond, shore, and inhabitants adjust over time.

Bluebird box along the West Pond Trail

Out the back door of the visitor center, hike the wide gravel path and head left (clockwise) around the pond. A flowering shrub and vine thicket shapes the trail's border. Interpretive signs, bird and bat nesting boxes, osprey nesting platforms, and frequent benches slow your pace. The circuit gradually shares views of Jamaica Bay with its mudflats, saltwater marsh, and open water. Cross-bay views include the Manhattan skyline.

With the change of seasons comes a change in residents: warblers in spring, snowy egrets followed by the shorebirds in summer, and snow geese and raptors in fall. Throughout the year a vibrant harmony of melodic and raucous notes rides the coastal breeze, with trills, honks, squawks, pipings, and plaintive screeches. Depending on the season of your visit, American kestrel; white and glossy ibis; red-winged blackbird; least, gull-billed, common, and Forster's terns; herring, great black-backed and laughing gulls; brant and snow goose; more than twenty species of ducks; great blue, little blue, green, and tricolored herons; double-crested cormorant; white-eyed, red-eyed, and warbling vireos; and twenty-five warbler species are all possible sightings, especially in May or September.

The setting grows more exposed at the outwash plain. Here, the more desertlike soils give rise to cactus and yucca, which bloom in June.

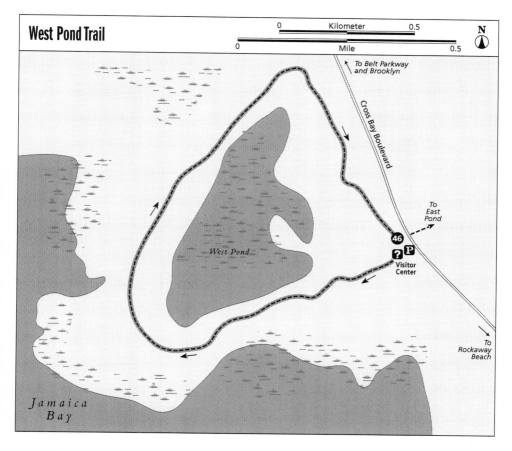

West Pond Trail

0   Kilometer   0.5

0   Mile   0.5

N

To Belt Parkway
and Brooklyn

Cross Bay Boulevard

To
East
Pond

46

P

Visitor
Center

To
Rockaway
Beach

West Pond

Jamaica
Bay

Snags may provide cormorants with convenient drying posts. The periodic roar of an airplane amplifies the serenity of the refuge. In breeding season Canada geese waddle the paths with their young, sometimes enforcing their right-of-way with a hostile hiss. The return path to the visitor center may reveal salt-spray roses along the trail, especially in spring.

Miles and Directions

0.0   Starting at the visitor center, hike the wide gravel trail, heading left at the loop.

1.5   Approach Cross Bay Boulevard. Keep right, still following the gravel loop trail.

1.8   End back at the visitor center.

HIKING WITH CHILDREN

Hiking with children is all about seeing and experiencing nature through their eyes. Kids like to explore and have fun. They like to stop and point out bugs and plants, look under rocks, jump in puddles, and throw sticks. If you're taking a toddler or young child on a hike, start with a trail that is familiar to you. Trails that have interesting things for kids, like piles of leaves to play in or a frog pond to investigate, will make the hike much more enjoyable for them and will keep them from getting bored.

Have a strategy before starting on the trail. Using games is not only an effective way to keep children's attention, it's also a great way to teach them about nature. Quiz children on the names of plants and animals. If your children are old enough, let them carry their own daypacks filled with snacks and water. Let them lead the way and set the pace. Playing follow-the-leader works particularly well when you have a group of children. Have each child take a turn at being the leader.

Hike Information

Local Information
New York City Tourism + Conventions, www.nyctourism.com

Local Events/Attractions
The **Jamaica Bay Unit of Gateway National Recreation Area** has beaches, other natural areas, and historic sites to visit. Dunes, upland, lawn areas, and Atlantic and bay shores offer experiences in nature, while Jacob Riis Park, Fort Tilden (a coastal defense site established in 1917), and Floyd Bennett Field all provide insights into the area's history. Canarsie Pier, Plumb Beach, and Frank Charles Park sit off Shore Parkway. Many are popular with birders. Gateway National Recreation Area, www.nps.gov/gate.

47 Rocky Point Pine Barrens State Forest

For $1, New York State purchased this nearly 6,000-acre pine barrens and oak-wooded parcel formerly used by Radio Corporation of America (RCA) for transatlantic broadcasting. Only the concrete footings of the transmission towers remain, while color-coded hiking trails crisscross sandy woods roads and firebreaks, some of which double as mountain-bike or horse trails. The northern reaches of the state forest feature gently rolling hills, while the southern extent flattens for easy walking. Rocky Point Road slices the area into east–west halves.

Start: At the Whiskey Road trailhead
Distance: 10.9-mile lasso-shaped hike
Approximate hiking time: 5.5 to 7.5 hours
Difficulty: Easy
Elevation change: The trail has a 100-foot elevation change.
Trail surface: Sandy path, woods road, and firebreaks
Seasons: Open year-round, but a daily permit is required. Spring through fall is best for hiking.
Other trail users: Mountain bikers and horseback riders (on separate intersecting or parallel trails), hunters
Canine compatibility: Leashed dogs permitted (Carry water for your animal and clean up after your pet.)
Land status: New York State Department of Environmental Conservation (DEC)

Nearest town: Rocky Point
Fees and permits: No fees but permit required; call (631) 444-0270 or email R1info@dec.ny.gov.
Schedule: Daylight hours
Map: www.dec.ny.gov/docs/regions_pdf/rphiking.pdf
Trail contact: New York State DEC, Region 1, Stony Brook, 50 Circle Rd., Stony Brook; (631) 444-0270; www.dec.ny.gov
Special considerations: Rangers recommend all users wear blaze orange during hunting season (Nov–Jan). Because ticks are present and numerous in some areas, stay on trails, wear long sleeves and long pants, use an insect repellent that contains permethrin, and make frequent tick checks while at the management area and immediately after you return home.

Finding the trailhead: From the junction of Rocky Point Road (NY 21) and NY 25A in Rocky Point, go south on Rocky Point Road for 2.5 miles, then turn left (east) onto Whiskey Road. In 1.1 miles turn left (north) to enter the trail parking lot. GPS: 40.908137, -72.921540

The Hike

Cross the stair stile into the state forest and follow the footpath north into a pine stand that later fills out with oak and huckleberry. Red trail markers and Paumanok Path symbols mark the way. At the loop junction, bear right for a counterclockwise tour, staying on the red trail. The blue trail concludes the loop. Part company with the Paumanok Path, a 125-mile-long trail traversing Long Island's pine barrens from Rocky Point to Montauk Point. The flatness of the hike ahead and the sameness of the forest can lull you into relaxation.

Spatially open forest pairs with the trail at Rocky Point Pine Barrens.

Crossing over woods roads and passing firebreak clearings, the trail ascends and tops Sand Hill. The hill likely owes its start to a stream that flowed over a glacier, depositing silt over time. When the glacier receded at the end of the last ice age, this modest hill remained. You trace a curve left over the sandy summit, which extends no views, to again find the red trail. It leads you on a brief, sharp descent before it turns left. The yellow trail straight ahead rolls over the next rise to reach a trailhead on NY 25A.

The well-marked loop continues through oak woodland, crossing fire grades and woods roads, with pines once more winning a place in the forest. Throughout the tract, bountiful ferns announce recently burned areas. Fire regenerates the pine forest, so prescribed burns take place here as a matter of course. Because an ever-encroaching society objects to such burns, the survival of this habitat depends on setting aside large intact tracts. Pine barrens once covered 250,000 acres of Long Island; now only one-third of the barrens remains.

A narrow footpath leads to the crossing of Rocky Point Road and the western half of the preserve, clad in oaks and huckleberry bushes. At the upcoming junction, continue straight on the red trail. The gently rolling route passes through firebreak field and pine-oak woods.

The state forest boundary appears as you emerge at an open flat with concrete walks and roads, an old foundation, and an untamed border of maple, chokecherry, and dogwood. Skirt the site, following the broken paved route to the right. Where the abandoned avenue forks, go left for the loop. To the right lies NY 25A. Keep an eye out for the blue-blazed path, which continues the loop.

The trail now passes through varied woods of red cedar, ash, cherry, oak, and pine, with an understory of grass, Virginia creeper, and fern. Pass a pair of rocks, formerly identified as Sitting Rock on an old map. The lone rocks on the circuit do indeed suggest a seat, but check first for any ants or errant poison ivy.

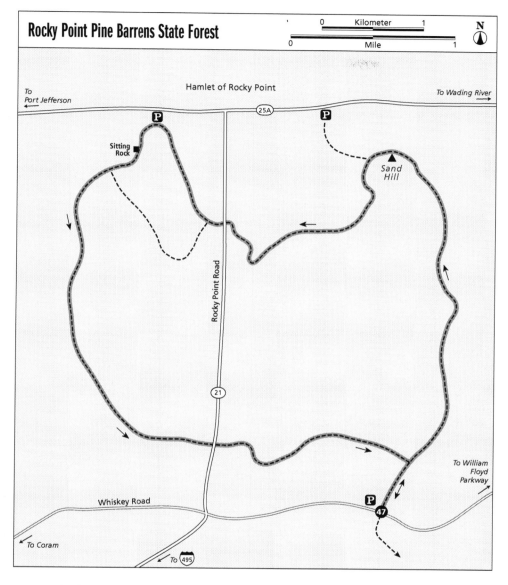

Rocky Point Pine Barrens State Forest

Kilometer 0 — 1

Mile 0 — 1

N

Hamlet of Rocky Point

To Port Jefferson

To Wading River

25A

P

P

Sitting Rock

Sand Hill

Rocky Point Road

21

P

47

To William Floyd Parkway

Whiskey Road

To Coram

To 495

At the junction with a yellow trail, continue following the blue-marked route, encountering more road and trail crossings. Ant mounds riddle the forest. Where the trail bottoms out, it again travels long straightaway through a pine stand with an open cathedral and only patchy shade. Scarlet tanagers can capture attention with their color, while cinquefoil and violet in springtime edge the porous sand. After taller oaks fill out the forest, follow the blue trail back across Rocky Point Road.

The trail continues much as it has through pine barrens to close the loop. Turn right on the red trail, retracing the hike's start to Whiskey Road.

Miles and Directions

0.0 Start from the Whiskey Road trailhead and hike north.

0.5 Reach the loop junction. Bear right, following red markers.

2.9 Top Sand Hill and begin a descent.

3.0 Reach a junction. Follow the red trail as it turns left. *Note:* The yellow trail straight ahead crosses the next rise to reach NY 25A.

4.5 Cross Rocky Point Road to the western half of the preserve.

4.6 Reach a junction. Continue straight on the red trail.

5.4 Where the abandoned avenue forks, go left, round the foundation flat, and seek out and follow the blue-blazed path, which continues the counterclockwise loop.

5.6 Pass Sitting Rock.

5.9 Reach a junction; continue following the blue markers. *Note:* The yellow trail journeys left 0.5 mile to Lookout Point for an uninspired woods view overlooking a firebreak corridor.

8.7 Cross back over Rocky Point Road.

10.4 Complete the loop. Turn right to return to the trailhead.

10.9 End back at the Whiskey Road trailhead.

Hike Information

Local Information

Port Jefferson Chamber of Commerce, 118 West Broadway, Port Jefferson; (631) 473-1414; www.portjeffchamber.com. **Discover Long Island,** 330 Motor Parkway, Suite 203, Hauppauge; (877) 386-6654; www.discoverlongisland.com.

Local Events/Attractions

Port Jefferson's 5.1-acre **Jeanne Garant Harborfront Park** provides a multipurpose park and public waterfront access at the head of the Port Jefferson Harbor. A playground, picnic area, promenade, public art, and seasonal events engage visitors. Contact the Port Jefferson Chamber, https://portjeff.com/harborfront-park/.

Accommodations

Wildwood State Park, east of the Rocky Point pine barrens, is open mid-April through late October and has 324 campsites. Reservations: (800) 456-2267; www .reserveamerica.com.

Organizations

The **Long Island Greenbelt Trail Conference** promotes Long Island trails. Long Island Greenbelt Trail Conference, PO Box 5636, Hauppauge, NY 11788; (631) 360-0753; www.ligreenbelt.org.

48 Fire Island National Seashore

Fire Island, Long Island's famed barrier island and a long-established summer destination for New Yorkers, extends for 32 miles along Long Island's south shore and protects it from the pounding surf of the Atlantic Ocean. But in its face-off with Hurricane Sandy in 2012, the island suffered a breach, altering the look of its welcome mat and trails. The island now holds two disparate-sized sections of beach and back bay between Smith Point and Watch Hill. Its Otis Pike High Dune Wilderness remains the only federally designated wilderness in New York State—at 1,380 acres and an interrupted 7 miles long, it is the smallest wilderness area managed by the National Park Service. Flowering beach plum and heather and wild rose accent the untouched dunes in spring. The toe of the seaward dune attracts nesting piping plovers and least terns April through August. A rich coastal landscape, wildlife, and Atlantic Ocean and Great South Bay views all make this a particularly pleasing stop.

Start: At the Smith Point Wilderness Visitor Center trailhead or at Watch Hill Ferry Landing

Distance: 3.6-mile out-and-back beach hike (Smith Point) or 10.6-mile out-and-back beach hike (Watch Hill), both with boardwalks and remnant sections of Burma Road through the dune swale to vary travel or add views

Approximate hiking time: 2.5 to 7.5 hours

Difficulty: Easy to moderate, depending on length and coast or swale

Elevation change: Beach portion is flat; back-bay swale has less than a 100-foot elevation change.

Trail surface: Sandy beach, swale track, boardwalk

Seasons: Year-round

Other trail users: Beachgoers

Canine compatibility: Given the access restrictions, it is best to leave dogs at home.

Land status: National park with public inholdings

Nearest town: Shirley or Patchogue

Fees and permits: No fees, but because the national seashore at Smith Point only has handicapped parking, you must park next door at Smith Point County Park, a fee area. For hikes entering the wilderness, rangers recommend you register at Smith Point Wilderness Visitor Center to alert them to your presence in this little-used area. To wilderness camp, a permit is required (obtain one from the Watch Hill Visitor Center).

Schedule: National seashore and Smith Point Wilderness Visitor Center, year-round; Watch Hill Visitor Center, mid-May through mid-Oct (typically closed Mon and Tues)

Map: www.nps.gov/fiis/planyourvisit/maps.htm

Trail contact: Fire Island National Seashore, 120 Laurel St., Patchogue; (631) 687-4750; www.nps.gov/fiis

Special considerations: Heed closures for nesting piping plovers and terns, and be sensitive to the primary dunes, crossing only at designated sites; no hiking on dunes. Because mosquitos are common, carry repellent. In vegetation be alert for poison ivy and, most especially, deer ticks (Lyme disease carriers). These ticks exist year-round, so take the necessary precautions. You will find drinking water at Smith Point and Watch Hill, but carry an ample quantity. Toilets can be found at the visitor centers (when open). Pack in, pack out.

Finding the trailhead: On Long Island at Shirley, take exit 58S from NY 27 (Sunrise Highway) and go south on NY 46 (William Floyd Parkway) for 5 miles, crossing over the bridge to reach Fire Island National Seashore and Smith Point Suffolk County Park. Park at Smith Point County Park, a fee area. GPS: 40.734524, -72.864628. A ferry operating out of Patchogue, New York, goes to the Watch Hill area to access the longer section of national seashore.

The Hike

Descend the seaward-stretching boardwalk at Smith Point Wilderness Visitor Center and turn right (west) onto the 150-foot-wide strand. The fine, light-colored crystalline sand tosses back the sun. Energy spreads along the wave crests, and churned foam slides up the beach.

Along the beach, staggered posts mark off the seasonal nesting sites, while protective covers safeguard the nests from foxes. Grant the birds a wide berth so as not to interfere with their nesting. The lower beach typically offers easier walking anyway, with tide-compressed sand. Gaps in the primary dune offer glimpses north toward Great South Bay.

Because Smith Point drew the short straw when Hurricane Sandy sliced the island, the hike's length suggests a leisurely stroll with frequent pauses to admire water and sand. The stop sign for this hike is the watery gap left behind by the hurricane. The National Park Service has adopted a hands-off policy, allowing nature to dictate the recovery here without any human interference. Take a moment to contemplate the force and healing here before turning back.

From Smith Point Wilderness Visitor Center, the westbound boardwalk suggests your taking another walk. It enters the back-bay dune swale, offering a look at and access to Otis Pike High Dune Wilderness. From the boardwalk, visitors find the lingering trace of the old Burma Road, which offers a walk into the wild. Remember to keep to the swale—no climbing on dunes. Stop where the alterations made by Hurricane Sandy have stolen the continuation of the trace. Here, you again have front-row seats to the recovery process. Return as you came.

Watch Hill, at Fire Island's west end, accesses the longer island break. From the developed area at the Watch Hill ferry landing, descend the boardwalk to the beach and turn left (east). Clam shells, skate egg cases, sea-polished pebbles, and gulls toying with horseshoe crabs amuse beachcombers seasonally. Again, markers or nest covers signal the nesting sites of the delicate little shorebirds. Keep well below the dunes and dune foot, walking the tide-washed sands. Calf muscles tire as the sandy beach slopes toward the ocean. Dunes bordering the beach fluctuate from a few feet to 20 feet high.

The inviting, undeveloped natural beach satisfies wanderlust and welcomes rambling meditations. Well past halfway, you might notice the hike's lone structural landmark, a covered picnic deck overlooking the beach. This is owned by the village of Bellport. Meanwhile, the Atlantic Ocean continues to mesmerize with its steady presence, and your quiet beach discovery continues until the watery breach signals an end

Dunes compose parts of Otis Pike Wilderness Area at Fire Island National Seashore.

to beach travel. Backtrack along the ocean shore, returning to the oasis of the Watch Hill area, with its campground, slat-roof shade, restroom/changing facility, showers, phone, drinking fountain, and snack bar. In July and August, lifeguards oversee the area's swimming beach.

Back at the Watch Hill area, the boardwalk and traces of sandy Burma Road offer additional hiking opportunities. The attractive boardwalk fashions a loop less than a mile long that explores the back-bay habitat between the campground and the ferry terminal. Eastbound, passing behind the seaward dunes, the trace of Burma Road alternately tours loose sand or overgrown track through shrub swale with beach plum, beach grass, sweet pepperbush, and salt-spray rose.

Caches of tall, feathery-headed phragmites, springtime puddles pulsing with toads, and a lush, green estuary vary viewing. After rolling, the trail levels to traverse areas of beach grass and beach heather, sandy plains, and pockets of pitch pine. Beware of poison ivy and brier, common beneath the pines, and make frequent inspections for ticks.

Wooden debris, an old cable route, and seashells are possible findings, but the shifting sand frequently rewrites the discovery. Again, with no signs for guidance, halt where the trace becomes faint and backtrack to the ferry landing. This sampler gives you a taste, at least, of the High Dune wilderness, allowing you to consider if you'd like to return here for a more in-depth exploration.

Miles and Directions

0.0   Start from Smith Point Wilderness Visitor Center, descend to the beach, and turn right to hike it west.

1.8   Arrive at the island breach, then return as you came along the ocean beach.

3.6   End at Smith Point Wilderness Visitor Center.

Options

At Smith Point, following the 0.2-mile boardwalk northwest away from the center into the back swale, you can admire the barrier island's dune habitat and gain access to Fire Island's Burma Road, a trace that traverses the back-bay swale of **Otis Pike High Dune Wilderness.** With no signs in the wilderness, turn around where the trace grows faint (before the breach).

From the Watch Hill Visitor Center and Ferry Landing, you have a trio of options: beach, boardwalk, and Burma Road. For the beach hike, follow the 0.2-mile boardwalk to the beach and hike 5.1 miles east along the strand to the breach, before turning back for a 10.6-mile round-trip hike. For a shorter hike, the Village of Bellport's covered picnic shelter above the beach at 3.8 miles signals a turnaround for a 7.6-mile round-trip hike.

The Boardwalk at Watch Hill offers an easy 0.8-mile walk through back-bay habitat, traveling a loop with spurs to the ferry landing. From the Watch Hill campground area, the eastbound Burma Road trace travels swale behind the seaward

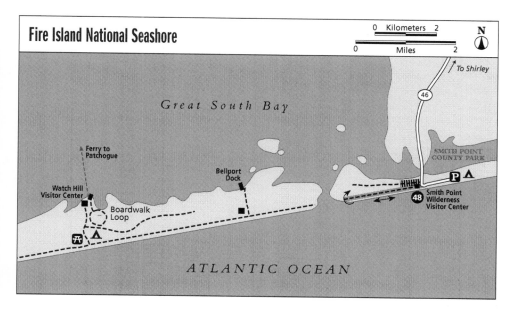

Fire Island National Seashore

0 Kilometers 2

0 Miles 2

N

Great South Bay

To Shirley

46

Ferry to
Patchogue

Bellport
Dock

SMITH POINT
COUNTY PARK

Watch Hill
Visitor Center

Boardwalk
Loop

P A

48 Smith Point
Wilderness
Visitor Center

ATLANTIC OCEAN

dunes, traversing the Otis Pike High Dune Wilderness, offering glimpses at its shifting landscape, windblown features, wetlands, and pitch-pine woods. The intermittent trace fades from the landscape after about a mile. Turn back here.

Hike Information

Local Information

Discover Long Island, 330 Motor Parkway, Suite 203, Hauppauge; (877) 386-6654; www.discoverlongisland.com

Local Events/Attractions

The **William Floyd Estate,** donated to Fire Island National Seashore in 1965, records three centuries of American life and consists of the ancestral home (the twenty-five-room "Old Mastic House"), attractive grounds, and the Floyd family cemetery. William Floyd, a general in the Revolutionary War and signer of the Declaration of Independence, was born in this house in 1743. Guided tours introduce the home and cemetery. William Floyd Estate, 245 Park Dr., Mastic Beach; (631) 399-2030; www.nps.gov/fiis.

Accommodations

Watch Hill Campground serves tent campers mid-May through mid-October and is concession operated. For access information, contact the National Park Service, (631) 687-4750; www.nps.gov/fiis.

Smith Point Suffolk County Park campground is open year-round and has 279 campsites. (631) 852-1314; www.suffolkcountyny.gov/Departments/Parks/Our-Parks/Smith-Point-County-Park.

49 Mashomack Preserve

Covering the southeastern third of Shelter Island, this 2,039-acre preserve of the Nature Conservancy (TNC) encompasses a maritime environment of tidal creeks, woodlands, fields, swamps, freshwater ponds, and 12 miles of stirring but inaccessible coastline. Four interlocking color-coded trails and the wheelchair-and-stroller-friendly 1-mile Joan Coles Trail introduce the preserve. A nature garden displays common vegetation, and the preserve supports a natural osprey nesting colony and a rare pine swamp.

Start: At the preserve visitor center trailhead

Distance: 12.0 miles out-and-back (Hike travels each of the 4 interlocking loops in its entirety, backtracking on itself only once between junctions G and H.)

Approximate hiking time: 6 to 8 hours

Difficulty: Easy

Elevation change: Despite only a modest elevation change, this rolling hike accumulates elevation 10 to 20 feet at a time.

Trail surface: Earthen path, woods road, boardwalk, and management (service) road

Seasons: Year-round

Other trail users: Birders and, when sufficient snow, cross-country skiers and snowshoers

Canine compatibility: Dogs not permitted

Land status: Private preserve

Nearest town: Greenport or North Haven

Fees and permits: Fees for the ferry service to the island; suggested donation to TNC

Schedule: Trails are open year-round daily, dawn to dusk

Map: www.nature.org/content/dam/tnc/nature/en/documents/Mashomack-Trail-Map-Summer-2021-r.pdf

Trail contacts: Mashomack Preserve, PO Box 850, 47 South Ferry Rd., Shelter Island, NY 11964; (631) 749-1001, www.nature.org

Special considerations: Keep to the trail and obey posted rules, which include no pets, no bikes, and no horses. There is no beach access for humans; beaches are for wildlife only. As TNC has marked the trails for just one direction of travel, follow the flow pattern indicated on the preserve map to avoid losing your way. Take the necessary precautions for ticks—they are prevalent here. There is no hiking access to the preserve on January weekdays because of hunting.

Finding the trailhead: From North Haven, take the South Ferry to Shelter Island and go 1 mile north on NY 114, turning right (east) to enter the preserve. Arriving from the North Ferry out of Greenport, follow NY 114 south 3 miles to the entrance. GPS: 41.057328, -72.324769

The Hike

Near the visitor center, the color-coded trails head east off the entry road into a rich woodland of mixed oak, red maple, hickory, beech, dogwood, and black locust. Approaching a service road, bear right per the red arrow. The trail merges with a wide woods lane, rounding to a gazebo overlooking Miss Annie's Creek—a tidal marsh bay with sandy strands and a treed island. Views stretch south, overlooking Shelter Island Sound and the South Ferry crossing.

Attractive woodland contributes to the tapestry of Mashomack Preserve.

At junction C, bear right for the yellow, green, and blue trails. A boardwalk continues the hike, crossing a salt meadow extension of the marsh. Here keep an eye out for the osprey nesting platform. After crossing a management road, twisted oaks and an open field precede the descent to junction F. Here the yellow trail heads left to close its loop, the blue trail heads straight, and the green trail bears right.

Follow the blue-marked trail through a field to explore the largest of the preserve loops. Before long, enter the shade of a beech-climax woods. The trail changes direction a couple of times before following a semishaded woods road as it curves east toward the bluff rim for sunnier travel. Pass a bench overlooking Gardiners Bay and Island. As the blue trail travels the outskirts of Great Swamp, a foot trail takes the baton; keep to the rim. Bullbrier entangles the woods as the open trail rolls south, trading looks at Gardiners Bay for looks at Northwest Harbor. Dogwoods lend their signature beauty.

Plum Pond Overlook extends a fine Northwest Harbor view, although Plum Pond itself may be masked by a leafy shroud. The trail then rounds above a kettle depression, bearing right and coming to a birding blind. Set back in the woods and camouflaged by phragmites, the blind overlooks the upper estuary of Bass Creek, at the edge of Katherine Ordway Wildlife Refuge, a restricted area of sensitive habitat. At the blind you might spy a sapsucker-drilled tree trunk, its circumference ringed by holes every few inches.

Where the blue trail tags the green loop at junction H, bear right to stay on the marked trail and follow the flow pattern indicated on the preserve map. The trail passes through mixed woods and crosses a service road to reach junction G (the head of the green trail loop). Here you bear left to add the green loop. The green loop passes through diverse woodland, overlooks the blue waters of Smith Cove, and reaches a blind looking out at Log Cabin Creek.

> A rare pine swamp, recognized for its uniqueness by the New York State Department of Environmental Quality, occupies the western edge of this preserve. Rimmed by swamp azalea, water willow, and highbush blueberry, the pines spring from a floating mat of sphagnum moss.

Turn right on the management road, passing through the staff residence area with its wood-shingled buildings, groomed lawns, shade trees, tidal ponds, and freshwater Sanctuary Pond. The buildings are off-limits to the public, but they provide an attractive addition to travel. The road becomes a doubletrack as it reenters woods, skirting the Bass Creek estuary. An upland woods ascent leads back to junction H. Go left, retracing the stretch between junctions H and G.

Once again at junction G, follow the green trail, ascending the steps to the right, now heading toward the visitor center. Scenic oaks lend shade as the trail traverses a coastal bluff. Below the trail sits a pristine, thin pebble beach reserved for wildlife (off-limits to the public). Upon crossing the management road, pass through woods and fields to junction F. Take the right fork of the yellow trail, tracking the yellow and red arrows back to the visitor center.

Miles and Directions

0.0   Start from the visitor center trailhead and head east off the entry road for the red trail.

0.3   Approaching a service road, bear right per the red arrow.

0.8   Reach junction C. Bear right for the yellow, green, and blue trails. *Note:* The red trail hooks left, returning to the visitor center.

1.2   Reach junction F. Hike the blue trail straight ahead. *Note:* The yellow trail heads left to close its loop; the green trail bears right.

3.1   Reach Gardiners Bay Overlook.

5.6   Reach Plum Pond Overlook.

6.0   Reach the wildlife blind at Bass Creek.

6.6   Reach junction H and the green trail. Bear right, following the mapped flow pattern.

7.3   Cross a service road to junction G (the head of the green trail loop) and bear left. *Note:* Going right here returns you to the visitor center.

7.5   Reach the wildlife blind at Log Cabin Creek.

8.8   Return to junction H. Go left, retracing the trail between junctions H and G.

9.5   At junction G, follow the green trail up the steps to the right toward the visitor center.

10.3   Reach junction F. Take the right fork of the yellow trail.

11.0   Cross the management road, and in 0.1 mile bear right on the red trail.

12.0   End at the visitor center.

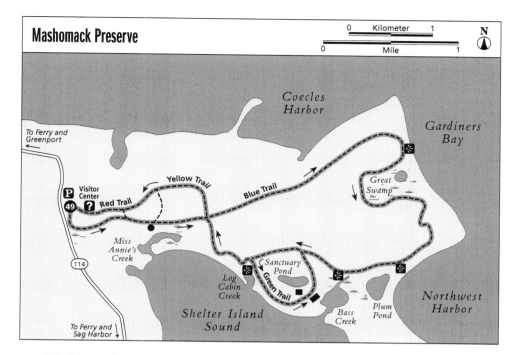

Mashomack Preserve

Kilometer

Mile

N

Coecles Harbor

Gardiners Bay

To Ferry and Greenport

Yellow Trail

Visitor Center

Red Trail

Blue Trail

Great Swamp

Miss Annie's Creek

114

Sanctuary Pond

Green Trail

Log Cabin Creek

Shelter Island Sound

Bass Creek

Plum Pond

Northwest Harbor

To Ferry and Sag Harbor

Hike Information

Local Information

Discover Long Island, 330 Motor Parkway, Suite 203, Hauppauge; (877) 386-6654; www.discoverlongisland.com

Local Events/Attractions

Shelter Island Kayak Tours offers guided trips on the pretty creeks and harbors of Shelter Island. Shelter Island Kayak Tours, Shelter Island; (631) 749-1990; www.kayaksi.com.

    Greenport's East End Seaport Museum and Marine Foundation together with the town's annual Maritime Festival in September keep the area's nautical roots intact. The museum offers you the chance to ride aboard a 1906 sailing schooner and has a wind exhibit demonstrating the physics of sailing, models of local sailing ships, sail-making artifacts, fishing and oystering memorabilia, and more. The museum is open mid-May through September, varying days and times. East End Seaport Museum and Marine Foundation, Third Street at the ferry dock, Greenport; (631) 477-2100; www.eastendseaport.org.

Accommodations

Cedar Point Suffolk County Park campground in East Hampton is open mid-May to mid-October and has 189 campsites. (631) 852-7620; www.suffolkcountyny.gov.

50 Hither Hills State Park

On Long Island's east end just before Montauk Point, this 1,755-acre state park brings together a superb lineup: walking dunes, "phantom forests," a pristine mile of Atlantic beach, the cobbled shore of Napeague Bay, and Goff Point, where piping plovers, least terns, and American oystercatchers nest. An interior region of pine barrens, dune heath, and maritime grassland completes the offering. The selected hiking loop travels the Napeague shoreline and makes an interior return via the Paumanok Path, Long Island's premier long-distance trail linking the island pine barrens between Montauk Point and Rocky Point Pine Barrens State Forest.

Start: At the Napeague Harbor Road harbor/dunes trailhead

Distance: 14.5-mile loop (13.5 miles when nesting season closes Goff Point)

Approximate hiking time: 8 to 9 hours

Difficulty: Moderate

Elevation change: The hike has about a 50-foot elevation change.

Trail surface: Sand and cobbled beach, sandy path, jeep grade

Seasons: Best for hiking fall through spring (Summers are hot and humid; carry extra water.)

Other trail users: Mountain bikers (on interior trails), horse riders, hunters

Canine compatibility: Leashed dogs permitted. Keep dogs tightly restrained and away from nesting sites or, better yet, leave them at home during nesting season. Carry water for your pet.

Land status: New York State Park

Nearest town: Montauk

Fees and permits: None for selected hike; park entrance fee at developed area of park and for Atlantic shoreline access

Schedule: Year-round, daylight hours

Map: https://parks.ny.gov/documents/parks/HitherHillsTrailmap.pdf

Trail contact: Hither Hills State Park, 164 Old Montauk Hwy., Montauk; (631) 668-2554; https://parks.ny.gov/parks/hitherhills/details.aspx

Special considerations: Obey all posted closures. Avoid Goff Point during nesting season (late May through June) and to give seals ample space when they haul out on the Atlantic beach in winter. On the Walking Dunes, the shifting canvas of sand can alter your course. Hunting occurs weekdays in December and January, so confine hiking to weekends during those months. Should you choose to hike weekdays, wear blaze orange. Carry ample drinking water.

A jeep trail between the Napeague Bay shore and the Paumanok Path offers a way to vary the featured loop. During nesting season, high tides, or strong winds, it can replace bay travel.

Finding the trailhead: From Amagansett, go 6 miles east on NY 27 (Montauk Highway) and turn left (north) on Napeague Harbor Road to find the Paumanok Path on the right in 0.4 mile (no parking). The shared trailhead for Walking Dunes and Napeague Shoreline is at road's end, in another 0.3 mile. Even though drifting sand reduces parking here to a few spaces, do not block the limited-use vehicle access to the beach. GPS: 41.010968, -72.037640. For Atlantic beach access, from Amagansett drive 7.2 miles east on NY 27 and Old Montauk Highway, turning south to enter the park, a fee area. GPS: 41.008757, -72.011144

Walking Dunes offer a nature walk where sands bury a former forest.

The Hike

From the end of Napeague Harbor Road, hike the harbor shoreline north, traveling an avenue of pinkish-orange sand and cobbles. A scattering of open-hinged scallops may record the recent activity of a ruddy turnstone.

At the neck of Goff Point, the season will determine your course of travel. Because American oystercatchers, endangered piping plovers, and least terns each have nesting territories on Goff Point, you should skip the point altogether during nesting, late May through June, and instead cross at the neck to follow the bay shore east. When point travel is appropriate, its broad flat still attracts feeding piping plovers and resting terns. Sit quietly and watch their antics. Waterspouts can betray the presence of clams. Continue north around the spit, but keep below the high-tide line. At the head of Goff Point, gulls congregate, cormorants string offshore, and slipper and orange jingle shells collect in stringy deposits. You'll leave Goff Point opposite Skonk Hole, a wet depression, to continue east along the bay shore.

Dune breaches offer looks south at a maritime grassland of beard and switchgrass, with beach plum adorning the dune top in showy spring finery. Rounded cobbles and shells create a crunchy thoroughfare. Before long, looks northeast find the offshore pilings of a shellfish bed and distant Rocky Point. The beach eventually shows more sand, and the dune gives way to a 25-foot bluff with an abrupt slip face. Colonies of bank swallows nest in the solid seams. Boulders on the beach offer dry seating.

Cobbles reappear underfoot as you round Rocky Point, and a cliff rises above the beach. After you tag the point, your bay shore travel ends at Dyer's Landing, which affords eastern views of Fort Pond Bay and Culloden Point. Now seek out and follow the foot trail heading uphill to the right. The trail meets a road and follows the blazed Paumanok Path right. Regularly marked with white blazes or Paumanok Path markers, the route passes among tangled oaks.

At the upcoming Y junction, head right. Openings and spurs to the right present views of Block Island Sound; spurs left lead to Old North Road. Watch for blazes to point you through a series of T junctions. After a stretch in the brushy coastal thicket of the marine terrace, oak woodland again offers shade. Forest changes bring the additions of maple, hickory, and basswood. Soon you meet Old North Road and follow it right.

Comfortable and tree-draped, Old North Road pleasantly pieces together the segments of the Paumanok Path. At the road junction ahead, a right leads to Quincetree Landing. Keep to the Paumanok Path, which later turns right off Old North Road to pass closer to shore atop cliffs or the coastal slope. Although the path dips to shore level, you never actually reach shore.

Eventually the hike is back in oaks and passing parallel to a railroad track, usually hidden from view by dense forest. At the next crossroads, a detour to the right finds Waterfence Overlook, with its fine vantage and spur trails to the beach. For the Paumanok Path alone, proceed forward, drifting farther from shore. Keep an eye out both for the guiding blazes at junctions and for box turtles.

At the upcoming four-way junction, the Paumanok Path heads left to round Fresh Pond. A short detour right here leads to shore. Fresh Pond is a large, open bass pond rimmed by sweet pepperbush and high-canopy forest. The next crossroads offer another chance for pond access.

On the last leg, the pitch pines of the barrens make an appearance and eventually gain dominance. Sounds from NY 27 creep into the hike's peace. Where you emerge at Napeague Harbor Road, turn right to return to the trail's start.

Miles and Directions

0.0   Start from the harbor/dunes trailhead and hike the harbor shore north.

1.2   Reach the neck of Goff Point. Round the point when appropriate. Late May through June (nesting), cross at the neck and hike east along the bay shore.

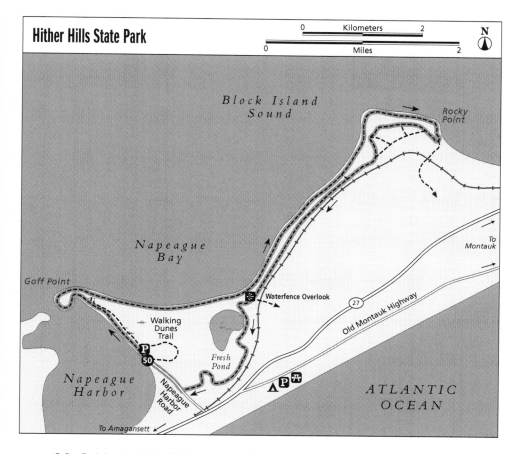

Hither Hills State Park

| 0 | Kilometers | 2 |
| 0 | Miles | 2 |

N

Block Island Sound

Rocky Point

Napeague Bay

Goff Point

To Montauk

Waterfence Overlook

27

Old Montauk Highway

Walking Dunes Trail

P 50

Fresh Pond

Napeague Harbor

Napeague Harbor Road

A P

ATLANTIC OCEAN

To Amagansett

2.2 End the stroll of Goff Point opposite Skonk Hole. Hike the bay shore east.

5.9 Begin to round Rocky Point.

7.4 Reach Rocky Point.

7.5 End bay shore travel at Dyer's Landing and turn inland.

7.6 Reach the Paumanok Path. Turn right.

7.8 Reach a Y junction. Head right.

9.0 Meet and follow right Old North Road.

9.5 Reach the Quincetree Landing junction. Continue forward on Old North Road, following the Paumanok Path, which later turns right off the road to pass closer to shore.

11.5 Reach a crossroads. Proceed forward on the Paumanok, drifting farther from shore. **Option:** A 0.5-mile detour to the right finds Waterfence Overlook, with its fine vantage and spur trails to the beach.

11.9 Reach a four-way junction. Follow the Paumanok Path left, skirting Fresh Pond.

14.2 Emerge at Napeague Harbor Road. Turn right.

14.5 End at the harbor/dunes trailhead.

Options

The 1-mile **Walking Dunes Trail,** with its 40-foot dunes and buried forests, fits naturally with a Napeague Shoreline–Paumanok Path hike, offering a pleasant start or cap. Head right (east) off the end of Napeague Harbor Road, following a sandy path into a maritime corridor of mixed oak, beach grass, beach plum, pitch pine, and poison ivy. Next enter the rare zone of shifting sand that "walks" over trees 30 feet tall. Only the crowns of the nearby oaks clear the burying sand. With a gust of wind, the sands go walking. The trail contours and gradually ascends the dunes, with first forest and then wetland sweeping away to the right. Minerals can streak the sands purple or black. Where the hike tops the dune, enjoy a grand area overview. The trail then descends to a western bowl and phantom forest, where snags record past forests overtaken and ultimately killed by the sand. Counterclockwise, skirt a native cranberry bog. Stay left. After passing through bayberry, aim for the wide sand track ahead and follow it over a rise and into the next bowl to reach the harbor beach (0.8 mile). Turn left to return to your vehicle (1 mile).

Hike Information

Local Information
Discover Long Island, 330 Motor Parkway, Suite 203, Hauppauge; (877) 386-6654; www.discoverlongisland.com

Local Events/Attractions
Montauk Point Lighthouse Museum and Light, a National Maritime Historic Landmark, will entice you to the eastern tip of Long Island. The museum's exhibits, video, and tower climb introduce you to the oldest lighthouse in New York, established in 1796. The light with its 80-foot sandstone tower occupies the spot where the British Royal Navy lit signal bonfires to guide its ships during the Revolutionary War. Montauk Point Lighthouse Museum and Light, 2000 Montauk Hwy., Montauk; (631) 668-2544; www.montaukhistoricalsociety.org.

Accommodations
Hither Hills State Park's oceanside campground, open early April to mid-November, has 168 sites. Reservations: (800) 456-2267; www.reserveamerica.com.

Organizations
The **Long Island Greenbelt Trail Conference** maintains and promotes Long Island trails and leads hikes, including here at Hither Hills. Long Island Greenbelt Trail Conference, PO Box 5636, Hauppauge, NY 11788; (631) 360-0753; www.ligreenbelt.org.

Honorable Mentions

AA   David A. Sarnoff Pine Barrens Preserve

South of Riverhead in Suffolk County, this preserve of more than 2,700 acres features classic pine barrens, wetlands, and kettle depressions. County Road 104 divides the preserve into east–west tracts, with the larger piece sitting west of the highway. A loop trail explores each tract. A round-trip on the Western Loop measures 5.4 miles; the Eastern Loop is 3.6 miles. The pleasant, mostly level trails lead through the pine-oak mixed forest, with subtle changes in the size of the trees and the thickness of the canopy. Access is by permit only. Request the free permit from the New York State Department of Environmental Conservation in Stony Brook. The preserve is closed to hiking during the January deer season.

Pine barrens clad much of the remaining natural areas on Long Island.

For the Western Loop, from the NY 24 rotary in Riverhead, drive 0.7 mile south on NY 104 (Riverleigh Avenue). The trailhead is on the west side of the road. GPS: 40.905870, -72.655382. For the Eastern Loop, from the NY 24 rotary, go south on NY 104 for 2.2 miles, finding off-road parking on the west side of the highway. GPS: 40.885980, -72.643059. Contact New York State Department of Environmental Conservation, Region 1, SUNY at Stony Brook, 50 Circle Rd., Stony Brook; (631) 444-0200; www.dec.ny.gov.

BB Connetquot River State Park Preserve

Color-coded primary and unmarked secondary trails explore this 3,500-acre state park preserve west of Oakdale. The site's previous life was as a private trout and hunting reservation for an elite sportsman's club, whose membership included such names as Tiffany, Vanderbilt, Belmont, and Carnegie. Ulysses S. Grant, Daniel Webster, and General Sherman were honored guests. A fish hatchery, a restored gristmill, and the rustic buildings of the historic lodge recall the era. The river springs from an aquifer beneath the pine barrens. Big trout swim in its pools. Deer, swan, fox, osprey, heron, hawk, and box turtle contribute to the menagerie.

A lazy 9.8-mile loop follows former carriage roads and trails through this unique natural area. It travels along the river from the historic park and Mill Pond, past the fish hatchery and Deep Pond, and across the preserve past Collins Junction, before reaching Veterans Highway and turning east. It then follows Cordwood Road southward, again swinging west past Slade Pond to end back at the historic area.

A vehicle entrance fee is charged. Fishing is by permit only. No pets are permitted.

From Oakdale on NY 27 (Sunrise Highway), go 1.4 miles west and turn north, entering the park. Eastbound traffic must make a U-turn in Oakdale, as there is only westbound access. GPS: 40.749201, -73.151972. Contact Connetquot River State Park Preserve, PO Box 505, Oakdale, NY 11769; (631) 581-1005; https://parks.ny.gov/parks/connetquotriver.

A historic sports club formerly occupied the grounds of Connetquot River State Park Preserve.

Appendix: Clubs and Trail Groups

Adirondack Mountain Club (ADK) is a nonprofit membership organization that protects wild lands and waters through a balanced approach of conservation and advocacy, environmental education, and responsible recreation. It carries out its mission in New York State forest preserves, parks, and other wild places. Adirondack Mountain Club, 814 Goggins Rd., Lake George, NY 12845; (518) 668-4447; adkinfo@adk.org; www.adk.org.

Appalachian Mountain Club (AMC), the nation's oldest outdoor recreation and conservation organization (active since 1876), promotes the protection, enjoyment, and wise use of mountains, rivers, and trails in the Appalachian region. Appalachian Mountain Club, AMC Main Office, 5 Joy St., Boston, MA 02108; (617) 523-0636; fax: (617) 523-0722; www.outdoors.org.

Appalachian Trail Conservancy (ATC), formerly known as the Appalachian Trail Conference, is a volunteer-based, private nonprofit organization dedicated to the conservation of the 2,175-mile Appalachian National Scenic Trail (AT) and its 250,000-acre greenway extending from Maine to Georgia. The ATC has done so since 1925 and also provides AT information and education. It works in unison with the National Park Service, thirty maintaining clubs, and a host of partners and volunteers. Appalachian Trail Conservancy, PO Box 807, 799 Washington St., Harpers Ferry, WV 25425-0807; (304) 535-6331; https://appalachiantrail.org.

Catskill Mountain Club, a community-based volunteer organization, promotes responsible, safe, and sustainable outdoor recreation in the Catskill region through its outdoor recreational programs, educational programs, volunteer stewardship, and environmental and recreational advocacy. Catskill Mountain Club, PO Box 404, Margaretville, NY 12455-0404; info@catskillmountainclub.org; https://catskillmountain club.org.

Finger Lakes Trail Conference (FLTC) has the mission to build, protect, and enhance the Finger Lakes Trail, a continuous footpath across New York State. Volunteers annually log about 15,000 hours of trail work. But more than physical labor, the FLTC supports and promotes the trail and provides services to members, partners, and the general public. The conference also maintains and markets up-to-date maps for the Finger Lakes Trail. FLTC, 6111 Visitor Center Rd., Mount Morris; (585) 658-9320; https://fltconference.org.

Long Island Greenbelt Trail Conference is a nonprofit grassroots organization dedicated to preserving open space and developing trails on Long Island. With a dedicated core of volunteers, the group has established more than 200 miles of hiking trails (including two National Recreation Trails), offers guided hikes, and produces and sells Long Island trail maps. Long Island Greenbelt Trail Conference, PO Box 5636, Hauppauge, NY 11788; (631) 360-0753; fax: (631) 980-4009; www.ligreenbelt .org.

New York–New Jersey Trail Conference is a federation of member clubs and individuals that takes a leadership role in building, maintaining, marking, and promoting trails and advocating for open space in the New York–New Jersey region. The constituent clubs have a combined membership of over 100,000. The network's handiwork touches 1,600 miles of foot trails from the Delaware Water Gap north to beyond the Catskills. New York–New Jersey Trail Conference, 600 Ramapo Valley Rd., Mahwah, NJ 07430; (201) 512-9348; info@nynjtc.org; www.nynjtc.org.

Parks & Trails New York, founded in 1985, has grown from a handful of park advocates to a statewide organization of over 5,000 members and supporters. The group helps promote, expand, and protect trails, parks, and open spaces across the state. They advance both traditional and newly conceived parks and trails between villages and natural spaces. Parks & Trails New York, 29 Elk St., Albany, NY 12207; (518) 434-1583; fax: (518) 427-0067; ptny@ptny.org; www.ptny.org.

Sierra Club is a nonprofit membership organization that promotes conservation of the natural environment through grassroots advocacy, public education, outdoor activities, and lobbying. Founded in 1892, the club has 700,000 members nationwide. The Atlantic Chapter applies the principles of the national organization to environmental issues facing New York State. Sierra Club, Atlantic Chapter, 744 Broadway, Albany, NY 12207; (518) 426-9144; https://atlantic2.sierraclub.org.

Taconic Hiking Club helps maintain trails and the trail register sheets throughout the Capital District. The club welcomes members interested in hiking, cycling, canoeing, kayaking, snowshoeing, and cross-country skiing. Their newsletter lists activities and projects. Taconic Hiking Club, www.taconichikingclub.org.

Hike Index

About the Authors

Writer **Rhonda Ostertag** and photographer **George Ostertag** have collaborated on twenty outdoor guides and travel books over the last two decades and, more recently, on coffee-table photography books. Their bylines appear on thousands of articles in national and regional publications, almost always on topics of nature, travel, and outdoor recreation. Their books include *Our Washington, Our Oregon, Backroads of Oregon, California State Parks: A Complete Recreation Guide, Best Short Hikes in Northwest Oregon*, and the FalconGuides *Hiking Connecticut and Rhode Island* and *Camping Oregon*.

Randi Minetor is the author of more than ninety books, including more than fifty books published by Rowman & Littlefield. Her books on New York State include *Hiking New York's Lower Hudson River Valley, Hiking through History New York*, and three editions to date of the bestselling *Hiking Waterfalls New York*, as well as two editions each of four books in the Best Easy Day Hikes series about Rochester, Buffalo, Syracuse, and Albany. She and her husband, photographer Nic Minetor, have collaborated on books including *Backyard Birding & Butterfly Gardening, Birding New England, Birding Florida, Birding Texas, Best Easy Birding Guides for Acadia and Cape Cod*, and *Scenic Driving New York*, as well as their many hiking books. Randi is the author of seven books in the Death in the Parks series, on Glacier, Rocky Mountain, Acadia, and Zion National Parks, and the Everglades, as well as *Death on Katahdin* and *Death on Mount Washington*. Her work also appears in *Birding* magazine, *Building Stone, Projection, Lights and Staging News; Lighting and Sound America; Western New York Physician;* and *North American Birds*, as well as in e-zines in the live entertainment technology, medicine, and birding trades. Randi is a W. T. Grant Scholar and earned an MA from the University of Rochester and a BA from the University at Buffalo. She and Nic live in Rochester, New York.

THE TEN ESSENTIALS OF HIKING

American Hiking Society

American Hiking Society recommends you pack the "Ten Essentials" every time you head out for a hike. Whether you plan to be gone for a couple of hours or several months, make sure to pack these items. Become familiar with these items and know how to use them. Learn more at **AmericanHiking.org/hiking-resources**

1. Appropriate Footwear

2. Navigation

3. Water (and a way to purify it)

4. Food

5. Rain Gear & Dry-Fast Layers

6. Safety Items (light, fire, and a whistle)

7. First Aid Kit

8. Knife or Multi-Tool

9. Sun Protection

10. Shelter